Sharon Crawford
Jason Gerend

Windows experts and popular
computer book authors

Faster
Smarter

Microsoft®
Windows® 98

Take charge of your Web code—
faster, smarter, *better*!

PUBLISHED BY
Microsoft Press
A Division of Microsoft Corporation
One Microsoft Way
Redmond, Washington 98052-6399

Library of Congress Cataloging-in-Publication Data
Crawford, Sharon.
    Faster Smarter Microsoft Windows 98 / Sharon Crawford, Jason Gerend.
       p. cm.
    Includes index.
    ISBN 0-7356-1858-5
    1. Microsoft Windows (Computer file)   2. Operating systems (Computers) I. Gerend,
Jason. II. Title.

QA76.76.O63 C72478 2002
005.4'469--dc21   2002033713

Printed and bound in the United States of America.

1 2 3 4 5 6 7 8 9   QWE   8 7 6 5 4 3

Distributed in Canada by H.B. Fenn and Company Ltd.

A CIP catalogue record for this book is available from the British Library.

Microsoft Press books are available through booksellers and distributors worldwide. For further information about international editions, contact your local Microsoft Corporation office or contact Microsoft Press International directly at fax (425) 936-7329. Visit our Web site at www.microsoft.com/mspress. Send comments to *mspinput@microsoft.com*.

Acquisitions Editor: Alex Blanton
Project Editor: Kristen Weatherby
Series Editor: Kristen Weatherby

Body Part No. X08-95126

Table of Contents

Acknowledgments . . . . *vii*
Introduction . . . . *ix*

Chapter 1:   Making Windows Work for You 1
   Which Windows? 2
   A Quick Lap Around Windows 98 2
   Instant Gratification: 5½ Ways to Make Windows Easier Right Now 5
   Starting and Stopping 9
   Deciphering the Start Menu 12
   Customizing the Start Menu 18
   Taskbars Translated Here 19

Chapter 2:   Covering the Desktop 25
   The Desktop Icons 25
   Making and Using Shortcuts 31
   Windows Explorer and My Computer 36
   Changing the Desktop Display 38
   Choosing Screen Savers 42
   Help on the Spot 44
   Help on the Web 46

Chapter 3:   Running Programs 49
   Opening and Switching Between Programs 49
   Closing Programs 52
   Installing Software 55
   Uninstalling Software 58
   Running Non-Windows 98 Programs 59
   Essential Software That's Free (or Cheap) 64

Chapter 4:   Working with Files and Folders **67**
Using Folders. 67
Selecting Files and Folders 78
The Association Between Files and Programs 79
Copying and Moving Files and Folders 83
Learning to Recycle 84
Working with Floppy Disks 90

Chapter 5:   What *IS* That File? **93**
What You See on the Hard Disk Drive 93
File Name Extensions and What They Mean 97
Meet the Registry. 97
Registry Tricks 99
Getting Rid of Unnecessary Files 103
Files You Must Not Delete 106

Chapter 6:   Fearless Web Browsing. **111**
Choosing an ISP 111
Using the Internet Connection Wizard. 115
Connecting and Disconnecting from the Internet. 117
Getting Around with Internet Explorer 120
Keeping Track of Web Pages. 124
Searching on the Web 132
Downloading Files 135

Chapter 7:   Using E-mail and Newsgroups **137**
Setting Up and Personalizing Outlook Express 138
Reading E-mail 147
Writing and Formatting E-mail 153
Using the Address Book. 156
Dealing with Large Amounts of E-mail 159
Newsgroups: All the News That's Fit to Print (and Then Some) 167

Chapter 8:   Printing **173**
Installing and Removing Printers 173
Getting the Most from Your Printer 175
Managing the Print Queue 182
Installing and Using a Network Printer 184

Chapter 9:   Conquering Computer Hardware 189
    Hardware and Windows 98 189
    Using the Device Manager 190
    Adding a USB Port 193
    Installing a Scanner 194
    Connecting a Digital Camera 194
    Configuring Modems 196
    Configuring ISDN 200
    Making DSL (Digital Subscriber Line) and Cable Connections 201
    Display Hardware and Settings 202
    Changing a Mouse 207
    Working with Game Controllers 207
    Hardware Profiles 209

Chapter 10:   Making Use of Control Panel Tools 211
    Training a Mouse 211
    Using Keyboard Options 215
    Improving Accessibility 217
    Multimedia Means Audio and Video 220
    Using Media Player 223

Chapter 11:   Playing It Safe 227
    Stopping Hackers and Viruses 227
    Maintaining Your Privacy 229
    E-mail Security 240
    Safe Shopping 243
    Cover Your Tracks 245
    Restricting Access to Objectionable Content 248

Chapter 12:   Maintaining a Healthy Computer 251
    Keeping Your Software Updated 251
    Housecleaning 252
    Optimizing System Performance 256
    Backing Up Your Files 269
    Dealing with Startup Problems 279
    Dealing with Shutdown Problems 285

Chapter 13:   Building and Using a Network 287
        Before You Begin: Designing a Network .288
        Building a Network. 293
        Sharing Files on a Network. 302
        Testing and Troubleshooting a Network. .304
        Protecting a Network from Hackers. 308

Chapter 14:   Connecting from Home or On the Road 313
        Working with Dial-Up Connections 313
        Working with VPN Connections. 316
        Dialing In to Your Computer While Away .321

Index 325

Acknowledgments

Our thanks to Alex Blanton and Kristen Weatherby at Microsoft Press. Alex got the project started and Kristen did the heavy lifting after that. As the series editor, Kristen has a task no sensible person would want—trying to keep everyone happy and the work moving in a situation involving many people and intrinsically fraught with stress, conflict, and the occasional attack of high dudgeon. She did a great job.

Thanks also to Neil J. Salkind of Studio B Productions. He's both tireless and soothing, a great combination in an agent.

Jason would like to thank Brian Hodges and Mercea Strecker for their input and support.

And Sharon thanks Jason, a great coauthor through rough times, as well as the usual suspects, and the late Dr. Rudolph S. Langer, who couldn't have imagined what he started.

Introduction

Microsoft Windows 98 continues to be one of the most popular operating systems in use today. It's fast, easy to use, works with all your existing applications, and runs on just about every computer under the sun. If you're a home user, you might use it on your faithful old computer that you can't bear (or perhaps afford) to replace. If you're a business user, you might not have a choice—there's a computer in your office and it's got Windows 98 on it whether you like it or not.

Whatever your reason for using Windows 98, this book will help you get the most from this venerable operating system. Make no mistake, this is no dusty bargain-basement book written back in the 1990s. This book was written from cover to cover in 2002 to be the most up-to-date, knowledgeable, and relevant book on the market.

This Book Could Be for You

Faster Smarter Microsoft Windows 98 is specifically tailored for knowledge workers and other folks who've used Windows 98 before, but never up to its full potential. You might know some aspects of Windows well, and others not at all. Because of this, our strategy is to briefly cover the basics, bring everyone quickly up to speed, and then delve into truly useful tasks that might have eluded you until now. We present these tasks in a way that's easy for everyone to understand and chock-full of invaluable information, minus unnecessary fluff and condescending chatter. We also cover all the latest and greatest aspects of computers and software, digital cameras, and photo printers, as well as wireless networks, cable and DSL Internet technology, and how to keep hackers and viruses at bay.

In general, we introduce a topic or task briefly so that you understand why you might want to perform the procedure, and then we show you how to accomplish the task through a series of steps. We also pepper the book with tidbits of useful information in the following formats:

■   **Tip**   Useful information for putting Windows to better use or just generally making your computing life easier. For example, tips cover everything from how to find a good DSL provider to the proper method for cleaning your mouse ball.

- **Note**   Something that you should be aware of but that might not directly impact what you're doing. For example, we might tell you that a particular search technique doesn't work the same way in all search engines.

- **Caution**   Information that you need to avoid trouble. For example, we might warn you about files you shouldn't delete and advise on how to protect yourself against viruses.

- **Lingo**   Geekspeak to English translations. This is where we bring you up to speed on necessary acronyms and technical terms, such as TCP/IP and cookies.

- **Try This!**   Tasks that you can perform to achieve a better understanding of a concept, have fun, or use Windows in a different way. For example, one Try This! explains how to get thumbnail views of your photos instead of boring icons.

- **Sidebars**   Concepts that perhaps aren't necessary right now but that will serve you well in the future. For example, you'll find sidebars on what causes computers to slow down and how to keep your passwords secure.

- **See Also**   Provides additional references so that you can get more information on a topic if you want to. We might reference other parts of this book, Web sites, other books, or the Microsoft Knowledge Base (which is available for free online).

System Requirements

In order to run Windows 98 or Windows 98 Second Edition, you need a 486-based computer running at 66 MHz or faster, with 16 MB of memory, 200 MB of hard disk space, a monitor, keyboard, and CD-ROM drive (or a network connection to one). Although any computer with these specifications is fine if you like to file your nails while waiting for things to load, most people are happier with a computer somewhat more powerful—a Pentium-based system running at 100 MHz or faster, with at least 32 MB of RAM and 1 GB of hard disk space. This is a more realistic minimum these days and available dirt-cheap if you're willing to buy a used computer.

See Also   *Chances are pretty good that you're already running Windows 98, in which case system requirements are irrelevant. However, we do discuss optimizing and upgrading computers in Chapter 12, "Maintaining a Healthy Computer," should you find that your system has lost the spring in its step.*

Support

Every effort has been made to ensure the accuracy of this book. Microsoft Press provides corrections for books at the following address:

http://mspress.microsoft.com/support/

If you have comments, questions, or ideas regarding this book, please send them to the authors at FasterWin98@scribes.com or to Microsoft Press via e-mail to mspinput@microsoft.com or via postal mail to:

Microsoft Press
Attn: *Faster Smarter* Editor
One Microsoft Way
Redmond, WA 98052-6399

Please note that product support is not offered through the above addresses.

Chapter 1

Making Windows Work for You

If you have Microsoft Windows 98, you've probably been using it for a while, or perhaps you just inherited a computer with Windows 98 installed from someone further up the technological food chain. Either way, if you're like most people and see a computer as a tool and not a religion, you've learned just enough about Windows 98 to do what you want to do and not a bit more.

And why not? If you want to use e-mail only, why should you clutter up your brain with stuff you'll never use? You shouldn't. However, even for sending and receiving e-mail, many tips that you probably haven't encountered could make your Windows experience better. No matter what you actually do on a computer, you also need to know how to do simple maintenance chores, how to make a wayward printer work, and how to guard against viruses and hackers—just for starters.

In this book we aim to cover all the tricks, tips, and techniques to help a user of Windows 98, whether you spend your computer time playing games or writing a thesis on game theory. Some of the points covered are things you've already learned. If you long ago mastered making a shortcut, skip that section—but perhaps not entirely. Take a look at some of the other aspects of shortcuts because you could come across a tip that's just perfect for you. Similarly, some notes and comments might be too advanced for someone just starting out with Windows 98. Our advice is to skip any section likely to give you a headache (the ones with lots of acronyms like BIOS and SCSI) and come back to it later if you need to.

This chapter covers basic information. Someone who just started using Windows 98 can find lots of help, but even grizzled veterans should scan these pages because we've tucked in a number of valuable and little-known facts here and there.

Which Windows?

Not long after Windows 98 was released, along came Microsoft Windows 98 SE (Second Edition). To the naked eye, the two appear to be identical, though Windows 98 SE includes a number of fixes for minor problems in Windows 98 and some improved functionality. Some of the items in Windows 98 SE that aren't in regular Windows 98 include upgrades to Microsoft Wallet, Windows Media Player, and Microsoft NetMeeting. Additional improvements are mostly components that work behind the scenes.

Note   If you truly want to know all the differences between Windows 98 and Windows 98 SE, go to Microsoft's online Knowledge Base (*http://support.microsoft.com/default.asp* and click Search the Knowledge Base). Search for article *Q234762*.

To determine if Windows 98 SE is installed on your computer, right-click My Computer and then click Properties. If "Second Edition" is listed under System on the General tab, Windows 98 SE is already installed. Just about everything in the Second Edition can be downloaded from the Microsoft Download Center (*http://www.microsoft.com/downloads/search.asp?*).

A Quick Lap Around Windows 98

In the world of computing, as with every other subject, the ability to call things by their proper names is a distinguishing characteristic of people who know what they're doing—or who at least appear to. For example, no one who expected to pass zoology would persistently refer to *Ursus horribilis* as "that great shaggy creature with the enormous claws." In the next sections we'll describe parts of Windows 98 and the "correct" (or at least most-used) names for each. We'll use these names consistently throughout the book to ensure we are all speaking a common language.

Note   Completely familiar with Windows talk? Feel free to skip ahead to a later section. No hard feelings.

The Desktop

The first thing you see on the screen after Windows 98 completely launches is called the desktop—the screen being analogous to a real desk, that is, a work surface with papers (documents) and various tools (programs). It's an apt analogy. Just as with real desks, some desktops are surprisingly neat and others are incredibly cluttered. Critical components of the Windows 98 desktop are the Start button, icons, and the taskbar.

Figure 1-1 shows how the desktop looked back when it was first installed. It may not look like this on your computer, but the basic elements are probably still there.

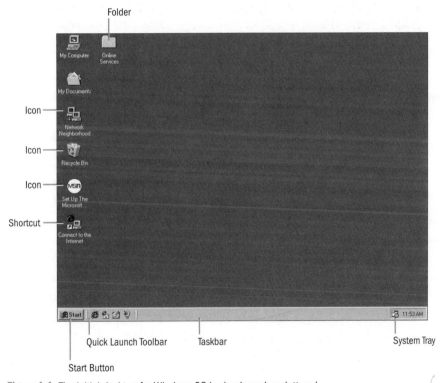

Figure 1-1 The initial desktop for Windows 98 is simple and uncluttered.

The Start Button

Click the Start button to open the Start menu. Just about *everything* you need to do in Windows 98 can be done from some part of the Start menu, although it's the long way 'round for many operations. For this book, we've ferreted out the most direct routes for every task.

Icons and Shortcuts

The little pictures on the desktop are called *icons*. The ones with the arrow in the lower-left corner are called *shortcuts*. The difference might appear small but it's significant. Icons represent actual objects and when you delete the icon, you delete the function or object it represents. For example, delete the icon for a printer and you can no longer use that printer. Delete a program icon and the program is deleted.

A shortcut, on the other hand, is a tiny file that has no function of its own— it merely points to the real object. Clicking a shortcut to a program redirects you to the actual program. The whole process is instantaneous, as if you clicked the program file directly. Because they're only pointers, you can create and delete shortcuts any time.

If you're not clear on creating, deleting, and otherwise modifying shortcuts, the whole story is in Chapter 2 in the section entitled "Making and Using Shortcuts."

Lingo   Until Windows 95, the term *shortcut* always referred to a keyboard shortcut—in other words, a combination of keys that would produce some action on screen. But now we have short-cuts meaning pointers, and the shortcut menu (the one you see when you right-click an object). In this book, *shortcut* means a pointer, *shortcut menu* refers to the menu that appears when you right-click, and *keyboard shortcut* indicates a key combination.

The Taskbar

The taskbar spans the bottom of the screen (unless someone's clicked and dragged it to another part of the desktop). The area to the left is called the Quick Launch toolbar because it acts as a launching pad for programs you access all the time. In the middle is the main body of the taskbar, and that's where the icons representing each open program reside. On the other end of the taskbar is the system tray. Think of it as a notification area showing system processes that could be of interest. For example, when the modem or printer is active, you see a modem or printer icon in the tray.

See Also   Brush up your taskbar skills a little later in this chapter in the section entitled "Task-bars Translated Here."

Instant Gratification: 5½ Ways to Make Windows Easier Right Now

If you've used Windows 98 at all, you can take advantage of five big tips (plus a small one) to make your time with Windows more trouble-free now—not later.

1. Let Wizards Do the Work

Windows 98 comes equipped with more than a dozen wizards to guide you through some potentially vexing procedures. Sometimes the wizards start themselves—for example, when you select Modems in Control Panel. If you're not sure how to do something, click Start and select Help. On the Index tab, type **wizards** in the text box and a list appears. Select one and the instructions for starting the wizard display in the right pane (as shown in Figure 1-2).

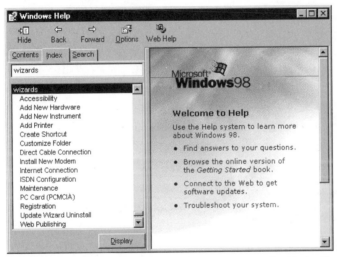

Figure 1-2 Select a wizard from the list in the left pane and click Display. Then follow the instructions; it couldn't be easier.

2. Organize Your Shortcuts

Because shortcuts take up so little space and are so useful, they are a convenient way to get the things you need quickly. For example, on my desktop, I have a shortcut to the folder shown in Figure 1-3. As you can see, inside the folders are more shortcuts to postage programs and Internet shortcuts to the postal service and other shipping companies.

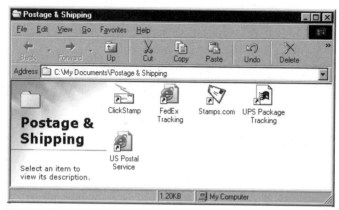

Figure 1-3 Organizing sets of shortcuts into like-minded groups helps you find items quickly.

Organize other files into folders, such as *Finances*, which could include financial software, a spreadsheet, budget records, and so on. While you're at it, add a shortcut to your printer and an Internet shortcut to your bank's online services. The best part is that none of this has to make any sense to anyone else— you're free to arrange everything to suit yourself.

3. Get One-Click Access to All Your Favorite Folders

Create a folder in My Documents (or another location) and give it an imaginative name like *My Stuff*. Put shortcuts to all your favorite folders inside this folder. Make a shortcut to the folder and then drag and drop the shortcut to Start. The shortcut is now on the Start menu (see Figure 1-4), and with a single click you have access to all your favorite folders without cluttering up the desktop.

Figure 1-4 Drag and drop a shortcut to Start to add the shortcut to the Start menu.

See Also   *Unclear about the role of folders in the larger scheme of things? Enlightenment awaits in Chapter 4, "Working with Files and Folders."*

---

4. Make Use of the Keyboard

For programs or folders you open frequently, set up a key combination that starts a program or opens a folder for you. First, make a shortcut to the program or folder then follow these steps.

1   Right-click the shortcut and select Properties.

2   On the Shortcut tab, select the Shortcut Key field.

3   Type a single letter and Windows adds Ctrl+Alt (see Figure 1-5). For example, if you enter a *K*, the keyboard combination becomes Ctrl+Alt+K.

4   Click OK when you're finished.

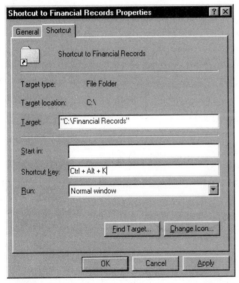

Figure 1-5 Click the Shortcut Key field and enter a single letter. The instant you do, the letter is turned into the keyboard combination of Ctrl+Alt+*<Yourletter>*.

To remove a keyboard shortcut, select the Shortcut Key field and press the Backspace key.

Tip   It's best to limit the number of these keyboard shortcuts because they have precedence in Windows. For example, if you define a keyboard combination that's also used *in* a program, the program loses the ability to use that key combination.

A list of keyboard shortcuts already assigned in Windows 98 can be found in the "Using Different Keyboards" section of Chapter 10.

---

5. Take Advantage of Your Mouse

Everyone who's ever used any version of Windows up to and including Windows 98 knows the drill when it comes to using a mouse or other pointing device. It's click once to select, double-click to open. In Windows 98, at long last, you can change the mouse settings to a single click for everything. That is, you point at an item to select it and click once to open it. Here's how to make the change.

1 Click Start, select Settings, and then click Folder Options.

2 On the General tab, click Settings.

3 At the bottom of Custom Settings dialog box (Figure 1-6), change the Click Items As Follows settings to the single-click option.

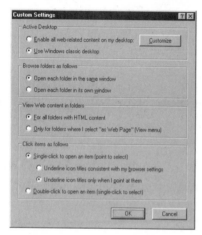

Figure 1-6 Set the mouse to use just a single click.

If you're an accomplished mouser, it might take some time to get used to the new setting. On the other hand, there's no disgrace in staying with the traditional way or in switching back to it later.

Note Throughout this book, we assume you're using the traditional click once to select and double-click to open. If you use this tip, you'll have to make the mental translation.

---

5 ½. Use the Right Mouse Button

By the *right* mouse button, we don't mean the *correct* button; we mean the button on the right side of the mouse. If you are a left-handed mouser, the button we're talking about is on the left side of the mouse.

If you're stuck and don't know what to do, try the right mouse button first. Click it when your cursor is almost anywhere on the desktop, and a helpful shortcut menu opens. The choices on the menu vary depending on the context. It's surprising how often some useful information pops up.

Starting and Stopping

Turning your computer on and off is a simple process, but what's going on inside is a good deal more complex. The next sections of this chapter cover how to do these tasks. If you are content not knowing these details, feel free to go on to something you find more interesting.

In the Beginning

There are actually two separate startup processes, and they run one after the other. First the computer goes through its own startup and then the operating system starts. The whole process is called *booting* and may take up to several minutes.

Lingo   When a computer is turned on (a *cold boot*) or reset (a *warm boot*) it launches software that then launches the operating system. The name *booting* comes from the notion that the computer is pulling itself up by its own bootstraps.

If you have more than one operating system installed, the system pauses for you to select the one to be started. The system checks your network connections (if any) and your individual computer settings.

When Windows 98 finishes loading, a logon box appears on the screen. If the computer is a single machine, not connected to others through a local area network (LAN), you can use a password, although it's pointless. A password provides an illusion of security. Whereas it's true that no one can log on as you without your password, it's also true that anyone can sign on using another name (or no name) and no password at all. If you want your computer to be safe from that sort of incursion, you must make the computer itself *physically* secure.

See Also   See Chapter 11, "Playing it Safe," for ways to make your Windows 98 computer more secure.

If your Windows 98 machine is connected to a network, enter your user name and password in the boxes provided. The log on is then validated against the list of user accounts stored on the nearest domain controller (if you belong to a Windows 2000 or Windows NT domain). If the log on is validated, the Windows 98 desktop appears. Otherwise, you're prompted to enter your user name and password again (correctly this time).

Caution   If you enter an incorrect password several times (sometimes as few as three times, depending on the password policy in effect on the network), the system locks you out, and you have to go to a network administrator to get your password reset. Most embarrassing.

One Computer, Many Users

Everyone sets up Windows in a slightly different way. This is great—until you must share your computer with someone else. If you're the sort of person who likes a plain and tidy desktop and you have to share with your sister who likes Day-Glo colors and fifty icons scattered around, you will surely go mad. Fortunately, something called Profiles keeps everyone sane. You must log on with a password, but once you do, the desktop that appears is yours and yours alone. The color scheme, icons, shortcuts, and fonts are all just as you arranged. When your sister with lurid tastes logs on, her desktop appears the way she likes it.

Setting Up a User Profile

On installation, Windows 98 assumes that the computer has a single user. Therefore, if you share the computer, you need to tell Windows to allow user profiles.

1   Click Start, select Settings, and then Control Panel. In Control Panel, double-click Passwords to open the Password Properties dialog box.

2   Click the User Profiles tab. Select the Users Can Customize Their Preferences… option.

3   Select the options or settings you want individual users to be able to change and save:

   ● Desktop icons and Network Neighborhood settings

   ● Start menu and Program groups

   You can allow either, both, or none of these. Changes that other users make affect only their profiles.

4   Click OK when you're finished.

Once user profiles are enabled, every user has to sign on with a user name and password. The first time a new user logs on, the desktop looks the same as it did at the time user profiles were enabled. Nevertheless, all changes, subject to the restrictions you set in step 3 above, are saved for that user.

Removing a User Profile

To delete a user profile, log on with a username and password other than the one to be deleted. Select Users in Control Panel. Highlight the user profile you want to remove (Figure 1-7) and click the Delete button.

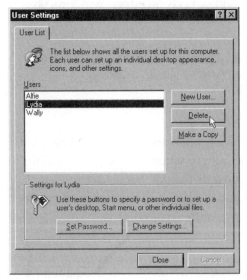

Figure 1-7 Deleting a user account is even easier than adding one.

You can bypass all user profiles at startup by clicking Cancel in the dialog box that asks for name and password—so don't be misled into thinking that profiles are security devices; they're strictly for convenience.

Shutting Down

All versions of Windows are persnickety about being shut down properly. It is the nature of Windows to have pieces of itself all over your memory and hard drive. Windows programs are similarly prone to wandering. The shutdown procedure allows Windows to delete temporary files and shut down the many processes working in the background.

Click Start and select Shut Down from the menu. Click Shut Down and then OK in the dialog box; Windows takes it from there. After the programs and Windows gear is properly stowed, the message It Is Now Safe To Turn Off Your Computer appears. (Some computers—particularly laptops with advanced power management features—turn themselves off.)

Alas, sometimes the best plans go awry and you accidentally or deliberately hit the computer's reset button, making it impossible for Windows to do its required housekeeping. When you start the computer again, a screen announces that the computer wasn't shut down properly, and a program called Scandisk checks your hard drive for errors. After Scandisk finds no errors, Windows 98 starts as usual.

See Also In the event that Scandisk finds errors, you are asked what you want to do about it. See Chapter 12, "Maintaining a Healthy Computer," for help in making that decision.

Deciphering the Start Menu

The Start menu is the door into just about every nook and cranny of Windows 98. However, it's not always the most direct route to where you're going and the road signs aren't the clearest. The next sections include details about major entries on the Start Menu and referrals to more extensive information. If you feel you've mastered the Start Menu and all its features, pass on by.

The Run Command

The Run command is a quick way to the *command line*. If you need a full DOS window, you can open one by selecting Start and then Programs and then the MS-DOS Prompt.

Lingo The *command line* is where a user enters a command to the system. The command can be as simple as the name of a program or as complex as a long list of instructions. Windows was invented to do away with the command line, so you rarely need to use it.

If you don't know which path you want, use the Browse button to look around. Click the down arrow next to the text box to view a drop-down list of recent Run command entries.

See Also   *If you're having trouble running old DOS programs, you can obtain a little sympathy and a lot of assistance in "Running DOS Programs" in Chapter 3. Confused about paths? See "All About Paths" in Chapter 3.*

Finding the Lost

Losing files on a computer is common. Hard drives are immense, programs can save files in odd places if you're not paying careful attention, and some files just seem to have a will of their own. Therefore, it's obligatory that a Windows 98 user become adept at using the Find tool. Fortunately, it's a good deal easier than trying to find a misplaced paper file in a filing cabinet.

For a general system-wide search of your computer, use the Start menu approach. Click Start, then Find, then Files Or Folders to open the dialog box shown in Figure 1-8.

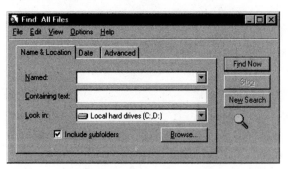

Figure 1-8 Use this dialog box to conduct system-wide searches.

Exactly how you use Find depends on what you already know about the lost or strayed item, as you'll learn in the following sections.

When You Know What You're Looking For

If you already know the file or folder's name—or even part of the name—you can use that in your search.

1   Click Start, then Find, and then click Files Or Folders.

2   Type in the file name—either whole or in part. You don't need to know how the file begins or ends. For example, a search for files with *part* in their names yielded the results shown in Figure 1-9 on next page.

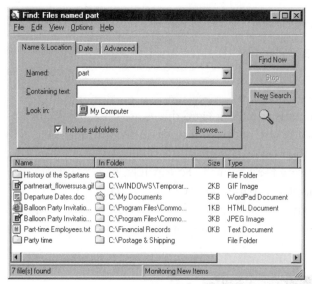

Figure 1-9 A search for files with *part* in their names yields a widely divergent list.

3   The Look In box tells the program where to search. If you haven't a clue, use the drop-down list or Browse to select My Computer. The program searches everywhere on the system.

4   Click Find Now to start the search.

Tip   To force the program to search for the name exactly as you enter it, including uppercase and lowercase letters, select Case Sensitive from the Options menu.

When You Don't Know Enough to Search by Name

Occasionally you don't know enough of the name to make a search, or all you know is enough to get hundreds of results. If you have an idea when the file was created or when it was last opened or worked on, you can use the Date tab of the Find dialog box. You can specify a search between two dates or look for files dated within some previous number of months or days. Specifying a search between two dates is made easier by the calendar that appears when you click the drop-down arrow of either date box. Base the search on the date the file was last modified, or the date of last access, or on the date it was originally created.

When You Know Practically Nothing

Perhaps it's even worse than the previous scenarios—perhaps all you know is that the document you're seeking was written using Microsoft Word and addressed to a company in Schenectady. In that case, you're actually in luck. Select Start and then Find and click Files or Folders. Type **Schenectady** in the Containing Text field on the Name and Location tab. Then click the Advanced tab and select the file type (see Figure 1-10).

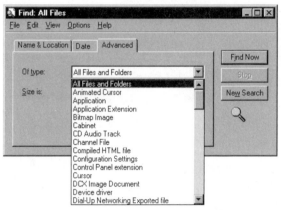

Figure 1-10 Searches will be faster if you can narrow your objective to a single file type.

Searches can be based on any combination of the choices in Find. Of course, the more you can tell the program, the faster the search.

Tip   Search for multiple files or file types. For example, to search for all files with names that begin with Sat, Sun, and Mon, type **Sat*.*, Sun*.*, Mon*.*** in the Named text box. A comma is necessary between entries. A space is optional.

Saving Search Results

When you've made a particularly long and complex search, you might have several results that you want to check out. To avoid repeating the search, save the results by choosing Save Search from the File menu. The search results are saved in the form of an icon on the desktop. Select the icon to re-open the Find dialog box with the search results displayed.

Tip   Press F3 to open a Find dialog box wherever you are.

The Documents Folder

Whether you spend much of the day working with many documents or just a few, click Start and select Documents to display a list of files you've worked with recently. To open one, select it and the file opens in the application that created it.

To clear the Documents menu follow these steps.

1   Click Start and select Settings, followed by Taskbar & Start Menu.

2   Click the Start Menu Programs tab and then click Clear in the Document Menu frame.

The Documents folder is emptied and starts reconstructing a list of recent documents as you use them.

But what if you want to remove some of the files in the Documents menu and leave others? That's a little more complicated because the content of the Documents menu is in a hidden folder; nevertheless, it is possible. Just follow these steps:

1   Click Start, select Settings, and then Folder Options.

2   In the Folder Options dialog box, click the View tab. In the Advanced Settings window, under Hidden files, select Show All Files. Click OK.

3   Next, right-click Start and click Explore.

4   In the left pane, click the plus sign next to the drive Windows is installed on and then click the plus sign next to the Windows folder to open the subfolders.

5   Click the Recent folder. The contents of the Documents menu appear in the right pane of Windows Explorer. Delete the files you choose.

When you return to the Documents list on the Start menu, the deleted files are no longer listed. To return hidden files to their former unseen status, return to Folder Options and change the hidden files option back to Do Not Show Hidden or System Files.

Note   Clearing the Documents list does *not* delete the files from the hard disk because the list is made up of shortcuts to the documents, not the documents themselves.

Using Windows Update

To use the Windows Update feature, you need to upgrade to Windows Internet Explorer 6. Internet Explorer 5 or 5.1 work also—but not Internet Explorer 4. However, if you have version 5 or 5.1, it's worth the few minutes it takes to download and install Internet Explorer 6. To see which version you have now, launch Internet Explorer and then choose About Internet Explorer from the Help menu.

See Also   *For help in upgrading Windows Internet Explorer, see Chapter 6, "Fearless Web Browsing."*

Apart from the slight hiccup of upgrading Windows Internet Explorer, Windows Update couldn't be simpler. You choose Windows Update from the Start menu and Internet Explorer connects you to the Windows Update site. Click the Product Updates link for a list of available updates (Figure 1-11).

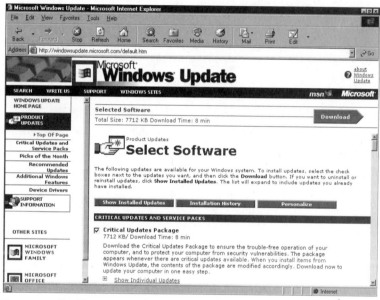

Figure 1-11 The Windows Update site looks slightly different each time you visit. The categories remain the same, but the content changes.

If you haven't used Windows Update before, you have some catching up to do. The list of updates is fairly daunting, but fortunately you won't want or need all of them. Definitely spend some time perusing the entries under Critical Updates and Service Packs. These sections are the most vital.

The next most important entry is Recommended Updates. Inspect these with an eye to which ones would be helpful to you. Other categories, Picks Of The Month, Additional Windows Features, and Device Drivers, may or may not be of interest.

Select the updates you want and then click Download. Don't worry about tracking which ones you accepted because the next time you connect to Windows Update, the site shows which updates you've already installed.

Tip   Do download Windows Critical Update Notification in the Recommended Updates section. You won't have to remember to visit the Update site periodically, because when you're online this small program checks to see if there are any Critical Updates that you don't have and notifies you when they're available.

Customizing the Start Menu

Everyone has a stable of programs used every day. It might be as few as two or as many as a half-dozen or more. Undoubtedly, you'd like to access some of these programs without searching around the desktop or through the menus. The Start menu and the Quick Launch toolbar (see "Toolbars on the Taskbar" later in this chapter) are the best spots for programs you use every day.

Adding to the Start Menu

To add a program to the top of the Start menu, click a shortcut, drag it to the Start button, and drop it on top. Then when you next click Start, the program is instantly available.

If the program is buried several folders deep, it's easier to use these steps.

1   Click Start, then Settings, and then Taskbar & Start Menu.

2   Click the Start Menu Programs tab and then click Add.

3   If you know the location of the program, enter it in the Command Line text box. Otherwise, click Browse and poke around until you find the program. Select the program file and then click Open.

4   Click Next, then select the Start folder for the new program, and click Next.

5   Accept the suggested name for the menu item or provide a new one. Click Finish.

Tip   The Advanced button on the Start menu Programs page opens Windows Explorer so you can do more extensive browsing for items you might want to add to the Start menu.

Deleting from the Start Menu

You remove programs from the Start menu by reversing the add process. Right-click the item and drag it to the desktop, then choose Move Here from the short-cut menu that appears. If the program can't be dragged from the Start menu, follow these steps.

1   Click Start, then Settings, then Taskbar & Start Menu.

2 Click the Start Menu Programs tab and then click Remove.

3 Select a program you want to remove and then click Remove. Repeat these steps for any additional programs.

Taskbars Translated Here

The taskbar is at the bottom of the screen—although you can move it to the top or either side of the screen by clicking and dragging it to the new location. The taskbar is a handy repository for your open programs and can be set up to help you conveniently use programs you need most often, connect to the Internet (or an intranet) address, and track what's going on in the system.

To save desktop space, you can choose to hide the taskbar. It'll reappear when you move the mouse pointer over the area where it normally appears. To hide the taskbar, click Start, select Settings, then Taskbar & Start Menu. Click the Auto Hide check box.

To reverse the setting and make the taskbar always visible, even when a program is running full screen, follow the previous procedure and click the Always On Top check box.

Changing the Taskbar's Appearance

Many elements of the taskbar can be changed to suit your preferences. For example, you can choose to make the following changes to your taskbar:

■ Click and drag the edge of the taskbar to make it wider or narrower.

■ Right-click a blank area of the Quick Launch toolbar and choose View from the shortcut menu to choose between displaying large or small icons.

■ To save precious taskbar space, right-click any other visible toolbars and clear Show Text and Show Title.

Toolbars on the Taskbar

Usually, you have to use Windows 98 for a while before you discover the toolbars that are configured through the taskbar. Use as many or as few as you want, though using several can crowd the taskbar.

To display a particular toolbar, right-click a blank spot on the taskbar and select Toolbars from the shortcut menu. In the list of available toolbars, click a toolbar name to select it. Toolbars with check marks are already displaying. To remove a toolbar, click the name to remove the check mark.

Quick Launch Toolbar

By default, one of the toolbars—the Quick Launch toolbar—is already dis-played when Windows 98 is installed. It's even more useful than the Start menu as a place providing instant access to popular programs. The shortcuts on the Quick Launch toolbar can be dragged off the toolbar, and other shortcuts can be added. In fact, you can make the Quick Launch toolbar as large as you want, but at a certain point expanding the toolbar leaves too little space for the other func-tions of the taskbar.

   Everyone who is upgrading from Windows 95 to Windows 98 welcomes the Desktop icon on the Quick Launch toolbar.

   At last, you can minimize all the open windows on the desktop with one click. Just click the Desktop icon and everything open is minimized to the task-bar. Click the Desktop icon a second time to restore all the minimized windows, or you can restore them one at a time from the taskbar. Normally, many dialog boxes won't minimize—file properties and wizard dialog boxes, for example. Even these, however, are forced to the taskbar when you click the Desktop icon.

Address Toolbar

To display the Address toolbar, right-click a blank spot on the taskbar and select Toolbars from the shortcut menu. Select the Address toolbar and an address text box displays on the taskbar.

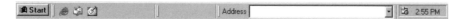

   Enter Internet addresses or local intranet addresses for a quick connection. You can even enter local addresses to quickly open a folder on your hard drive. Click the arrow to the side of the text box to open a list of past addresses you've entered.

Links Toolbar

To display the Links toolbar, right-click a blank spot on the taskbar and select Toolbars from the shortcut menu. Select Links to display the same links that appear on the Internet Explorer Links toolbar. Like the Address toolbar, this is another way to make quick connections—in this case to the sites represented by the links.

See Also   *Links are properly a part of Internet Explorer. Check Chapter 6 for information about how to make and use links.*

Desktop Toolbar

Although it's true that you can always access the desktop by clicking the Desktop icon in the Quick Launch toolbar, you can also make a toolbar where every icon on the desktop is represented.

A Desktop toolbar looks like this when it's first set up.

You might well ask, what's the purpose of this? Not much. However, if you right-click this toolbar and clear Show Text and Show Title, the toolbar becomes small enough to be used.

Custom Toolbars

To create a toolbar with content of your own making, right-click the taskbar, select Toolbars, and then click New Toolbar. A dialog box opens like the one shown in Figure 1-12. Select a folder.

Figure 1-12 Select the folder to be displayed as a toolbar.

Tip   Earlier in this chapter, the third tip under the "Instant Gratification" heading described making a folder of shortcuts to go on the Start menu. Similarly, you can make a folder containing shortcuts to your favorite programs, and folders can be made into a custom toolbar and placed on the taskbar instead of the Start menu.

To delete a custom toolbar, right-click the taskbar and select Toolbars from the shortcut menu. A checkmark next to the name of a toolbar indicates that it's active. Select a custom toolbar to delete it. The default toolbars remain available on the toolbar menu whether selected or not. A custom toolbar evaporates when cleared, so you must recreate the custom toolbar if you want to use it again. (In contrast, a folder of shortcuts dragged to the Start menu remains on the menu until dragged off again.)

Adjusting Toolbar Size and Location

If you don't care for the default size or location of the toolbar, change it. On the taskbar, toolbars are set apart from one another by two vertical bars.

Move the mouse pointer until it's over a set of bars and the pointer changes to a two-headed arrow. Drag the bars to the left or right to make the toolbar larger or smaller.

To change the *location* of individual toolbars, click the vertical bars next to the Start button and drag the Quick Launch toolbar to the right side of the taskbar. To change locations again, grab the same vertical bars next to Start and drag to the right.

Click a blank spot towards the left on a Links, Address, or Custom toolbar, and you can drag it onto the desktop.

Note   The Quick Launch toolbar can be dragged to change its location on the taskbar, although it stubbornly refuses to be dragged onto the desktop.

Key Points

■ Starting Windows involves two processes—first the computer goes through its own startup (basically hardware checking), and then the operating system starts.

■ Through the use of user profiles, several people can share a single computer.

■ The Start menu is the gateway to just about every function in Windows 98, although it might not be the only, or even the best, way to perform a task.

■ The Start Menu can be made more useful by adding and removing entries.

■ Taskbars and toolbars can be made even more useful tools by configuring them according to the way you want to use them.

Chapter 2

Covering the Desktop

Generally, there are two approaches to the desktop. One maintains that the desktop is best kept clean with all files put away in their proper location (such as the My Documents folder). We call this the "a place for everything and everything in its place" approach.

The second viewpoint has it that everything useful (or potentially useful) should be placed on the desktop for easy access. It may look untidy but it's functional. These two philosophies are unlikely to be reconciled any time soon, so Microsoft Windows 98 takes the middle ground and starts with a minimalist approach, allowing users to add as much clutter as they like and making each approach equally easy to use.

The Desktop Icons

Windows 98 installs a number of icons on the desktop during setup. Depending on how Windows 98 was installed and how it's been used, some icons will remain on your desktop and others may have been removed. The icons that are sure to be there are My Computer, My Documents, Recycle Bin, and possibly Network Neighborhood.

■ **My Documents** My Documents is the default location for documents created by most applications, and this icon is a shortcut to this folder, even though it lacks the arrow in the lower-left corner that normally indicates a shortcut. Because it's convenient to have this folder at hand, the icon stays on the desktop unless removed.

- **Internet Explorer**   Starts Microsoft Internet Explorer.

- **Online Services**   Contains software for connecting to companies that provide Internet access.

- **Outlook Express**   Starts the Internet mail and newsgroup client that comes with Windows 98.

- **Set Up The Microsoft Network**   Microsoft gives its own online service a prominent position on the desktop.

The permanent desktop icons—as distinguished from the removable ones above and the transient shortcuts that come and go at your whim—are My Computer, Recycle Bin, and Network Neighborhood. These, plus My Documents, are also called System icons. Although you may have more than a casual acquaintance with these tools, stay tuned. They have more powers than you might imagine.

My Computer

The My Computer icon is on every Windows 98 desktop. Double-click My Computer to see icons for all your drives, plus folders for Control Panel, Printers, Dial-Up Networking, and perhaps a few other items, depending on configuration choices made either during installation or later. My Computer is one of several ways to acquire information about all these subjects.

See Also   See the section "Windows Explorer and My Computer" later in this chapter for a discussion of My Computer and Microsoft Windows Explorer as navigational tools.

If the name My Computer is just too Mr. Rogers for your taste, right-click the icon and select Rename from the menu. Type a new name.

Network Neighborhood

The Network Neighborhood icon is on the desktop if you're connected to a Local Area Network (LAN). It opens to reveal the network resources available to you—drives or folders on other computers and network printers, for example.

See Also   Using an existing network or building your own is covered in Chapter 13, "Building and Using a Network."

If you're not connected to a network and have no expectation of ever being connected to one yet you still have a Network Neighborhood icon hanging around bugging you, see the section in Chapter 5 entitled "Getting Rid of Network Neighborhood."

Recycle Bin

The Recycle Bin is a permanent icon on the desktop representing a storage area on the hard disk for deleted files. It's insurance against the inevitable accidental deletion of an important file.

Despite the name, the deleted files aren't actually recycled unless you rescue them from the bin before they're deleted permanently. Nevertheless, the Recycle Bin provides a nice margin of safety. When you delete a file you have days or even weeks (depending on how you set things up) to change your mind and retrieve it.

Remember two important facts about the Recycle Bin:

- The Recycle Bin icon can't be renamed or deleted—though you can change the icon.

- Files that are deleted using DOS programs or any program that is not an integral part of Windows 98 are not sent to the Recycle Bin. They're just deleted—forever and ever.

The Recycle Bin retains your deleted files for as long as you want, and you can adjust the security level from "just a little" to "all I can get" to match your personal comfort level.

See Also   See the section entitled "Learning to Recycle" in Chapter 4 for all the details on configuring the Recycle Bin for your own using pleasure.

Managing Icons

The rules for altering icons depend on the type of icon being modified. (Wouldn't you just know it?) Shortcut icons are generally configurable. Program icons can sometimes be changed. File and folder icons usually can't be changed. System icons, My Computer, the Recycle Bin, My Documents, and Network Neighborhood can be changed but require a special method.

See Also   More than any sensible person needs to know about shortcuts, including how to make them, starts in the section entitled "Making and Using Shortcuts" in this chapter.

Changing System Icons

Because system icons live on the desktop, changes to them are done through desktop properties.

1 Right-click a blank spot on the desktop and select Properties from the shortcut menu.

2 In the Display Properties dialog box, click the Effects tab. In the Desktop Icons pane, select the icon you want to change and then click Change Icon.

3 Select an icon from the Change Icon dialog box and then click OK.

To return to the original icon, you need only to select the icon on the Effects page and then click the Default Icon button.

Just What Are Properties? Just about everything on the desktop (and everywhere else in your Windows 98 system) has properties attached to it. To display the properties for an object in a dialog box, right-click the object and select Properties.

What you find can vary from the single sheet of information attached to a typical file to the multi-page extravaganza for display properties. The role of the Properties dialog box is to provide you with information on the object and allow modification of some settings.

If the object is a file or a folder, you'll get information about the object's size, location, dates created and modified, and attributes. If the object is a piece of hardware or the desktop (or anything on the desktop, like the taskbar or the Recycle Bin), the Properties dialog box has multiple tabs and covers all the possible settings for the object in question.

As a rule, when you see something you don't understand or just want to know more about, try the Properties dialog box first. You can often find as much as you need to know right there and save yourself a trip to the Help system.

Adjusting the Icon Arrangement

By default, the icons on your desktop can be dragged hither and yon and will stay where you put them. To have your icons snap to a grid, right-click the desktop and select Line Up Icons from the shortcut menu.

For a tidier look, right-click the desktop and point to Arrange Icons and then click Auto Arrange on the shortcut menu. This adds a check mark to Auto Arrange and all your icons will be organized in neat rows and columns.

Changing Icon Spacing

In general, the Auto Arrange function produces a good alignment of icons in columns and rows. In some cases, however, your icons may appear to be too close together, particularly if some icons have long names.

To adjust the amount of space between icons without rearranging them one by one, follow these steps. Auto Arrange must be turned on.

1   Right-click a blank spot on the desktop and select Properties from the shortcut menu.

2   In the Display Properties dialog box, click the Appearance tab. In the Item drop-down list, select Icon Spacing (Horizontal) or Icon Spacing (Vertical).

3   Adjust the number down or up (the default setting for both is 43 pixels). Make modest changes and click Apply after each change to test the new setting.

4   Click OK when you're finished.

Changing the Size of Icons

Your monitor's resolution or your eyesight might require a change in the size of desktop icons. To enlarge desktop icons, follow these steps:

1   Right-click the desktop and select Properties from the shortcut menu.

2   Click the Effects tab.

3   In the Visual Effects frame, click the Use Large Icons check box.

4   Click Apply to see if the effect is what you wanted. (Figure 2-1 shows the screen with large icons.) If you don't like it, clear the check box and try the next effect.

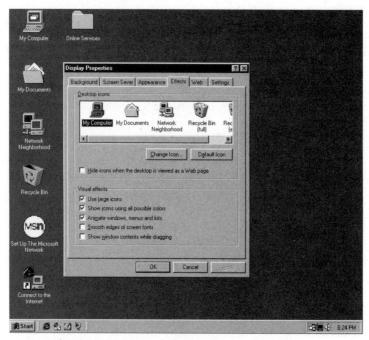

Figure 2-1 Try the large icons if the default ones are too puny.

For a more precise method of enlarging or shrinking desktop icons, follow these steps.

1 Right-click the desktop and select Properties from the shortcut menu.

2 In the Display Properties dialog box, click the Appearance tab. Select Icon from the Item drop-down list.

3 Change the number in the Size box to something larger or smaller than the default size of 32 pixels. (The minimum size is 16 and the maximum is 72.)

4 Click Apply to check what the new size looks like. Click OK when you're satisfied.

Bear in mind that if you make the icons much smaller than the default, the resultant spacing may be too tight—even if you don't change the horizontal and vertical icon spacing settings. Figure 2-2 shows icons at 20 pixels. Even if there appears to be lots of space between icons, many of the names are truncated. If you want smaller icons, you'll undoubtedly need to change the spacing settings as well.

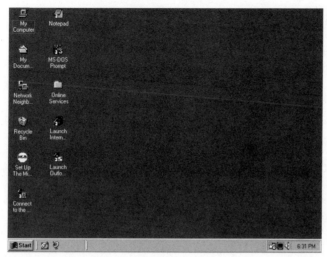

Figure 2-2 Very small icons may require a change in icon spacing if you're to see the whole name.

Making and Using Shortcuts

Windows 98 rarely offers only one way to do something. Most of us find one method of doing a task and never realize other—perhaps better—ways are available to us. For example, you can open the Start menu and click the program application you want to start. You can also create a shortcut for that program, place it on the desktop or the Quick Launch toolbar, and click it when you want to launch the program. Alternatively, you might put a shortcut to the program in a folder where you often work.

Shortcuts introduce a new level of convenience and customization to Windows. They're meant to be easy ways to access everything on your computer or network: documents, applications, folders, printers, and so on.

When you right-click and drag and drop an object from one location to another, a menu opens asking whether you want to move, copy, or create a shortcut, as shown below.

A shortcut is identified by the small arrow in the lower-left corner of the icon. The arrow is a reminder that the icon is only pointer to a real application or file or device. The distinction is important because you can delete a shortcut at will with no consequences (other than having to create it again if the need arises). Deleting an original program or file (not a copy) requires reinstallation or rummaging around in the Recycle Bin to retrieve it. Moreover, if it's a while before you notice it's missing, the Recycle Bin may have been emptied and the object would be gone.

If you put a shortcut to a file on your desktop and later delete it, the file on the hard drive remains. If you delete the file on the hard drive, the shortcut is still there but there's nothing for it to point to. On the other hand, if you move the file to another folder or even another drive and then click the shortcut, Windows searches for it—and usually finds it.

Shortcuts are an excellent tool for configuring your Desktop. Create shortcuts to folders, to programs, and to individual files—in fact to any Windows 98 object. Arrange shortcuts any way you want on the desktop, inside other folders, or on menus.

Creating Shortcuts

The Create Shortcut option appears in many places, including:

- On an object's shortcut menu.
- On various drop-down menus.
- On the desktop shortcut menu. Right-click the desktop and select New and then Shortcut.

Because shortcuts are pointers to objects, you need to either find the object you want to create a shortcut for or be able to tell Windows 98 where the object is located.

The easiest way to create a shortcut is to use My Computer or Windows Explorer to locate the object. Then right-click the object and select Create Shortcut. A new icon named Shortcut appears. However, some special circumstances apply, depending on the object's location, as discussed in the following section.

Creating a Shortcut When You Can See the Object

To create a shortcut when you have the original object or a shortcut to the object in view, right-click the object or shortcut and select Create Shortcut from the shortcut menu. The new shortcut includes the name of the program or file.

Note Shortcuts made from other shortcuts are clones and work identically.

Creating a Shortcut When You Can't See the Object

If the original object isn't handy or you don't want to go hunting for it (which means you probably can't remember where it is or never knew in the first place), you can still create a shortcut if you follow these steps.

1   Right-click the Desktop and click New and then Shortcut on the shortcut menu.

2   In the dialog box, type the location and name of the original object. If you don't know the path (and who ever does?), click Browse.

3   Using the Browse dialog box, mouse around until you find the file or object you want. You might have to change the Files Of Type item in the Browse dialog box to the All Files option.

4   Select the file (its name appears in the File Name text box) and click Open. The Command line box now contains the path and name of the object.

5   Click Next and accept or change the name for the shortcut.

6   Click Finish and the shortcut appears on your Desktop.

Renaming a Shortcut

When you create a shortcut, Windows 98 gives the shortcut the name of the object the shortcut is pointing to. In most cases, Shortcut To precedes the name. Because you already know how a shortcut looks, you might want to shorten the name or alter it. To rename the shortcut, right-click the icon and select Rename from the menu. Type the name you want and click a blank spot on the desktop when you're finished.

What to Name Shortcuts

When renaming a shortcut, take full advantage of long file names (up to 255 characters). No need to get carried away, but you might as well call a folder March Budget Reports rather than MAR_BUD. As with any file name, certain characters aren't allowed in shortcut names, such as / \ < > | : " ? *. All other keyboard characters are acceptable, including spaces.

Shortcut Settings

As we mentioned earlier in this chapter, every Windows 98 object has properties associated with it—including shortcuts. (To learn more about properties, see the sidebar "Just What Are Properties?" earlier in the chapter.) The configuration options for shortcuts to Windows objects are on the Shortcut tab of the Properties dialog box, as shown in Figure 2-3.

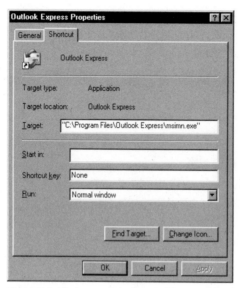

Figure 2-3 Like every other object in Windows 98, each shortcut has properties.

Finding the Target

Need to find the object represented by the shortcut? The path or address for the target, or the object from which the shortcut was created, is available in the Target text box on the Shortcut tab of the Properties dialog box.

If you want to actually go to the shortcut's target, click Find Target. The folder containing the application or file the shortcut represents is displayed. (The target file is highlighted as well.)

Try This! Shortcuts to programs usually display the icon associated with that program. However, you can change the icon for a shortcut by following these steps:

1 Right-click the shortcut icon and select Properties from the shortcut menu.

2 Select the Shortcut tab and click Change Icon. If you want to use one of the icons displayed, select it and click OK. Otherwise, go on to step 3.

3 Use Browse to look in other files. (Moricons.dll in your Windows folder has numerous program icons. Many other icons for printers, dial-up connections, and so forth, are in the shell32.dll file located in the System folder inside the Windows folder.)

4 Select the icon to use. Click OK twice and the new shortcut icon is displayed, taking the place of the old icon.

More icons are available in the form of icon libraries or shareware programs for making your own icons. Try *http://shareware.cnet.com* or *http://www.tucows.com* and search on icons.

Adding a Shortcut to the Send To Menu

When you right-click most files in Windows 98, one of the choices on the short-cut menu is Send To. By default, the Send To menu includes your floppy drive, the My Documents folder, and the Desktop. It might also include shortcuts to mail and fax recipients. You can add other useful items to the menu, such as a printer. Right-click a file icon and select the printer. The application associated with the icon opens and the document prints. Pretty nifty.

The Longer Version

If you're not going to make a habit of adding lots of items to the Send To menu, use the following method to add a shortcut to Send To. With this method you add only the item you specify.

1 Click Start, select Programs, and then Windows Explorer.

2 Locate the Windows folder in the left pane of the Explorer and open it.

3 Locate the SendTo folder and open it.

4 Now drag a shortcut to the item you want to appear on the Send To menu into the SendTo folder.

You may have to open a second instance of Windows Explorer to get at other folders if the shortcuts you want are not on the Desktop. As soon as the shortcut is in the SendTo folder it appears on the Send To menu.

Note   Yes, the folder is called *SendTo* and the menu is called *Send To*. I don't understand either, but there it is.

The Slightly Shorter Version

If you want to add stuff to the Send To menu without going through the previous steps every time, just do the following once.

1 Open a Windows Explorer window and select the Windows folder.

2 Right-click the SendTo folder and select Create Shortcut from the menu. Right-click the new shortcut and select Cut.

3 Open the SendTo folder under Windows.

4 Right-click inside the SendTo folder and select Paste (Figure 2-4).

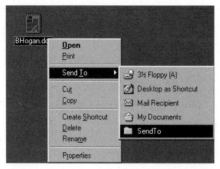

Figure 2-4 Inside the SendTo folder, you can change the name of the new shortcut, getting rid of the Shortcut to SendTo.

Now when you highlight an object and open the Send To menu using the right-click shortcut menu, there's a shortcut to Send To as an option on the menu. You can right-click a program, folder, printer, click Send To, and then click SendTo. The program, folder, or printer is added to the Send To menu.

When the menu becomes too crowded, open the SendTo folder in the Explorer and delete any extra clutter.

Tip   If you add a shortcut to \windows\system\viewers\Quikview.exe to your SendTo folder, you can use the Send To menu to view any file. If the file you select isn't supported by QuickView, the default viewer appears.

Windows Explorer and My Computer

Windows Explorer and My Computer offer the same access to your computer's innards, except with quite different views. Double-click My Computer and a single window opens. Open Windows Explorer and a two-paned window opens. See Figure 2-5.

Figure 2-5 When My Computer (left) and Windows Explorer open by default, they look quite different.

However, if you right-click My Computer and select Explore, when My Computer opens it looks just like Windows Explorer. If you're confused, don't worry about it. Just remember that they're basically the same tool with slightly different looks.

Windows Explorer and My Computer can both do just about anything you need to do, from copying a file to another folder to examining how much space is available on your hard drive. When you install a program, the program's folders are placed on the hard drive—usually in the form of a main folder and subfolders (folders inside the main folder). In Windows 98, most new applications are installed in the folder named Program Files.

In the left pane, folders may have either a plus or minus sign next to them. A plus sign means there are subfolders—click directly on the plus sign to expand the view. When expanded, the plus sign turns into a minus sign.

Tip A desktop shortcut for Windows Explorer can prove very useful. To create one, click the Start button, point to Programs, and then point to Windows Explorer. Right-click Windows Explorer and drag it to the desktop. Release the mouse button and select the option for creating a shortcut, which is Create Shortcut(s) Here. Leave the shortcut on the desktop or drag it to the Quick Launch toolbar so it will always be available.

Using Two Explorers at Once

If you're working with and moving around a number of files or folders, it's easier if you can have two Windows Explorer windows open at once—just select Windows Explorer from the Programs menu for each copy you want.

To arrange the Explorer windows so you can access them easily, right-click the taskbar and select Tile Horizontally or Tile Vertically. Figure 2-6 shows two instances of Explorer tiled vertically.

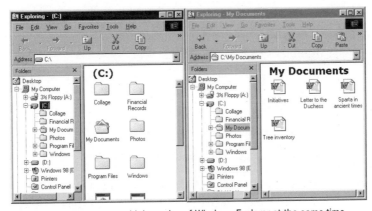

Figure 2-6 You can use multiple copies of Windows Explorer at the same time.

Navigating the Desktop Using Windows Explorer

If you've been using Windows Explorer for a while, you surely don't need the navigational basics; however, some of the tips in the next sections may be news to you.

As mentioned before, when you see a plus sign next to an icon in Windows Explorer, it means that at least one subfolder is inside that folder. Click the plus sign to expand the view. Click a minus sign and the subfolders collapse inside the main folder. You can slide the scroll boxes to view items that are outside the pane view.

Scroll boxes are proportionate in Windows 98. That is, the scroll box shows how much of the pane's content is being displayed. A scroll box that fills half the bar tells you that you're looking at half of what there is to see (in that particular pane).

To open a new folder on the Desktop displaying the contents of a folder, double-click a folder in the left pane of Windows Explorer to display the folder's contents in the right pane. You can also right-click the folder in either pane and choose Open from the shortcut menu.

Changing the Desktop Display

If you spend a lot of time at a computer, it's at least some comfort to know that you can tailor a custom fit for the Windows interface. A well-designed desktop can actually help you work more efficiently and comfortably. This section covers the nips and tucks you can make to the Windows display.

Choosing a Desktop Theme

A whole package of desktop themes comes with Windows 98. Each theme includes wallpaper, special icons and pointers, unique sounds, and a screen saver built around a single motif. Some of the themes are Mystery, Travel, Sports, and Science. Desktop themes aren't installed by default, so to add them, follow these steps. Note that you need to put the Windows 98 installation CD in the CD-ROM drive to install themes.

1   Open Control Panel and select Add/Remove Programs.

2   Click the Windows Setup tab.

3   Highlight Desktop Themes and click Details.

4   Put check marks next to the themes you want and click OK twice.

After the files are copied, close Control Panel and open it again. Select the Desktop Themes icon in the Control Panel. From the Themes drop-down box, select the theme you wish to preview. Figure 2-7 shows the theme called Underwater.

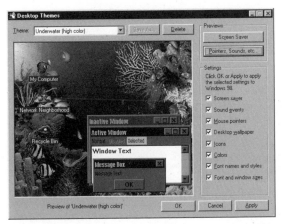

Figure 2-7 Playing with Desktop Themes can be a pleasurable way to waste many hours.

Customizing a Theme

Of course, you may not want an entire desktop theme package as it stands. You may like a particular theme but hate the fonts used or find the sounds annoying. Fortunately, you can get rid of elements you don't like. In the Settings frame, as shown in Figure 2-7, remove the check marks from elements you don't want included.

Rather than guess whether the sounds and pointers that come with a theme are acceptable, you can check them out by clicking Pointers, Sounds in the Previews frame. Figure 2-8 shows the dialog box that opens so you can check out the pointers, sounds, and icons (Visuals) that come with a theme. Highlight the element's name and you can see it in the Preview box. For sounds, click the right-pointing arrowhead to play the selected sound.

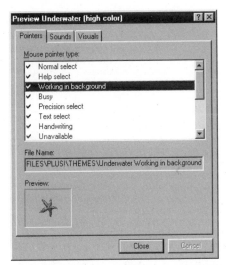

Figure 2-8 Review all the special pointers, sounds, and icons that come with a particular theme.

Some of the desktop themes require what's called High Color settings. If your display adapter can't render more than 256 colors, you might not obtain satisfactory results with the High Color themes. However, it does no harm to try.

Desktop Schemes

To change your desktop's color scheme, right-click the desktop, select Properties, and then click the Appearance tab. Select the Scheme drop-down list to see a long list of possible schemes, as shown in Figure 2-9. Select a color scheme to see a preview.

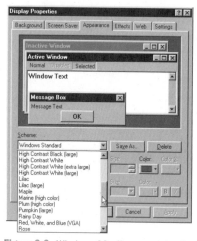

Figure 2-9 Windows 98 offers a variety of schemes to choose from.

Lingo   What, you may ask, is the difference between desktop *schemes* and desktop *themes*? Well, desktop themes, as described earlier, include sounds, special pointers, custom icons, and so forth. A desktop scheme is really just a *color* scheme with some changeable elements, such as font size and selection.

Modifying a Color Scheme

Perhaps you like a particular color scheme except for one or two colors. To change those elements, follow these steps:

1   In the preview box, click the element you want to change—the color of the desktop, the window title bar, or something else.

2   The name of the element appears in the Item drop-down list.

3   What can be changed about the element shows to the right of the Item drop-down list, as shown in Figure 2-10. (Dimmed items can't be changed in the selected color scheme.)

Figure 2-10 In the Slate scheme, many elements have customizable colors and sizes.

4 Click the up and down arrows in the Size box to change the dimensions of the element. Click the Color button(s) to select different colors.

5 If the element you're changing has modifiable text, you can change the typeface, its size, color, and whether it's bold or italic.

When you're done customizing the desktop scheme, click Save As to save the scheme under a name you choose. It is added to the Scheme drop-down list so that you can change schemes later and return to the customized one at any time.

Selecting Wallpaper

Wallpaper is actually the background for your desktop. How a *desktop* setting got to be called *wallpaper* is anyone's guess, but the term has been around as long as the graphical interface. Anyway, Windows 98 comes with a supply of wallpaper—mostly boring, in our opinion. The real fun of wallpaper is in providing your own pictures of your kids or your dog or that beach in Bora Bora that you're determined to visit one day. We'll get to that in a minute. To set up wallpaper available on Windows 98, follow these steps:

1 Right-click a blank spot on the desktop and choose Properties from the shortcut menu.

2 Select the Background tab, if it's not already showing. Click any of the choices in the Wallpaper list and the selection previews in the screen at the top.

3 Experiment with Center, Tile, or Stretch in the Display drop-down list to find the effect you like.

4 Click OK when you're finished.

Note   Most of the wallpaper designs appear different depending on whether you're showing them as centered, tiled, or stretched. The more complicated the design, the more distracting it can be when shown full screen. Everyone's taste is different; experiment to see what you like.

Supplying Your Own Wallpaper

Almost any graphic file format works as wallpaper, although Windows bitmaps are the most common. By default, the only pictures shown in the Wallpaper list are bitmaps that are also in the main Windows folder on your hard drive. To use another picture, you'll need to tell Windows 98 about it.

Here's how to use your own graphic as wallpaper:

1 Right-click a blank spot on the desktop, choose Properties from the shortcut menu, and then click the Background tab.

2 Click Browse. Locate the file you want to use, and click Open.

3 If you like the way the file looks in preview, click OK.

Sometimes a picture selected this way won't appear after a reboot. If that happens, just move the picture file into the Windows folder on your hard drive. Select it again using the above steps, and it should be permanently on the desktop—at least until you decide to change it.

You can use almost any graphics file as wallpaper—look for files with extensions such as .bmp, .gif, .jpg, .tif, or .pcx. However, you're not limited to conventional graphics files. You can also use any HTML page (look for files with the extension .htm). To make any picture into wallpaper, right-click it and select Set As Background.

Choosing Screen Savers

Add screen savers to the list of computer misnomers. At one time—long ago— it could be argued that the constant motion of a screen saver protected your monitor screen from burn-in—that is, the permanent etching of your screen by whatever picture was left on the screen too long.

Burn-in hasn't been a problem for many years, yet screen savers continue to be popular. One reason is that they are the equivalent of covering your work when you leave your desk. The other is that they're entertaining, a good enough reason in itself.

To select one of the screen savers that come with Windows 98, follow these steps:

1 Right-click a blank area of the desktop and choose Properties from the shortcut menu.

2 In the Display Properties dialog box, click the Screen Saver tab.

3 Select a screen saver from the drop-down list box. A sample displays, as shown in Figure 2-11.

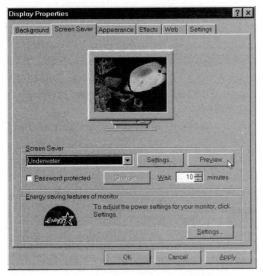

Figure 2-11 Select a screen saver to see a preview.

4 To see the one you've selected in full-screen, click Preview. Move the mouse when you want to return to the dialog box.

5 Click Settings to see what's configurable. This varies depending on the screen saver chosen.

6 Click OK to close the dialog box when you're done.

Adding a Password to the Screen Saver

In general, moving the mouse or pressing any key on the keyboard clears a screen saver. If you're the least bit paranoid about leaving your computer unguarded while you go down the hall to cadge some jelly beans, add a password to the screen saver. Then when the mouse is moved or a key is pressed, a dialog box prompts for the password, and the screen saver won't clear until the correct password is entered.

Caution   It's important to understand that the screen saver password represents only the most minimal level of security. A determined intruder can just reboot your computer and bypass the screen saver password entirely.

To add a password to the screen saver you select, put a check mark in the Password Protected box on the Screen Saver tab shown previously in Figure 2-11. Click Change, type the password twice, and then click OK.

If you want to stop using the password, clear the check mark in the Password Protected box. When you want to start using it again, click to place a check mark in the box again. The password you've typed stays the same until you change it.

Tip   Even though this password is not case sensitive, make no assumptions about other passwords. In general, passwords are *always* case sensitive, so you need to remember whether you used uppercase or lowercase or a mixture of the two.

Help on the Spot

Who needs Help with Windows 98? Sooner or later, *everyone*. Windows 98 has an extensive Help system. If you had all the time in the world, you could undoubtedly find darn near anything. Alas, no one has that kind of time, and if people did, they probably wouldn't want to spend it poking around in Windows. It's important to focus your search for help. The best help is help that is nearest to the problem and context aware. Start your search for answers close to where the problem occurred and only gradually move to a larger area as needed. The following sections are listed in the order they should be tried.

First Press F1

Windows has always allowed the user to press the F1 key to access Help on a selected dialog box option. Well, this easiest of Help methods is still alive and well. At anytime in any Windows 98 dialog box, you can press F1 and access Help on the desktop or the current action you are undertaking. It's quick, it's convenient, and it frequently works.

Click the Right Mouse Button

No luck with F1? Point to the item in question and right-click. If a button labeled What's This? opens, click the button for a description. Not all items have a What's This? button, but it never hurts to ask.

Click the Question Mark

Another Help source is the question mark found on some dialog boxes. Click the question mark, move the pointer to the area you're questioning, and click again. Like the right-click Help, it's in some locations and not others.

Select Help from the Menu Bar

Some windows and dialog boxes have a Help menu or a Help button. Try these next. These Help sources broaden the search possibilities. Nevertheless, it's still confined to the program or dialog box, so the total amount that has to be sorted through is small.

Start Menu Help

No joy? Now it's time to get out the big guns. Select Help from the Start menu. Figure 2-12 shows the three tabs in Windows Help: Contents, Index, and Search. Here's how each works.

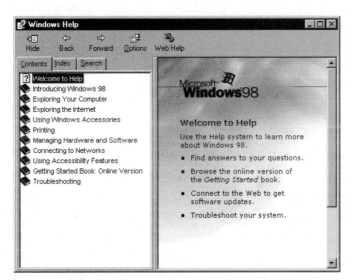

Figure 2-12 Windows Help includes three ways to search for what you need.

On the Contents tab, Help is grouped by overall topic. If you have a question about printing, for example, click that topic to display a list of possible answers. These won't be all the answers about printing, just the most common ones.

The Index tab, not surprisingly, has content arranged like an index. The index content is still listed by keyword but with many more keywords to choose from. This tab works best when searching for an overall topic narrower than the ones displayed on the Contents tab. Therefore, a search for *printing* turns up a long list of subjects, even though what you're looking for may be under *print* or *printer*. Remember to check under other forms of the keyword.

Sometimes you don't know the overall topic your question might be listed under. Let's say you want to know how to hide the toolbar in Windows Explorer. Certainly you can look under hide or toolbar or Windows Explorer on the Index tab, but it's often faster to use the Search tab. Type a word or phrase and click List Topics. Every help item that contains that word or phrase is listed.

Tip   The Search tab isn't the place to type a general topic such as *print* or *display* because every Help entry with the word in it is listed—and that's a lot of entries to look through.

Help on the Web

If you find no help locally, it's time to branch out to the Internet. The place to start is Windows Update (at the top of the Start menu). If you're missing any Windows 98 updates, now is the time to get them.

If your question isn't something that's solvable by an update, click Support on the Windows Update home page banner and select Microsoft Product Support. If you're not visiting by way of Windows Update, type *http:// support.microsoft.com* in the Internet Explorer address bar. On the Help and Support page, click the link for Search The Knowledge Base. Select Windows 98 from the Select A Microsoft Product drop-down menu (Figure 2-13).

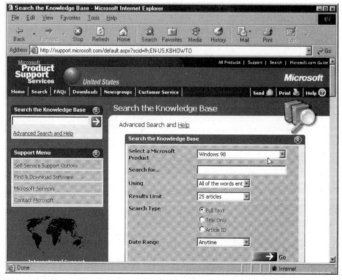

Figure 2-13 Searching the Knowledge Base for Windows 98 Help.

Provide some search words and be as specific as you can. Try for a combination of words or a phrase that's unlikely to be in a zillion different articles, then select The Exact Phrase Entered or All Of The Words Entered in the dialog box. For example, you want to find an article explaining why your scanner can't connect to Windows 98. If you search just for *scanner*, the search identifies 139 articles. Search for *HP scanner* (using the All Of The Words Entered option) and the search identifies 42 articles—still too many. So try *HP scanner not available* and the selection is down to a manageable 3 articles.

If you're having trouble getting a good number of responses, scroll down the page and select from the search alternatives.

The ability to make efficient searches is extremely valuable when you're dealing with the volume of information on the Microsoft support site. It's even more important on the Internet as a whole. However, it's a skill that takes practice, practice, practice, so don't be discouraged if you're not a whiz at it immediately.

Newsgroup Help

Newsgroups are the last place to try—not because they're a poor source of information—to the contrary. However, you should try first to find an answer on your own because the volunteers who answer questions in newsgroups are a limited resource. These folks need to spend their time answering the hard questions.

This is not meant to discourage you from using newsgroups. If you've tried all the above steps and haven't found the answer, you definitely have a hard question.

The easiest way to get to the newsgroups is to type *http:// support.microsoft.com/newsgroups* in the address bar of Internet Explorer. In the Community Newsgroups list, select Windows and then Windows 98. Select a newsgroup that covers your subject.

An important rule for posting a question in a newsgroup—any newsgroup—is to be thorough. If you must, compose your query in advance offline, so you have time to get the information together. It saves time in the end.

If you post something like "How do I make my scanner work with Windows 98?" you may not get an answer at all, and if you do, it'll just be a request for more information. A good question would include the brand and model number of your scanner, how it connects to your computer (serial port, USB port), what error messages you get when trying to scan, how much RAM your computer has, and if the scanner has ever worked, never worked, or works intermittently.

If you don't receive an answer in a day or two, post again. Politely. With even *more* information. Someone will come to your aid.

Key Points

■ The desktop is your working surface; set it up any way that's comfortable for you.

■ The rules for altering icons depend on the type of icon being modified.

■ Shortcuts offer an easy way for documents, applications, folders, and printers to be in many places at the same time.

■ Windows Explorer and My Computer offer the same access to the contents of your computer but with different views.

■ A well tailored desktop can help you work more efficiently and comfortably. Use desktop themes and schemes to enhance your computer use.

■ The Help function begins with the nearest problem. Gradually move to a larger area when necessary.

Chapter 3

Running Programs

Computers exist to run programs. Without programs, computers are just expensive space heaters—although they can function quite well in that role (especially in the summer). Technically speaking, everything that runs on your computer is a program, including Microsoft Windows, which is a special type of program called an operating system.

Lingo *Operating systems* provide an environment for running other programs, as well as providing a file system and various services, such as printing, communications, and networking.

If you've been using Microsoft Windows 98, you probably already know something about running programs—how to start and stop them, how to install new software, as well as how to switch between running applications. If you're a pro at these tasks, just skim through this chapter, keeping your eyes open for useful bits (especially in the Closing Programs section).

Toward the end of the chapter, you'll find sections on running high-performance games and programs not designed for Windows 98.

Opening and Switching Between Programs

Everyone has to open multiple programs and then switch between them. Doing so is easy, although it sometimes takes some tricks to do it efficiently. Background information can increase your understanding of what's going on.

Mechanics of Programs

To use a program, you must start it. Starting a program is also called opening, loading, or launching the program. The program starts when you double-click the program's main executable file (identified by the extension .exe) or, more likely, click an icon in the Start menu that represents the executable file. The program's various parts are retrieved from the hard drive and loaded into *RAM* (Random Access Memory)—where they'll stay until the program is closed. When you're finished using a program, close it so that the memory is freed up for other programs (some memory is also released when you minimize a program).

Lingo *RAM* (Random Access Memory), also called memory, is the computer equivalent of the brain's short term or working memory. RAM is much faster than a hard drive, although more expensive, and it stores data only temporarily. RAM is wiped clean when the computer shuts down.

Launching Programs

To start a program, click the Start button, point to Programs and then select the program you want (it may be located in a subfolder), as shown in Figure 3-1. Here are some other methods and locations from which you can launch programs.

Figure 3-1 The Start menu is the first place to go when starting almost any program.

■ **On the desktop** To create a shortcut for a program on the desktop, right-click the program on the Start menu and drag it to the desktop. When you release the mouse button, choose Create Shortcut Here. Double-click the newly created shortcut to open the program.

- **On the Quick Launch toolbar, located next to the Start button**
  To create a shortcut on the Quick Launch toolbar, drag and drop a program icon to a blank space in the toolbar. Click the newly created shortcut to open the program.

- **In the Startup folder**   Programs in the Startup folder launch every time you start your computer. To add a program to the Startup folder, right-click Start and select Open. Double-click Programs and then Startup. Using the right mouse button, drag and drop a shortcut to the program into the Startup folder.

- **Other methods used more rarely**   One approach is to double-click the program file (for example, Word.exe) in My Computer or Windows Explorer. Or you could type the program file's complete name, *Notepad.exe* for example, in the Run dialog box or an MS-DOS Prompt window. Sometimes you must enter the entire path (for example, C:\Program Files\ Microsoft Office XP\Office 10\Word.exe).

All About Paths   Paths are aptly named because they describe a route through the thousands of files on the computer to your destination. Although you don't often have to type in a path, it's important to know what they are so you can read and understand one when you see it.

Ordinarily, in Windows 98, you navigate through folders graphically—that is, using windows and clicking folders to see their contents, then a folder inside that folder, and so on until you find your quarry. Paths are a text-only way of describing a particular file's location. They read from left to right and from the general to the specific. For example, the path C:\My Documents\Letter to Leander.doc translates to "On my hard drive named C is a folder named My Documents and inside that folder is a document named Letter to Leander.doc."

Switching Between Programs

Often you're running more than one program in Windows—in fact, it's rare not to—so you must be able to switch easily. Here are the methods at your disposal.

- **Click the Window**   The simplest method of switching between programs is to click inside the window you want to make active. This shifts the *focus*, turning the title bar of the window a brighter color. If you can't find the window you're looking for, move windows out of the way by dragging the title bar of the window.

> **Lingo**   *Focus* refers to which program or window is active. All keyboard input goes into the currently active window.

- **Use the Taskbar**   When you have several windows open on your desktop, each has an icon on the Taskbar along the bottom of the desktop, as shown in Figure 3-2. To make a window active, click the corresponding icon on the Taskbar.

Figure 3-2 Each open program has an icon on the Taskbar.

Too many windows open on your desktop? Use the handy Show Desktop button on the Quick Launch toolbar (next to the Start menu) to minimize all windows and herd them down to the Taskbar. To restore your windows to the desktop, click the Desktop icon again, or restore them one at a time by selecting individual icons from the Taskbar.

Tip   If you have a Windows keyboard, press the Windows key and the letter *D* simultaneously to minimize all windows, or to restore them.

- **Use the Alt and Tab Keys to Cycle Though Programs**   If you don't want to take your hands away from the keyboard to mouse around, switch between programs by holding down Alt and then pressing Tab. Each press of the Tab key changes the focus.

- **Use the Windows and Tab Keys to Cycle Though Programs**   If you have a Windows key on your keyboard, hold it down and then press Tab to cycle through the buttons on the Taskbar. Release the Windows key and then press Enter to switch to the selected program or window.

Tip   To move the focus backwards, hold down the Shift key while pressing Tab. Decide not to change the focus after all? Press Esc.

Closing Programs

Deciding when to close a program is like determining the right time to turn off lights when leaving a room. Going to be gone a while? Turn it off. You'll be freeing up memory and system resources for other programs. Just leaving the program for a short time? Leave the program open. The time you save by not repeatedly closing and reopening more than compensates for a brief freeing of resources.

Closing programs is easy—pick the method you prefer:

- Click the X in the upper-right corner of the program window. (If you see two Xs, the lower one closes the currently open document, but not the program.)
- Choose Exit from the program's File menu.
- Right-click the program on the Taskbar and choose Close.
- Press Alt+F4.

Caution Always wait for a program to start completely before closing it. Closing a program before it finishes loading in Windows 98, Windows 95, or Windows Millennium Edition (Windows Me) can cause a memory leak, which saps system resources and slows your computer down.

Programs That Refuse To Die

It's a sad fact of life that sometimes programs lose their grip on reality and enter a darker realm. Then the program refuses to respond to anything you do—it won't even close. At this point, all you can do is force it to close.

Lingo A program (or Windows itself) that stops responding to your actions is *hung*.

Save your work in any open programs if you can and then close the offending program by attempting the following tasks, in order.

- Press Alt+Tab, as described earlier, until the frozen application is selected. Release Alt+Tab and try to close the program as you normally would.
- If the program remains open, right-click the program on the Taskbar and choose Close.

Tip If you need to search the Microsoft Knowledge Base for information on programs that hang, use the keyword *hangs* in addition to your other keywords.

- If the program still refuses to close, press Ctrl+Alt+Delete. In the Close Program window, select the program that you want to close and click End Task, as shown in Figure 3-3.
- If Windows displays an error message announcing that the system is busy, you're probably out of luck in terms of an orderly shutdown. Press Escape and wait for a few minutes. If the system doesn't come back to life, press Ctrl+Alt+Del until the system reboots. Sadly, you'll lose any unsaved work.

Note Microsoft Office 2000 and later contain an Autorecover feature that does a pretty good job of rescuing your documents during a crash—though there is no substitute for saving early and often.

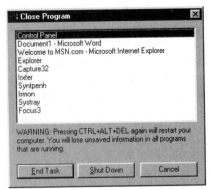

Figure 3-3 Use the Close Program window to kill programs that aren't responding.

What to Do About a Computer Slowdown Sometimes programs get a bit overzealous in their use of the computer's processor (the brain of the computer), greatly slowing down your system. When everything seems bogged down—not hung, just slow—and you can't figure out why, there's something funny going on.

To get to the bottom of it, click the Start button, choose Programs, Accessories, System Tools, and finally System Monitor. If System Monitor, shown in Figure 3-4, indicates that the Processor Usage is 100 percent, even when you're not doing anything, some process is taking more than its share of the computer's processing power.

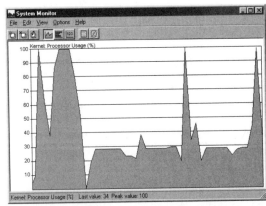

Figure 3-4 Use System Monitor to keep track of various components of your system's performance, most notably the processor.

Close programs one by one until the processor usage goes down—which will identify the culprit. If it never goes down, reboot the system and try again (this restarts the entire memory subsystem of Windows, wiping the slate clean).

When you find the culprit, put it on probation. Whenever you run the program, pay attention to your system's behavior (or open Performance Monitor and actively monitor it). If the program repeatedly steals (as opposed to borrows) all the processing power and your system seems to noticeably slow down, discontinue using the program, reinstall it, upgrade to a newer version, or take the matter up with the software manufacturer.

Note If System Monitor isn't already installed, install it by double-clicking Add/Remove Programs in Control Panel, clicking the Windows Setup tab, choosing System Tools, clicking Details, selecting System Monitor, and then clicking OK.

Installing Software

You can install software in several ways, as described in the following sections. You can uninstall it, however, in two ways only. If you've already set up lots of software without a problem, just skip merrily ahead. If you're just a tiny bit less sure of your skills in this area, read on to improve your confidence. But even experts are hereby reminded to use the Add/Remove Programs tool in Control Panel to uninstall software whenever possible—don't just delete programs from your hard drive.

Just Insert the CD

The easiest way to install a program is to insert the program's installation CD into the CD drive. Most programs automatically display a special AutoPlay window that includes the option to install the program. Click the option and follow the on-screen instructions to install the program.

If nothing happens when you insert the CD, right-click the CD-ROM or DVD-ROM drive in My Computer or Windows Explorer and choose AutoPlay.

Tip Most Windows 98 systems are rock solid—until too many programs and related device drivers are installed. You can help your system by installing only the software that you actually need and uninstalling what you don't. Programs you no longer use just add more clutter and potential instability to your system.

If AutoPlay Doesn't AutoMatically Play If a setup window doesn't appear auto-matically, see if AutoPlay is enabled for the CD-ROM or DVD-ROM drive by following these steps.

1 Double-click the System tool in the Control Panel. Then click the Device Manager tab in the System Properties dialog box.

2 Click the plus sign next to the CD-ROM icon, select your CD-ROM or DVD-ROM drive, and click Properties.

3 Click the Settings tab and select the Auto Insert Notification check box, as shown in Figure 3-5. Click OK.

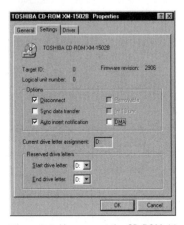

Figure 3-5 You can set the CD-ROM drive to automatically start when a disk is inserted.

Using Add/Remove Programs

Not all programs provide an AutoPlay option. For those that don't, use the Add/Remove Programs tool. To use this tool to launch a program's setup procedure, follow these steps.

1 From Control Panel, double-click Add/Remove Programs. Click Install.

2 Insert the program's installation CD-ROM, DVD-ROM, or floppy disk and then click Next. Windows looks for a setup program and displays the results in the next page of the wizard.

3 Verify that the setup program is indeed the correct setup program. (If the disk contains multiple programs, Windows may display the wrong one.) Then click Finish.

RTM (Read the Manual)

As bizarre as it may seem, one option for installing a program is to read the program's installation instructions. Sometimes the instructions tell you to click Start, choose Run, and then enter the setup program's name in the Open text box (for example, *\:DSetup.exe*).

You can also open up My Computer or Windows Explorer and look for the setup program. If you choose this approach, look for files named setup.exe or install.exe, and read any files with README in their file names before installing the program. They often contain useful, sometimes even critical information.

Downloaded Software

Not all software comes on a CD or floppy disk—many programs are available for download from the Internet. Some are even free. Others may require payment but even then they are probably cheaper than software from a store or catalog.

See Also   See the "Downloading Files" section of Chapter 6, "Fearless Web Browsing," for more on the general subject.

---

1   Open Internet Explorer and enter the URL or browse to the download location of the program you want.

Lingo   A *URL* (Uniform Resource Locator) is the address of a file on the Internet. For example, a page on the World Wide Web might have the URL *http://www.microsoft.com*.

---

2   Click the download hyperlink for the program.

3   In the File Download dialog box, choose Save:

- Choose Open if you don't anticipate reinstalling the program anytime soon. Windows saves the file to a temporary location and immediately launches the install program.

- Choose Save if you might want to reinstall the program later and downloading it again would be a nuisance (for example, if you purchased the software online or have a slow Internet connection).

Caution   Files that you download from the Internet can contain viruses. This isn't a concern for files from major companies such as Adobe and Microsoft, but is for files from companies that you don't trust or any files found on a personal Web site. If you're unsure of a file, save it to your hard drive and use your virus scanner to scan the file (usually by right-clicking the file and choosing Scan For Viruses, depending on your virus software vendor).

---

4   If you chose to save the program to your hard drive, use the Save As
dialog box to specify the desired location.

> **Tip**   If you want to make it easy to find downloaded files and keep your desktop
> clean in one fell swoop, create a folder on your hard drive called Downloads and save
> downloaded programs there.

5   If you click Open, the setup program starts automatically once the file is
downloaded. If you chose to save the file to your hard drive, click Open
to launch the setup program when the file is downloaded or Open
Folder to open the folder, so that you can first scan the file for viruses.

6   If the setup program asks where it should place extracted files, point it
to a new folder in your newly created Downloads folder.

Uninstalling Software

To uninstall software, you can use the program's own uninstall shortcut (if it
provides one), or you can use the Add/Remove Programs tool in Windows 98.

If the program has an uninstall icon on the Start menu, click that. The
program's uninstall routine is usually the most thorough about rooting out and
deleting the program's files. If the program doesn't have its own uninstall shortcut,
or if you prefer to use the Add/Remove Programs tool (you might get inspired to
uninstall other unused programs hanging around), use the following steps:

1   Open Add/Remove Programs from the Control Panel.

2   Select the program you want to uninstall from the list, as shown in
Figure 3-6.

Figure 3-6 The Add/Remove Programs tool keeps track of all properly installed programs written
for Windows 95 or newer.

3   Click Add/Remove and then use the uninstall wizard to uninstall the program. If given the choice between Automatic and Custom, choose Automatic.

4   If Windows asks whether to remove unused .dll files or leave them, make a choice: Remove them if you have a recent system backup and feel confident that other programs aren't reliant on the shared file, or leave them if you're unsure or want to play it safe.

5   Use My Computer or Windows Explorer to manually delete any folders and files that the uninstall program couldn't remove (often it can't delete the program's main folder, which is usually located in the *C:\Program Files* folder). Just be careful not to delete any of your precious data that might be lingering in these folders.

If the program isn't registered in Add/Remove Programs and doesn't have its own uninstall shortcut (such as is the case with Windows 3.*x* and DOS programs), manually delete the program's folder using Windows Explorer or My Computer. You might leave some files cluttering up the Windows folder, and there might be some registry entries that get orphaned, but the rule of thumb is this: if you're not sure what a file is for, leave it alone.

Manually deleting the program is a last resort because in Windows, programs put pieces of themselves all over your hard drive. Just deleting the program's folder doesn't do a full cleanup.

See Also   See the "Connecting to a Shared Folder on Another Computer" section of Chapter 13, "Building and Using a Network," for information on how to map a drive. "Capturing Printer Ports for pre-Windows 95 Programs" in Chapter 8, "Printing," has more on printer ports and Windows 3.x programs.

Running Non-Windows 98 Programs

Windows 98 can run the widest variety of programs of any version of Windows currently available—even more than Windows XP. Not only does it run Windows 95 and Windows 98 applications (and applications written for Windows 2000 or Windows XP, provided your computer is fast enough), it also handily runs almost every Windows 3.*x* application as well as most DOS applications. Windows NT and Windows 2000 just can't compete here, and although Windows XP makes an admirable attempt, when you need to run an old program, Windows 98 is the way to go.

The following sections cover running older programs, as well as newer programs and high-performance games. If your programs are running fine, you don't need these sections—just go about your business. However, if a problem pops up, come back for assistance.

Gamers should consult the Running High Performance Games section later in this chapter whether your games work properly or not. We can show you how to make them run faster.

Programs for Windows 3.1 and Later

Install and run older Windows applications just like newer applications—with a couple of important exceptions. Anti-virus and disk utilities designed for any operating system before Windows 95 crash and probably trash your system in a most unpleasant way. Trash *them* and get new ones.

Some other differences are less dramatic. Windows 3.*x* programs aren't network aware. To use a network drive in a program written for these operating systems, map the network location to a drive letter. And to use a network printer, you must capture a printer port.

> **See Also**   See the "Connecting to a Shared Folder on Another Computer" section of Chapter 13 for information on how to map a drive. "Capturing Printer Ports for pre-Windows 95 Programs" in Chapter 8, "Printing," has more on printer ports and Windows 3.x programs.

Try This! Many programs for Windows 3.x or DOS work even if you don't run an install routine. I have an especially old copy of PaintShop Pro that's registered and paid for, but the original installation disks vanished two or three computers ago. If you're in a similar situation, copy the program's entire folder to your new machine. You can use floppy disks or a network connection. If, when you run the program at its new location, you see an error message to the effect that a particular file is missing, look for it on the old machine. When you find the missing file, make sure you copy it to the corresponding location on your new computer. That is, if the file was in the Windows subdirectory on the old machine, that's where it belongs on the new computer.

Running DOS Programs

Despite all the fanfare surrounding the demise of MS-DOS (may it rest in peace), many users still have DOS applications that they find useful for one reason or another. Maybe it's an old accounting program that you've learned how to use and don't want to abandon, a custom designed business application that's one-of-a-kind, or perhaps it's the original Space Quest game that you fire up every once in a while to kick some alien butt.

In any case, Windows 98 runs your trusty old DOS programs (as well as the persnickety ones), but it might take a little finessing, so read on.

You install and run DOS programs just like Windows programs, except that you'll probably have to manually create shortcuts to the programs, as DOS based programs don't create shortcuts in the Start menu. Also, most DOS programs can be copied from computer to computer without installing—just run the program file from the proper folder.

Troubleshooting DOS Programs

Most DOS programs run perfectly well without any tweaking, but some don't—especially games. To optimize or troubleshoot how a DOS program runs, use the following procedures. Change only one thing at a time so you'll know which procedure solved the problem.

■ Use My Computer or Windows Explorer to locate the program file you want to run (it has an .exe, .bat or .com file extension). Right-click the file and choose Properties. Click the Screen tab, and select the Full Screen option to force the program to open full screen instead of in a window (DOS programs with graphics must be run full screen).

■ In My Computer or Windows Explorer, right-click the program file and choose Properties. Click the Misc tab, as shown in Figure 3-7. Clear the Allow Screen Saver check box (screensavers can interfere with DOS programs).

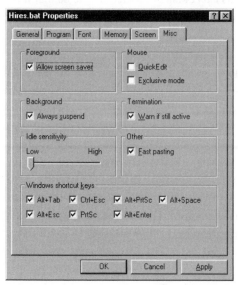

Figure 3-7 Use the Misc tab to disable screen savers, adjust the Idle Sensitivity and other options.

■ If the computer seems to slow down drastically when the DOS program is minimized or in the background, return to the Misc tab in the Properties dialog box and select the Always Suspend check box in the Background section. This stops the DOS program from running when it's in the background (when you're looking at another program).

■   If the program is running slowly or freezing, return to the Misc tab in the Properties dialog box and drag the Idle Sensitivity Slider to Low. This tells Windows to give the program more exclusive access to the processor, and is highly recommended for games.

■   If the program refuses to run (especially if it mumbles something about Windows), right-click the program file, choose Properties, and then click the Program tab. Click Advanced. Select the Prevent MS-DOS Based Programs From Detecting Windows check box.

How Can a DOS Program *Know* About Windows?   If DOS came before Windows (and it did), how can a DOS program even know that such a thing as Windows exists? The answer is actually easy once you think about it. Many, many programs were written for DOS after the introduction of Windows 1.0, in part because it was far from clear that this new-fangled Windows thing would ever get off the ground.

Tons of games were written during the era of Windows 3.x. Even for a year or two after Windows 95 came out, top-of-the-line game programs were written for DOS because for many game programmers, that was their expertise. These programs didn't want to have anything to do with Windows. They would pop up a message such as "Error, this program hates Windows. Please reboot into DOS and run the program again."

Eventually, the popularity of Windows, the introduction of DirectX (a Windows programming interface that allowed games faster access to hardware) and increasingly powerful computers won out. If you still use a program that hates Windows, it has to be tricked into thinking that Windows is nowhere to be found, which is what the Prevent MS-DOS Based Programs From Detecting Windows option forces it to do.

■   If you still have difficulty running the program, return to the Advanced tab and select the MS-DOS Mode check box. This instructs Windows to reboot into MS-DOS and run the program. (If necessary, choose the Specify A New MS-DOS Configuration and enter needed CONFIG.SYS and AUTOEXEC.BAT lines.)

> **Tip**   You can always reboot the system into DOS mode and run programs from an honest-to-goodness DOS prompt. To do so, click Start, choose Shut Down, and then Restart in DOS Mode. You can also make a DOS boot disk and boot the system from a floppy disk.

Running Newer Programs

Windows 98 runs almost every program written since Windows 95—a few Windows NT programs won't run in Windows 98, but almost all Windows 2000 and Windows XP programs work perfectly.

The only restriction you're likely to encounter is hardware. Computers that had plenty of memory and hard-drive space when Windows 98 was released (32 MB of RAM and a 4 GB hard drive) are hard-pressed by some newer applications.

Running High-Performance Games

Of all types of programs, games are the some of the most hardware and software intensive. They push computers to the limits in the attempt to achieve more appealing graphics, better sound, and faster action, so it's important to optimize your system to run them well.

Although optimizing your computer is covered in greater detail in Chapter 12, "Maintaining a Healthy Computer," here are some steps to take to maximize the speed at which you mow down those space aliens:

1 Download and install the latest device driver for your video display card (see the section entitled "Getting and Using Drivers" in Chapter 9 for more help on this).

2 Download and install the latest version of DirectX, available through Windows Update.

3 Perform "complete" or "full" installs of games to your fastest hard drive. This minimizes the amount of time wasted loading files from the CD.

4 Check the game manufacturer's Web site for patches or program updates.

5 Install and calibrate the game controllers you want to use in the game, such as a joystick or racing wheel.

> **Note** Games such as Solitaire, Minesweeper, and Hearts don't require any special attention—they run fine on any system, no matter what level of optimization.

6 Defragment your hard drive regularly (maybe once a month, or anytime that you add or delete a lot of data from your hard drive).

7 Close all other programs before running any full-screen games, unless the programs are needed to play the game, such as a network connection. Right-click any icons in the System Tray that aren't vital to the computer (or game's) functioning and choose Exit or Close to close them.

8 If the game is too sluggish, reduce display quality in the game and in your display drivers.

9 For online games, find servers that are 10 "hops" away or less (each hop is a router that information has to pass through, adding lag to your gameplay). If your game doesn't display hop counts, open an MS-DOS prompt and type **tracert IP_address**, where *IP_address* is the IP address for a game server you want to use, for example 216.254.0.164.

See Also *How and why to use Windows Update is covered in the "Using Windows Update" section of Chapter 1, "Making Windows Work for You." Steps for defragmenting are discussed in the "Scheduling Chores with the Maintenance Wizard" section of Chapter 12, "Maintaining a Healthy Computer." And for help setting up your game controller, see the "Working with Game Controllers" section of Chapter 9, "Conquering Computer Hardware."*

Essential Software That's Free (or Cheap)

Great as it is, Windows 98 won't solve every Internet dilemma. People send you files that you can't open because they're in some format your computer doesn't recognize. Web sites offer video that you're not able to play. The following list is by no means comprehensive—you might need other programs as well. However, you certainly should have the following items:

- **Winzip** A venerable program that creates compressed files (with the .zip file extension). Use Winzip to uncompress files and to compress files for e-mail. You can download an evaluation copy at *http://www.winzip.com* and use it free for 21 days. If you keep it—which you undoubtedly will—the price is modest.

- **Adobe Acrobat Reader** Use this program to view files with the *.PDF* extension. You can download this free viewer at *http://www.adobe.com/products/acrobat/readstep.html*.

Lingo *Portable Document Format* (PDF) is a file format developed by Adobe Systems. PDF captures formatting information from desktop publishing programs. That means when you view a PDF file, it looks like a published document just as the creator intended it.

- **QuickTime Player** The QuickTime player, also free, plays movie and video clips. You can download it at *http://www.apple.com/quicktime/download/*.

■ **Ad Aware**   This free program detects and removes a number of nasty programs known as *scumware, parasites, Trojan horses,* or *spyware.* You can download it at *http://www.lavasoftusa.com.* This program is not a substitute for a real antivirus program.

See Also   See the "Stopping Hackers and Viruses" section of Chapter 11, "Playing It Safe," for more on antivirus software.

Each of these programs comes with simple installation instructions.

Key Points

■ You start programs from the Start menu or by double-clicking their shortcuts on the Desktop or by double-clicking the programs themselves in My Computer.

■ Switch between programs using the Taskbar, Alt+Tab, or by clicking directly in the desired window.

■ Close programs when you're not using them; press Ctrl-+Alt+Delete to close programs that refuse to close properly.

■ Install and uninstall software using Add/Remove Programs in Control Panel—don't just delete programs.

■ Windows 98 runs Windows 3.*x* programs reliably, while DOS programs usually run fine, but can require some adjustments.

■ Before running a high-performance game, get the latest display drivers and software updates and close all other programs.

Chapter 4

Working with Files and Folders

Admittedly, reading a chapter about working with files and folders sounds about as exhilarating as watching paint dry. After all, everyone who uses Windows for more than five minutes learns the basics of files and folders, right? Perhaps. But you will need more than the basics if you don't want your computer to drive you mad. The specific skills of a power user (that's you) are needed, and they're needed now.

This chapter covers the basics but doesn't linger. Mostly, you'll find tips, tricks, advice, and information that you can put to use right away.

Using Folders

Folders are the basic organizational unit in Microsoft Windows 98. (Caution: Analogy Approaching!). Your computer is like a file cabinet. The drawers are hard drives. The folders are, well, folders. And the computer files inside the computer folders are like papers inside paper folders. The difference is that on a computer you can make, change, move, and throw away files and folders with a click of the mouse and without leaving your comfy chair.

Creating New Folders

There's really nothing easier than creating a new folder. Using Windows Explorer, navigate to where you want to put the new folder, right-click a blank spot, and select New and then Folder from the shortcut menu.

When you create a folder, Windows 98 automatically gives it the name New Folder. If you create more than one folder in the same location, without renaming the first one, then the second and third and so on are named New Folder (2), New Folder (3), and so forth.

To rename a folder, right-click the folder and choose Rename from the shortcut menu. To do it even more directly, slowly double-click the folder name and the name becomes highlighted. You can then enter the new name.

Setting Folder Views

The way items inside a folder are displayed is called the folder view. Files—and other folders—are usually displayed as large or small icons, as a list, or as a list with details (such as the date, file size, and so forth). An additional option in Windows 98 is to view folders as Web pages.

Folders as Web Pages

An option on the View menu of folders is As Web Page. This option is a toggle; a click changes it from on to off or vice versa. When you view a folder as a Web page, a hypertext template controls its appearance. The default template uses roughly the left one-third of the Windows Explorer folder pane to display the folder name and a variety of useful information.

Lingo   *Hypertext*, as defined by Ted Nelson, who coined the term, is *non-sequential* writing—text that branches and allows choices to the reader and is best read on an interactive screen. Hypertext is best at organizing a large amount of disparate information. When reading a document about Kenya, for example, a hypertext link can connect you to pictures of lions or a sound clip of Masaai chanting. Other links can take you further, or you can use a link to return to the original page.

When you select an object in the folder, information about the object appears in the left-hand side of the folder pane. The type of information depends on the object. For a document file, it may include such properties as the author's name in addition to the file date and time, as shown in Figure 4-1.

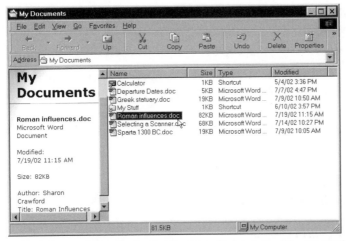

Figure 4-1 In the Web page view, information is displayed about the selected file.

For disk drives, the information includes space used and space available, along with a pie graph, as shown in Figure 4-2.

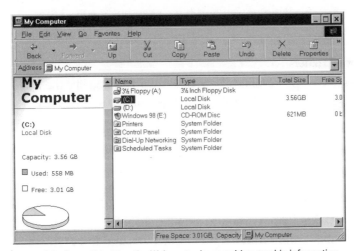

Figure 4-2 For a disk drive, the Web page view provides graphic information.

For system folders and other objects, a general description indicates the object's function.

To learn how to set all your folders to Web view, see the section entitled "Selecting System-Wide Folder Options" later in this chapter.

Customizing Folders

On each folder's View menu there is an option called Customize This Folder. Choosing it starts a Wizard of the same name that offers three choices.

■ **Create Or Edit An HTML Document** This controls the appearance of the folder when As Web Page is selected from the View menu. This sounds good, but as the next dialog explains, this involves working with a hypertext template and editing the *HTML*. If you're comfortable with HTML, go for it.

> **Lingo** *HTML* is the abbreviation for *Hypertext Markup Language*, the language used for authoring documents on the World Wide Web.

■ **Choose A Background Picture** A picture in .bmp, .jpg, or .gif format can serve as a background for the folder view.

■ **Remove Customization** Choose this to return to a plain background. This also returns you to the default template for the Web view if you're using the As Web Page option and have previously edited the HTML for the template.

Setting a Single View for All Folders

All your folders can be set to display identically. In other words, if you like the Large Icon view or the Details view, specify that all your folders are to use that view.

1   Open a folder and customize it so that it's set up exactly as you want all your folders to be.

2   Select Folder Options from the View menu.

3   On the View tab, select Like Current Folder.

4   A dialog box opens asking if you want to set all the folders on your computer to match the current folder's view. Click Yes and then OK.

Other folders that are open won't immediately adopt the change, but the next time you open any folder it displays what you specified.

Having a Different View for Each Folder

If you don't want all your folders to look the same, you're in luck. Windows 98 lets you have some folders using large icons, others showing the details view, and so on. All you have to do is open a folder and select the options you want from the View menu. Although this approach is a little more labor-intensive, you only have to do it once for each folder.

Tip If your setting doesn't appear to be sticking, select Folder Options from the View menu and click the View tab. Make sure the Remember Each Folder's View Settings option is selected.

Try This! When you have a folder full of photos, none of the ordinary views are particularly satisfactory. However, you can set a folder to display each file as a thumbnail.

1 Right-click the folder and select Properties.

2 On the General tab, select the Enable Thumbnail View option, and then click OK.

3 Open the folder and then select Thumbnails from the View menu.

You can get a similar effect by selecting the As Web Page option from the View menu. As you select a photo file, a small version of the picture is displayed in the Web pane.

Selecting System-Wide Folder Options

When you select Folder Options from a folder's View menu, Windows 98 opens a dialog box like the one shown in Figure 4-3. The settings you make here are global, unlike the View menu settings just described. In other words, you can't change the options for just one folder. Changes here affect your whole system.

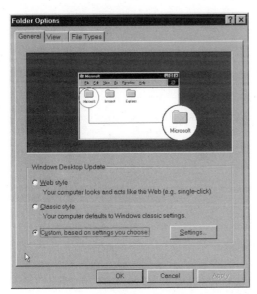

Figure 4-3 The Folder Options dialog box makes settings for all your folders.

The General Tab

The General tab is for setting the basic look and behavior of folders. You can choose the Web Style, which has the following characteristics.

- The folders you browse all open in the same window, rather than a new window for each folder.

- All folders default to the Web view.

- The names and icons of files and subfolders look and behave like hyperlinks. That is, the names are underlined, the icons are selected when you point at them, and they open with a single click.

  The Classic Style is the Windows 95 look and feel.

- Each folder opens in a new window.

- For a folder to have a Web page view, you must choose As Web Page on the folder's View menu.

- You click to select an item and double-click to open it.

  If you prefer some combination of these options (such as a classic Windows look with single-click file opening), choose Custom and click Settings to set your individual preferences.

The View Tab

The View tab is an important place to know about. In addition to the two buttons in the Folder Views area that allow you to give all folders the same view or reset them to the Windows 98 default view, the Advanced Settings list also allows you to toggle a variety of file and folder properties. Most of these settings really are self-explanatory, but here's a description of the not-so-clear ones.

- **Allow All Uppercase Names**   Want folders with NAMES ALL IN CAPITAL LETTERS? Check this box, and you can have them.

- **Display The Full Path In Title Bar**   Ordinarily, the title bar of a folder shows only the folder's name. If you like seeing just where on your hard drive a folder resides, select this option and the full path is displayed on the title bar of each folder.

  Some program and system files are hidden. These are usually files that should not be moved or deleted. The default setting is not to show either type, but you can change that to show all files or to hide only hidden files. If you choose to show hidden files, they show up in your folder listings with ghostlike icons—just so you remember that they are normally hidden. In general, it's best to keep hidden and system files out of view, but there are times when you need to see them. For example, if you're copying a folder that includes hidden files, you'll have to have the Show all files option selected to include the hidden files in the copying.

■ **Hide File Extensions For Known File Types**   By default, this option is selected. It means that you won't see the file name extensions for files that Windows 98 already knows how to use. With this option selected, the only files with extensions are those that have no associated application. (See the section entitled "The Association Between Files and Programs" later in this chapter for information on how to tell Windows 98 about an unrecognized file.)

■ **Show Map Network Drive Button In Toolbar**   This adds the button for mapping network drives to every toolbar.

■ **Show File Attributes In Detail View**   To include individual file *attributes* (whether a file is backed up or a system file, for example) in the Details view, check this box.

Lingo   Each file and folder has three configurable *attributes* that convey basic information. Attributes are visible on the file's property sheet. You can make the file read-only, make it into a hidden file, or change the archive attribute. The archive attribute is automatically marked when a file has changed since the last backup. A fourth attribute shows if a file is a system file. The system attribute can't be changed.

■ **Show Pop-up Description For Folder And Desktop Items**   This controls the descriptive boxes that appear when you move your pointer over icons such as My Computer. Remove the check mark when you've seen enough of them.

■ **Hide Icons When Desktop Is Viewed As Web Page**   With this option, you can hide your desktop icons for a better view of Active Desktop. Do not attempt to use Active Desktop. Of course, if you've had Windows 98 for a few years, you've already tried it and know that it's an idea whose time never came. Perhaps you recall the "Channel Bar" that automatically loaded on your desktop? You can still see it by opening Display Properties in Control Panel and clicking the Web tab. Select the options on the page and the Channel Bar will reappear on your desktop. Of course, none of the channels actually *work* any more and none worked very well even when Windows 98 was new. But that's not important. What's important is that we tell you all the facts about Windows 98—even the useless and embarrassing ones.

- **Show Window Contents While Dragging**   Disable this option if you notice an annoying jerkiness when you drag a window or if it takes a long time to drag a window.

- **Smooth Edges Of Screen Fonts**   Selecting this option improves the appearance of large fonts but might slow your computer.

Folder Properties

Not surprisingly, folders have properties, just as everything else has. Right-click any folder and select Properties from the shortcut menu to open a dialog box like the one in Figure 4-4.

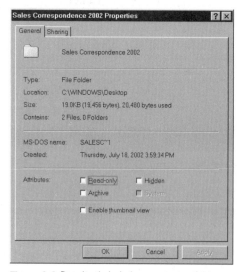

Figure 4-4 Despite their drab appearance, folder property dialog boxes include much useful information.

The General Tab

The General tab provides information about the folder, including its size and the number of files and other folders to be found inside. As on the property dialog boxes for individual files, you'll find check boxes for setting specific attributes:

- **Read-Only**   With this selected, the folder cannot be written to. This isn't a security measure (if you can change it, anyone else with access to your computer can change it back), but it makes it harder to alter a file accidentally.

- **Archive** A check in this box means that all the files in the folder have been backed up by a program that sets the archive bit. If the box appears dimmed, it means that some of the files in the folder are backed up but others are not.

- **Hidden** Folders and files that are hidden are unseen in the Windows 98 interface unless you specifically choose to display them. They operate as usual, but aren't visible in Windows Explorer or other programs.

- **System** System files are necessary to the operation of Windows 98. You don't want to delete them. In any case, a whole folder cannot be designated as System, so this box always appears dimmed on a folder.

Tip To change a file or folder from hidden to visible, select Folder Options from the View menu in any window. On the View tab, select Show All Files. Click OK. Now find the file you want to change, right-click it to open its property dialog box, and change the Hidden attribute.

Sharing Tab

If you're on a network, share a folder with others on the network by clicking the Sharing tab of the folder's property dialog box. Select Share As and decide which type of access to allow.

Note You can share a complete drive, but keep in mind that access is inherited. If you share drive C, *everything* on drive C is shared. Similarly, when you share a folder, all files and subfolders are also shared.

Keeping Your Files Under Control

It's not an exaggeration to say that simply organizing your files in a useful way can greatly reduce computing headaches. Windows 98 makes a contribution in that direction by supplying the My Documents folder as a default location. However, once you save a few dozen documents, you'll need additional tools. You can create new folders for different categories of files inside My Documents and then sort and move your files into those folders. Also, you can take advantage of long file names to make it easy to find and recognize documents.

Creating Files

The most direct way to create a new file is to right-click the desktop or a blank area inside a folder and select New from the shortcut menu. This opens a list of new objects you can create, as shown in the illustration.

In most programs you can create new files by opening the application and selecting New from the File menu. However, a fair number of applications create an option on the shortcut menu so you can also create new files with this option.

File Names

Those users who date back to the days of DOS or even Windows prior to Windows 95 doubly appreciate the ability to give long names to files. It's not that many of us want to use the full 250 characters allowed; it's just that the previous limitation of eight characters plus a three-letter file name extension (aka 8.3), was so confining.

File names can include spaces and characters like the comma, semicolon, equal sign (=) and square brackets ([]). In fact, you can use any letters or characters in file and folder names *except* \ / * < > : ? " |

File and folder names can have both uppercase and lowercase letters, and the system preserves them—but only for display purposes. When searching for a name, it's not necessary to remember whether some part of it is capitalized or not. Windows 98 finds it as long as the spelling is correct.

Note Although it's not necessary to worry about case when naming files, you must remember it when creating any of your passwords. Passwords are *always* case-sensitive, so a password such as Wormhead, while equally disgusting, is not the same as WormHead.

File Properties

The property dialog box should be your first stop when you have questions about characteristics of the folder or file you are dealing with. Properties dialog boxes for files can have one tab or many. Microsoft Word documents add several configurable tabs to the usual General one, as shown in Figure 4-5. The General tab, common to all files, describes the type, location, and size of the file and also includes information about the file's creation.

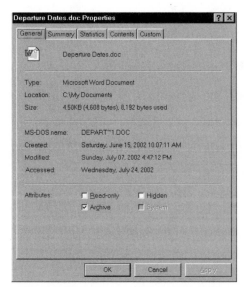

Figure 4-5 A Word document can include a lot of information about the document's properties.

Other types of files can include additional tabs on their property dialog box with information relevant to a specific file type, as shown in Figure 4-6.

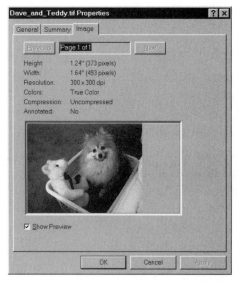

Figure 4-6   A graphic file in .tif format includes an Image tab in its property dialog box.

Selecting Files and Folders

Of course you already know how to select a file or folder—just point at the thing and click—but you may not know how to do more fancy selecting.

Selecting Everything

To select a bunch of files or folders, open the window showing the objects in question and then choose Select All from the Edit menu (or Ctrl+A on your keyboard). Everything in the window is highlighted. Right-click one of the highlighted icons, as shown in Figure 4-7, and choose the action you want from the shortcut menu.

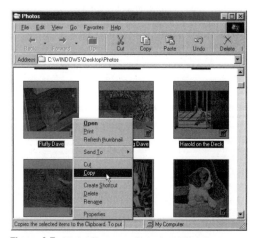

Figure 4-7   All the files are selected and the shortcut menu offers choices as to what to do.

Selecting Some but Not All

The easiest method for selecting some of the objects in a window depends on how you have the files and folders displayed.

If you have large icons displayed, you can simply lasso the items in question. Click an area near the first item and, holding the left or right mouse button down, draw a box around the icons you want to select. When you're finished drawing the box, right-click one of the highlighted icons and the shortcut menu displays a choice of actions. Figure 4-8 shows icons selected in just this way.

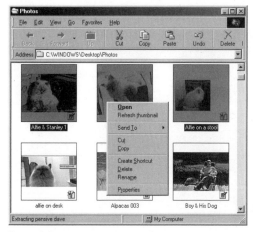

Figure 4-8 You can select icons for lassoing.

If the icons are displayed as a list or in the Details view, it's easiest to select them by holding down the Ctrl key while clicking each item in turn.

If you want all the files in a series, highlight the first one. Then hold down the Shift key and move the pointer to the last one and click it. All the objects in between and including the two files are selected.

The Association Between Files and Programs

When you click a file to open it, Windows 98 checks which application (or program) created the file. Ordinarily, when you install a program, Windows 98 registers the file types associated with the program in the *registry*. For example, files with the extension .doc are Word files, files with the extension .wpd are WordPerfect files, and files with the extension .pdf are Adobe Acrobat files.

Lingo The *registry* is a hidden file on your hard drive that keeps track of all sorts of configuration details including what kind of file goes with each application. Almost all installation programs are recorded in the registry, as are hardware installations and changes that you make to your system. Additional information about the registry can be found in Chapter 5, "What *IS* That File?"

In general, this works well; however, some annoying programs, when installed, change one or more associations without even asking (or they ask in a misleading way). So you might end up with your .jpg or .bmp files registered to open in a program other than the one you want.

Changing Registrations

To change the registration of a file type, select Folder Options from the View menu in any window. Click the File Types tab in the Folder Options dialog box to see a listing of all the file types that are registered on your machine. Select a file type to see details, as shown in Figure 4-9. This includes the extension or extensions used for the file type and the name of the program that works with the files.

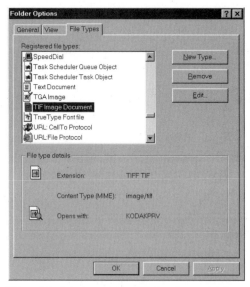

Figure 4-9 Select a registered file type to see details.

As you can see, Windows 98 has decided that all .tif graphics files should be opened in the Kodak Imaging program. That is, you double-click a file with the .tif extension and Windows 98 launches the Imaging program to display the file. But what if you want all .tif files to open automatically in Microsoft Photo Editor? Here's how to make the change.

1   On the File Types tab in the Folder Options dialog box select TIF Image Document under Registered File Types, and then click Edit.

2 In the Edit File Type dialog box under Actions, select Open.

Note In the Edit File Type dialog box, you can also change the icon associated with a file type and change other actions for the file type.

---

3 Click Edit. Browse for or enter the path for the application you want to use to open .tif files—in this case, Microsoft Photo Editor—as shown in Figure 4-10. Be sure to retain or replace the %1 notation at the end of the path. The first part of the path tells Windows to launch Photo Editor and the second part (%1) tells Windows to display the file that was just double-clicked. Without the %1 notation, the program starts but no file is opened.

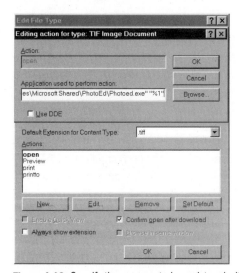

Figure 4-10 Specify the program to be registered with the file type.

4 Click OK, then Close.

Now when you return to the File Types tab, you can see that .tif files open with Photo Editor, as shown in Figure 4-11.

Note This doesn't mean you can no longer open .bmp files in Kodak Imaging. But once Imaging is no longer associated with that file type, you must launch the Imaging program and open the .bmp file using Open from the File menu.

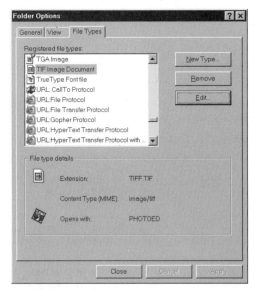

Figure 4-11 Now when you double-click a .tif file, Windows 98 launches Microsoft Photo Editor and displays the file.

How to Find the Desktop on Your Hard Drive

Windows 98 does its very best to convince you that the virtual desktop is just that—virtual. Open My Computer and there's no sign of anything called Desktop. Open Windows Explorer and slide the scrollbar up for the left pane and there it is at the top of the tree. Highlight Desktop, and sure enough the folders on the desktop are displayed, as illustrated.

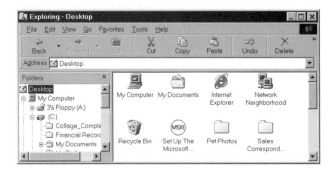

Alas, appearances are deceiving. Even the trick of using the Address drop-down list offers no clue. But in reality, the desktop is just another folder, albeit a special one in a special place.

The Desktop folder is inside the Windows folder. This is also the location of the Start Menu folder, and the Favorites folder, unless more than one person uses the machine. In that case, the individual folders are in Windows\Profiles.

Copying and Moving Files and Folders

At least three different methods for moving and copying files or folders are available. You can adopt one method and use it all the time, or pick and choose from the various methods, depending on the circumstances.

Move or Copy Using the Right Mouse Button

This is my personal favorite because it requires a minimum of thought:

1 Locate the file or folder using the Windows Explorer or My Computer.

2 Right-click the file or folder. Hold the mouse button down and drag the object to its new location.

3 Release the mouse button and choose Move or Copy from the shortcut menu.

For the shortest distance between two points, you might want to open a second instance of Windows Explorer so you can drag and drop directly. You can also move or copy the object to the desktop, and then open the destination folder or drive and drag the object a second time.

Move or Copy Using the Left Mouse Button

This method requires a bit more mental attention because when you use the left mouse button to drag and drop, the result is a *move* only if the source and destination are on the same drive letter. If they are on different drives, the result is a *copy*.

The basic procedure is much the same. Locate the file or folder using Windows Explorer or My Computer. Select the file or folder and hold the left mouse button down while dragging the object to its new location.

If you see a black plus sign in the transparent icon as you drag, that means that a copy is made when you release the left mouse button.

If you're dragging a *program* file (one with the extension .exe, .com, or .bat), Windows 98 creates a shortcut to the original file at the destination. You can tell that a shortcut is being made because a shortcut arrow appears in the transparent icon that you're dragging.

Tip   In any case, you can force a move by pressing and holding down the Shift key before you release the left mouse button.

Move or Copy Using Cut/Copy and Paste

Using the shortcut menu to move or copy files and folders is efficient because you don't need both the source and destination in view at the same time. To move or copy a file using Cut or Copy and Paste, follow these steps:

1   Locate the file or folder you want to move or copy, using My Computer or Windows Explorer.

2   Right-click the object and select Cut or Copy from the shortcut menu.

3   Find the destination folder and open it.

4   Right-click a blank spot inside the folder and select Paste from the shortcut menu.

Note   There are a few objects, such as disk icons, that you can't move or copy. If you try to, you'll get a message informing you of this fact and asking if you want a shortcut instead.

Learning to Recycle

The Recycle Bin, as you might imagine, is where deleted files go and hang out until you may need them again or until you send them to a quick and painless death (meaning they are no longer recoverable).

The Recycle Bin isn't a direct route to a landfill. You can rescue deleted files from the Recycle Bin until the bin is emptied. In this way, the Recycle Bin gives you a nice margin of safety. When you delete a file you have days or even weeks (depending on how you set things up) to change your mind and retrieve it.

Here are two important things about the Recycle Bin:

- The Recycle Bin icon can't be renamed or deleted.

- Files deleted over a network connection, using a DOS program, or directly from a program that is not part of Windows 98, are not sent to the Recycle Bin. If you proceed to delete a file and you're *not* asked whether you want the file to go to the Recycle Bin, the file will be deleted. They're just deleted—forever and ever—so be careful.

The Recycle Bin retains all your deleted files for as long as you want, and you can adjust the amount of security from "just a little" to "all I can get" to match your personal comfort level.

What the Recycle Bin Is

The Recycle Bin is a reserved space on your hard drive. When you delete a file or drag it to the Recycle Bin icon, the file is moved to that reserved space. If you have more than one hard drive, each drive has its own reserved space. There's an icon that represents the Recycle Bin on each drive—though the contents displayed when you double-click any icon are the same as the Recycle Bin on any other drive. If you want a deleted file back, double-click the Recycle Bin.

The Recycle Bin functions as a first-in first-out system. That is, when the bin is full, the oldest files are the first ones deleted to make room for the newest ones.

Sending a Floppy Disk's Files to the Recycle Bin

Normally, files that you delete from a floppy drive are *not* sent to the Recycle Bin. They're just deleted. However, if that strikes you as just a little too reckless, there's an easy way to make sure that the files on your floppy do go to the Recycle Bin.

1   Open Windows Explorer. Use the scroll bar for the left pane to move up so you can see the entry for your floppy drive.

2   Select the floppy drive icon. In the right pane, select the file(s) you want to delete and send to the Recycle Bin.

3   Right-click the file(s) and select Cut. Right-click the desktop and select Paste.

4   Highlight the file(s) on the desktop. (If there's more than one, hold down the Ctrl key while you click each one in turn.) Right-click a highlighted file and select Delete. You're prompted to confirm that you want to send the file(s) to the Recycle Bin.

There's no more direct way to do this because the Recycle Bin stubbornly refuses to see any files that are sent directly from a floppy.

Bypassing the Recycle Bin

If you have a file that you know for certain you want to delete and that you therefore don't want taking up space in the Recycle Bin, just hold down the Shift key when you select Delete. Just be sure that's what you want to do because there's no way in Windows 98 to recover a deleted file that's bypassed the Recycle Bin.

Tip   If you have the Norton Utilities for Windows 98, you can use the Norton Unerase program to recover deleted files that are not in the Recycle Bin. Again, you must do this quickly before another file overwrites the one you want to recover.

Some older programs (not written specifically for Windows 98) allow you to delete files from within the program. Files deleted this way are not sent to the Recycle Bin. Similarly, files you delete at the DOS prompt also disappear into the wild blue yonder rather than the Recycle Bin.

So it stands to reason that you should make all deletions through Windows Explorer or My Computer or on the desktop. If Windows 98 knows about the deletion, the file automatically goes to the Recycle Bin.

Recovering a File from the Recycle Bin

Retrieving a file from the Recycle Bins is remarkably easy. Just double-click the Recycle Bin icon. The Recycle Bin window can be set up in any of the usual choices on the View menu. The Large Icon view is shown in Figure 4-12.

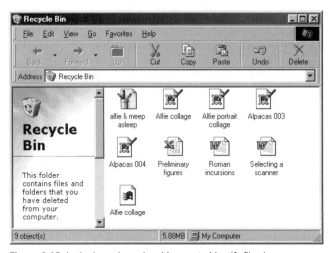

Figure 4-12 In the Large Icon view, it's easy to identify files by program.

Figure 4-13 shows the Details view, the best view if you're looking for a file recently deleted. Just click the Date Deleted bar to arrange the files in date order. A second click reverses the order. Similarly, if you know the name of the file, clicking the Name bar lists the files in alphabetical order.

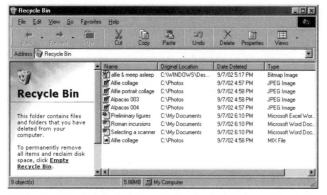

Figure 4-13 The Details view is useful if you're searching by date or name.

To retrieve a single file, click it with either the left or the right button and drag it to a folder or the desktop. If you just want to send it back to its original location, right-click the file name and select Restore from the shortcut menu.

More Than One File

To recover more than one file at a time, hold down the Ctrl key while selecting file names. Then right-click one of the highlighted files and select Restore. You can also use cut and paste to send the whole bunch to a different location. And of course, you can also click and drag (with either the right or left mouse button) the files to your desktop or another open folder.

To retrieve a number of files all in a series, click the first one and then hold down the Shift key while you select the last one in the series.

Let's say you deleted a whole folder and the only thing all the parts of the folder have in common is that all were deleted at the same time. Here's how to recover them.

1   Open the Recycle Bin.

2   Select Details from the View menu.

3   Click Date Deleted. Use the scroll bar to move through the list until you find the group of files you want to retrieve.

4   Click the name of the first file and then, while holding down the Shift key, click the name of the last file you want. All the files in between the first and last click are selected.

5   Right-click one of the selected files and choose Recover from the shortcut menu.

All the files are returned to their original home and even though the original folder is not listed in the Recycle Bin, the files are in the original folder.

Recycle Bin Settings

You can adjust the amount of space the Recycle Bin uses and change other settings that affect how the Recycle Bin works. Mostly you have to decide just how much safety you need to feel comfortable.

How Much Space?

Right-click the Recycle Bin icon and select Properties to see the dialog box shown in the following illustration.

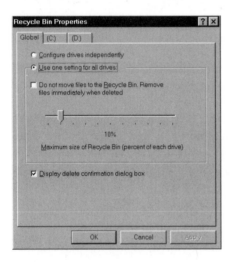

As you can see, the amount of space reserved for the Recycle Bin on each hard drive partition can be set individually, or you can make a global setting that applies to all drives.

By default, 10 percent of each drive is set aside for the Recycle Bin. On a large drive, that's a lot of megabytes, so you may want to reduce the size a bit. Click Configure Drives Independently and then select each drive's tab in turn. Move the slider until the maximum size of the Recycle Bin is to your liking.

There's also a field below the slider, showing the percentage of the drive that is reserved. If your drives are different sizes, you may want to make things easier for yourself by just reserving the same percentage on each drive.

Note   Remember that the Recycle Bin is first-in, first-out, so if you make the reserved space small, deleted files might pass into oblivion faster than you want them to.

Getting Rid of Confirmations

On the Global tab of the Recycle Bin Properties dialog box, there's a check box you can clear if you don't want to see a question like this every time you delete a file:

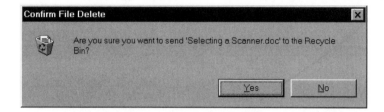

If there's a check in the box, you'll be asked to confirm each deletion, as shown here. This is just a little extra margin of safety that isn't necessary as long as all your deletions are going to the Recycle Bin and the Recycle Bin is large enough to hold deleted files for some time.

Doing Away with the Recycle Bin

Okay, you can't really do away with the Recycle Bin completely. As mentioned earlier, you can't delete it or remove it from the desktop. However, you can check Do Not Move Files To The Recycle Bin on the Recycle Bin Properties dialog box. If you have the Recycle Bin space configured separately for each drive, you can pick which drives you want this to apply to.

Bypassing the Recycle Bin completely is not recommended. Sooner or later, everyone deletes a file—an important file—by mistake.

Even if you have a program that rescues files deleted in error, it's still inadvisable to skip the Recycle Bin entirely because such programs are dependent on retrieving the deleted file before it is overwritten by another file. Overwriting can happen quickly in Windows 98, where there's almost always something going on behind the scenes.

If you begrudge giving up large portions of your hard drive, make the reserved space on the hard drive very small—5 or 10 megabytes. Check the box in the property dialog to disable the confirmation requests. Then the Recycle Bin is quite unobtrusive, even though you still have a margin of safety.

Emptying the Recycle Bin

To clear out the Recycle Bin, right-click the Recycle Bin icon and select Empty Recycle Bin. An option to Empty Recycle Bin under the File menu is also available.

To remove just some of the items in the Recycle Bin, select the file names, right-click one of them, and select Delete from the shortcut menu. You'll be asked to confirm the deletion (assuming you have the confirmation option turned on), and when you say Yes, the files are deleted permanently.

Working with Floppy Disks

Even though floppy disks have been largely supplanted by compact disks, like DOS, the reports of their demise are premature. So as long as floppies endure, they'll need to be formatted and copied.

To Copy a Floppy

To make an exact copy of a floppy disk, put the disk in the drive and open Windows Explorer. Right-click the icon for the floppy drive and select Copy Disk.

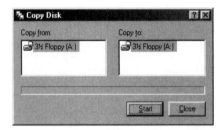

Although the dialog box doesn't say so, the Copy From and Copy To selections must be the same type of disk. For most people, that means the same drive (unless you have two identical diskette drives or two Zip drives). Click Start and follow the prompts.

Tip   If you do a lot of work with floppies, a shortcut to the drive can save you time. Just drag the floppy drive icon from the left pane of Windows Explorer to your desktop.

Formatting Floppies

Although floppy disks no longer have to be formatted before they can be used, when you do want to reuse one, reformatting the disk is the best way to start clean. Here's how to format a floppy disk:

1   Put the floppy disk in the drive and open Windows Explorer.

2   In the left pane of Windows Explorer, right-click the floppy drive icon and select Format from the shortcut menu.

3   Select the Format Type and Other options you want from the dialog
box.

- *Quick (Erase)*   A quick format changes the names of any files on
  the disk so that they disappear as far as the operating system is
  concerned. This format is fast (hence the name), but it doesn't
  check to make sure that the floppy disk is undamaged.

- *Full*   A full format is desirable because it checks for errors and
  defects on the disk. It's a lot slower, though.

- *Copy System Files Only*   This copies system files to a disk that's
  already formatted without removing any of the files already
  present. This function allows you to turn any floppy into a bootable floppy—providing there's room available on the floppy disk
  for the system files.

- *Label*   This lets you provide a label for the floppy.

- *Display Summary When Finished*   This option is on by default.
  When the formatting is complete, it displays the details of the formatted disk. Clear the box if you don't want to be bothered with
  this information.

- *Copy System Files*   Check this if you want system files copied to
  the disk to make the disk bootable.

4   When you're finished selecting options, click Start.

Tip   If Windows Explorer (or any open window) is showing the contents of the floppy
disk, Windows 98 concludes that the floppy disk is in use and therefore can't be formatted. If you get that message, click your drive C icon in Windows Explorer or close
the desktop window showing the contents of the floppy. Then right-click the floppy
disk icon and select Format from the shortcut menu.

Key Points

- Folders are the basic organizational units in Windows 98.

- Create new folders inside My Documents for different categories of
  files and take advantage of long file names to make finding and recog-
  nizing documents easy.

- Select Folder Options from the View Menu to set system-wide
  folder options.

- Some program and system files are intentionally hidden and shouldn't be moved or deleted.

- File associations tell the operating system that a particular file name extension is linked to a specific application.

- By default, Windows 98 is set up to deposit all deleted files in the Recycle Bin, a reserved space on your hard drive. Files deleted by mistake can be retrieved from the Recycle Bin.

- Files in the Recycle Bin are permanently deleted on a space-needed basis, so the Recycle Bin should be large enough to hold files for a reasonable amount of time.

Chapter 5

What *IS* That File?

When it comes to automobiles, some people really want to know what's going on under the hood, and an equally large number want to just turn the key and go. But even the turn-the-key-and-go folks admit that they have to do a *little* bit more—change the oil regularly, make sure the tires are inflated, and so on—if only to avoid becoming stranded or destroying their investment.

Similarly, some people positively yearn to know what's going on inside that computer box, while others shudder at the prospect. This chapter, along with Chapter 9, "Conquering Computer Hardware," and Chapter 12, "Maintaining a Healthy Computer," aims to provide what you need to know to keep from being stranded—plus a little bit more.

Those who claim no interest in computer innards can zip through this chapter, but Chapter 12 is required reading.

What You See on the Hard Disk Drive

What were directories and files in older operating systems are folders and documents in Microsoft Windows 95 and Microsoft Windows 98. But directories and files haven't really changed, just their names. You still hear the old names and probably will until the last DOS user has gone on to that great *X Files* convention in the sky.

By default, Windows 98 assumes you are the sort of user who doesn't want to be bothered by details, so many of the files and even whole folders on your computer are hidden from you. This does have the advantage of keeping you out of areas where you could do significant damage to the computer's operation. On the other hand, if you're reading this chapter, you're probably more curious than the average user and want to know more about what you're dealing with. For most situations, Windows 98 includes tools that you can use to save yourself, even if you do mess up.

Protected System Files

The operating system hides a whole series of files because moving, renaming, or deleting any of them can make your computer unstable. Table 5-1 shows the system files that should not be changed or moved.

Table 5-1   System Files to Leave Alone

File Name	Description
MSDOS.SYS	Boot configuration file
Io.sys	Real-mode operating system and system detection
Command.com	Command-line processor
Win.com	Real-mode stub to start Windows 98
Vmm32.vxd	Protected-mode Virtual Machine Manager
System.dat	Hardware specific information contained in the registry
User.dat	User specific information contained in the registry
Rb001.cab through Rb00n.cab	Registry backup files
Protocol.ini	Real-mode network configuration
System.ini	Windows environment system initialization file
Win.ini	Windows customization settings file
Explorer.exe	Shell executable file
Drvspace.bin	Compression support file

You should not delete any of these files. If you experience otherwise inexplicable errors, run the System File Checker to verify that all system files are okay. The System File Checker is on the System Tools submenu of the Accessories menu. If a system file turns out to be corrupted, the System File Checker can extract a clean version of the file from the Windows 98 installation CD. See the "If Windows 98 Will Start" section later in this chapter for more information.

Hidden Files and Folders

Hidden files and folders are unavailable because they are not in areas where most users need to venture. Deleting, renaming, or moving a hidden file probably won't make your computer stop working, but it might cause parts of Windows 98 to perform erratically or even fail.

When hidden files are not shown, you know of their existence by a report on the status bar, as shown in Figure 5-1.

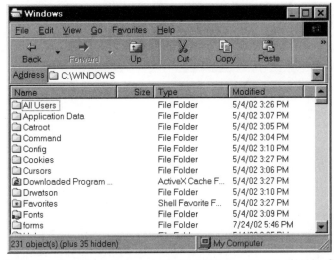

Figure 5-1 Even when not shown in the file listing, the presence of hidden files is reported in the status bar.

Other Files in the Windows Folder

In addition to the system files that Windows 98 hides by default, other operating system files are available to you. Some are utilities, some are programs in their own right, and some are simply files that are essential for normal operation of Windows 98.

By default, the normal installation directory for Windows 98 is in the Windows directory on your C drive. This directory, and its subdirectories, contain the literally thousands of files necessary for the normal operation of Windows 98. Ignore them.

Caution   Don't delete or change files in the Windows directory unless you know what you're doing and why you're doing it.

Program Files

Program files are installed by default into the Program Files folder on the same hard disk as the Windows folder (usually C). These files aren't hidden, but you should leave them alone. When you no longer want a program, remove it using Add/Remove Programs in Control Panel. This safely removes the unwanted files from your computer.

Simply deleting some or all of the files for a particular application doesn't completely remove it from your system and could cause problems. For example, if you delete some of the files for a program and later try deleting it using Add/Remove Programs, the operation fails and you may be stuck with a lot of stray files on your hard disk that are difficult to identify.

> **Note** To solve this little difficulty, see the section entitled "Getting Rid of Unneccessary Files" later in this chapter.

Temp Files

Temp files, as you might surmise, are temporary files created by programs and by the system itself. Each user has a Temp folder under his or her user profile. Another Temp folder is inside the Windows folder. Many temporary files have the .tmp extension, though other file types can show up in Temp folders.

Temporary files no longer in use can be deleted, but it's a tedious chore when done manually. A more efficient approach is to use Disk Cleanup periodically. Check the "The Disk Cleanup Solution" section later in this chapter.

> **Tip** Disk Cleanup seeks out and displays temporary files, compressible old files, temporary Internet files, and any other files cluttering your disks. You can then direct Disk Cleanup to delete some or all of those files.

What Are Cookies and How Did They Get Such a Silly Name?

A *cookie* is simply a small .txt file sent to your Web browser by a Web server. When you request a page from that server, the cookie is returned along with the page. The design is meant to benefit the user. Online sites such as Expedia, which require a user ID and password, store this information in the form of a cookie. When you return to Expedia, the cookie identifies you so that you don't have to enter your ID and password every visit; the server recognizes you. Similarly, online portals such as MSN and Yahoo! use cookies to "remember" users and offer customized news and services based on prior use. As another example, if you set up an account with an online retail store, cookies are used so you don't have to send your credit card information over the Internet repeatedly. The store reads the cookie and matches it to a stored profile that contains credit card data.

Cookies can't be malicious. They're just text files that you can delete at any time. Cookies can't spread viruses and they can't access your hard disk drive. However, any personal information that you give to a Web site, including credit card information, is probably stored in a cookie unless you have turned off the cookie feature in your browser. Cookies can only contain information that you voluntarily provide.

You can set Internet Explorer to accept all cookies, accept only per-session cookies (not stored on your computer), prompt you before accepting a cookie, or refuse all cookies. See Chapter 6, "Fearless Web Browsing" for information about setting cookie options.

Note   Internet Explorer 5 does not have the ability to regulate cookies—another reason to upgrade to Internet Explorer 6.

And how did cookies get that name? It seems to have originated in UNIX with magic cookies, which are a way of exchanging small tokens of information to help two programs (usually on separate computers) interact. And how did magic cookies get their name? Who knows? One can only point out that computer folk have always been fond of word play and fantasy fiction.

File Name Extensions and What They Mean

Though the term file format is used when talking about files with different extensions, it's not precisely accurate. The extension is what tells the operating system (and the program) what application is associated with the file. (See the section in Chapter 4 entitled "The Association Between Files and Programs" for more information on this topic.)

Inside the file, the actual file format may be similar or identical to any number of files with different extensions, but file format is still used as shorthand for file name extensions. Using this definition, there are thousands of different file formats.

Meet the Registry

Although it's not true that the registry is completely unmapped territory, it borders on it. The Help system in Windows 98 includes a few headings about how to backup and restore the registry but is tight-lipped about what the registry actually is.

See Also   *The almost 1800-page* Microsoft Windows 98 Resource Kit *kindly includes a chapter on the registry, but it's hardly a book for the average user.*

The reason for this peculiar reticence is that at the time Windows 98 was released, the registry was viewed as a dangerous place and none but the foolhardy would venture there. Opinions have changed somewhat, partly because many useful operations can be done only through the registry. Although there's no denying that it's *possible* to get into trouble changing the registry, it's also pretty easy to stay out of trouble.

Lingo   The *registry* is a binary hierarchical database that stores and maintains hardware and software information as well as user options. In other words, it keeps track of the programs on the computer and the types of documents each can create, user profiles, property sheet settings for folders and application icons, what hardware exists on the system, and which ports are in use. It's accessed indirectly when you make a hardware or software change.

Safeguarding the Registry

For all the dire warnings, the registry is really quite sturdy and robust. It can repair itself almost all the time. For the time not covered by "almost," you should always back up the registry before you make changes. The registry should also be backed up routinely along with other critical files on your computer. See Chapter 12, "Maintaining a Healthy Computer," for more on backups.

To make a quick backup of the registry, follow these steps.

1   Select Run from the Start menu.

2   Type **regedit** in the Open text box and click OK.

3   Select Export Registry File from the Registry menu. Enter a name for the file and click Save.

Tip   Include a date in the file name so that you can always recognize the most recent version, for example, 07-14.reg or 07-14-03.reg.

Software Problems? Check the Registry

The registry stores settings for programs installed on your computer. If these settings become corrupted or damaged, your programs and maybe even your computer won't run correctly.

Windows 98 comes with a utility called Registry Checker that checks the registry and backs it up every time you start the computer. If Registry Checker finds a problem in the registry, it automatically replaces the whole registry with the most recent backup copy.

To run the Registry Checker manually, follow these steps.

1   Click Start, select Programs, then Accessories, and then System Tools.
Click System Information.

2   Select Registry Checker from the Tools menu, as shown in Figure 5-2.

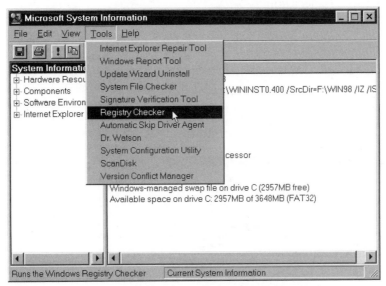

Figure 5-2 As soon as you select it, Registry Checker launches.

The tool checks your registry for errors and makes a backup of the registry
if you opt for it.

Registry Tricks

You can make most changes to the registry without ever using Regedit. For
example, changes in Control Panel and properties dialog boxes all change the
registry. However, some cool maneuvers require editing the registry directly. Just
be careful to backup first, and if the whole prospect makes you queasy, skip it.

Lingo   *Regedit.exe* is the program you run to actually access the Registry. To open Regedit, click
Start and then Run. Type **regedit.exe** in the text field and press Enter.

Getting Rid of the Network Neighborhood Icon

If you're not on a network and it annoys you to be reminded of that fact, eliminate the desktop Network Neighborhood icon with a simple registry edit. Follow these steps.

1 Click Start and select Run.

2 In the Open text box, type **regedit** and click OK.

3 In the Registry Editor, open the following path by clicking the plus signs next to each entry: `HKEY_CURRENT_USER\Software\Microsoft\Windows\CurrentVersion\Policies\Explorer`

4 In the right pane, right-click a blank spot and point to New and click String Value from the shortcut menu, as shown in Figure 5-3.

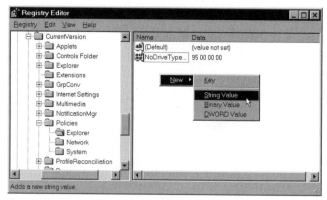

Figure 5-3 Add a new Value to the registry.

5 Type the new value **NoNetHood** in the New Value box.

6 Right-click the new value of NoNetHood and select Modify.

7 In the Edit String dialog box, type **1** in the Value Data box, as shown in Figure 5-4, then click OK.

Figure 5-4 Setting this value to 1 removes the Network Neighborhood icon.

Close the Registry Editor and reboot your system for the change to take effect.

Note   Change the value to 0 (zero) or delete the value entirely and the icon for Network Neighborhood returns with the next system reboot.

Getting Rid of the Recycle Bin on the Desktop

Yes, yes...we've repeatedly said that the Recycle Bin can't be removed from the desktop. Well, that was not exactly a lie, more like an exaggeration. You can actually eliminate the Recycle Bin with some effort. The Recycle Bin folder on every system remains, and you can right-click a file, select Delete, and send the file to the Recycle Bin, as usual. The only difference is that the icon is no longer on the desktop.

Caution   Once you delete the Recycle Bin icon from the desktop, you can't reverse the action. However, if you feel regretful, you can always make a shortcut to the Recycle Bin on the hard disk drive and put the shortcut on the desktop.

To delete the Recycle Bin from the desktop, follow these steps.

1 Start the Registry Editor (REGEDIT) as in the steps above.

2 Click the plus sign next to HKEY_CLASSES_ROOT and expand the levels to CSLID\{645FF040-5081-101B-9F08-00AA002F054E}\ShellFolder\, as shown in Figure 5-5.

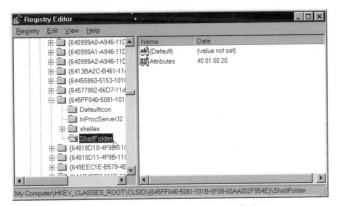

Figure 5-5 Locate the Registry entry for the Recycle Bin icon.

3 Right-click Attributes and select Modify.

4 In the Edit Binary Value dialog box, change 40 to 70. Click OK.

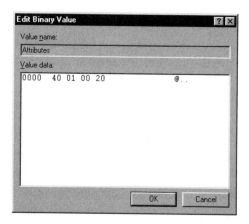

5   Close the Registry Editor.

6   Right-click the Recycle Bin icon and select Delete.

See Also   *If you're interested in plumbing the depths of the registry, you should try to find a copy of* Optimizing the Windows Registry *by Kathy Ivens, published by John Wiley & Sons, ISBN: 076453159X.*

Try This!   To reduce the amount of time it takes to reboot your computer, first select Folder Options from a View menu. Click the View tab and select the option to show all files. Then follow these steps.

1   Click Start, then Search, and then choose For Files Or Folders.

2   In the Named box, type **msdos.sys**; in the Look In box, select your C drive and click Find Now.

3   Once the file appears, right-click it and select Properties.

4   Deselect the Read-Only and Hidden attributes, and then click OK.

5   Right-click Msdos.sys and choose Open With from the shortcut menu. Select Notepad as the opening program.

6   Under Options, type **BootDelay=0** on its own line.

7   Save the file and close Notepad. Recheck the Read-Only and Hidden attributes for Msdos.sys.

8   Reboot your computer.

Getting Rid of Unnecessary Files

Windows 98 and the applications you run eventually create a shocking number of files on your hard disk drive. Over time, the ratio of useless files to useful ones grows higher and higher. The following sections cover the files you can delete with impunity as well as some files you can delete with caution.

The Disk Cleanup Solution

Before attempting anything tricky in the war against unnecessary files, start by running Disk Cleanup. Click Start, select Programs, then Accessories, then System Tools, and finally Disk Cleanup. Select the hard disk drive you want examined and the program reports on the files that can be deleted, as shown in Figure 5-6.

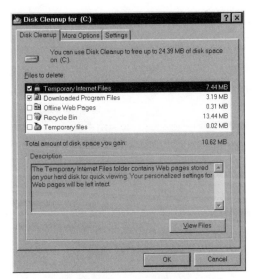

Figure 5-6 Check the boxes for actions you want.

Depending on your configuration, these files may include:

■ **Temporary Internet files**   To reduce loading time for Web documents, Internet Explorer stores copies of previously visited pages in a Temp directory. Each file is small but you can quickly accumulate hundreds of them.

■ **Downloaded program files**   Some Web pages cause program files to be downloaded and stored temporarily on your hard disk drive. These files cannot be automatically deleted when you close your browser.

- **Offline Web pages**   These are pages you've specifically requested to be stored on your computer so you can see them when you're not connected to the Internet.

- **Recycle Bin**   By default, this option is unchecked. Checking it permanently deletes all the files in the Recycle Bin. If this idea makes you nervous, leave the option unchecked and do a manual clearing of the Recycle Bin as described in Chapter 4, "Working with Files and Folders."

- **Temporary files**   Many programs deposit some files in a Temp directory and when you close the program, the files are usually deleted. However, if you shut down the system improperly (or more likely, the program crashes) the temporary files become permanent residents. Disk Cleanup can eliminate them.

Tip   If you're nervous about what might be deleted, click View Files and review the list of files scheduled for demolition.

Files You Can Delete

Disk Cleanup deals with some of the file types in Table 5-3, but not all of them. You can decide how to treat these files based on the table description and your needs for space.

Table 5-2   Disk Cleanup Files

Extension	What It Is
AVI	Video file. Usually very large.
BAK	A backup file. Older ones can be deleted.
BK!	WordPerfect backup document.
BMP, GIF, JPG, TIF	Graphics files. These can take up a lot of space. Delete the ones you don't need.
CAB	A type of compressed file used for software distribution. Delete if the application is installed and you have a backup of the program (in case you have to install it again).
CBT	Video training files. Huge and if you've seen them once, that's usually more than enough.
CHK	File fragments saved by Disk Defragmenter or Scandisk. Can also be a WordPerfect temporary file.
LNK	Shortcut.
MID, MP3, WAV	Sound files. Delete the ones you don't use.
TMP	A temporary file. Safe to delete any that don't have today's date.
ZIP	Archive. If you've extracted the files, you can delete the archive.

Clear Your Documents List

When you click Documents on the Start menu, you're presented with a list of short-cuts to the documents you've used recently. To clear the list of shortcuts from Documents, right-click a blank spot on the Taskbar and select Properties. Select the Start Menu Programs tab and then, in the Documents Menu frame, click Clear.

Automating the Search for Deletion Candidates

Certain types of files are always candidates for deletion, but you don't want to eliminate them without examination. For example, a file with a tilde (~) at the beginning of its name is probably suspect. Some LOG files are valid (such as the ones in Windows\System 32\Config). However, some applications (such as backup programs) generate many LOG files and may not clean them all up. Here's how to automate a search for these loiterers.

1   Open Notepad and type **dir c:\ *.log /s > c:\usual_suspects.txt**. The translation of this line is "Perform a listing of all the .log files on drive C, including subfolders (/s) and put the results in the usual_suspects file." Using the (>) character in this context is known as "piping" the results to a file.

2   On the second line type **dir c:\~*.* /s >>c:\usual_suspects.txt**. The second line translates to "Find files that begin with a tilde (~)" and to "add the list of these files to whatever is already in usual_suspects." It's important to use >> in the second and all subsequent lines. This appends the existing data, opposed to overwriting it."

3   Continue with separate lines for *.bak, *.tmp, *.~??, *.old or any other file types for which you want to search, as shown in Figure 5-7.

4   Save the file under a name you'll remember and give it the BAT (for batch) extension.

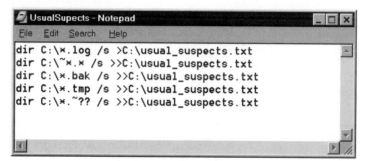

Figure 5-7 A batch file to search for stray files can be a bit tedious to write, but you only have to do it once.

Then when you feel the urge to do some spring-cleaning, double-click the BAT file. After the batch program completes, open the text file (in this case usual_suspects.txt) and review what the batch file has found. Figure 5-8 shows the results of a search. Use Windows Explorer to navigate to the locations of the main culprits and delete them.

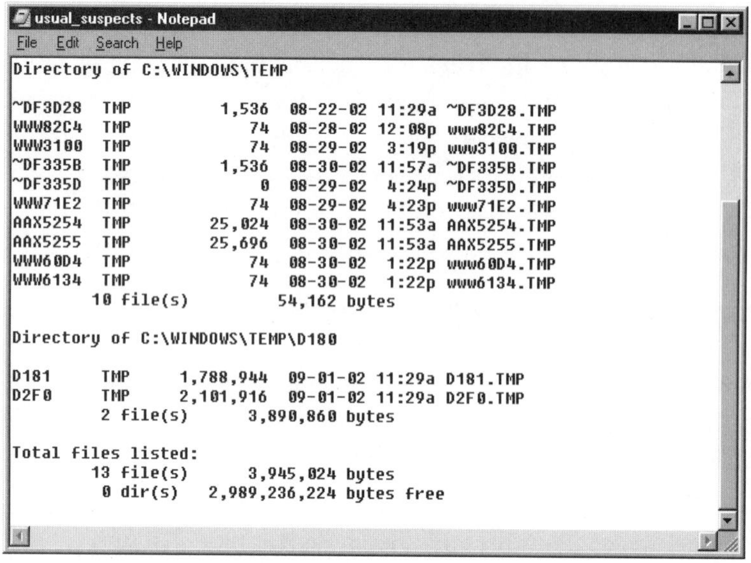

```
usual_suspects - Notepad                                        _ □ ✕
File  Edit  Search  Help
Directory of C:\WINDOWS\TEMP

~DF3D28   TMP        1,536   08-22-02  11:29a  ~DF3D28.TMP
WWW82C4   TMP           74   08-28-02  12:08p  www82C4.TMP
WWW3100   TMP           74   08-29-02   3:19p  www3100.TMP
~DF335B   TMP        1,536   08-30-02  11:57a  ~DF335B.TMP
~DF335D   TMP            0   08-29-02   4:24p  ~DF335D.TMP
WWW71E2   TMP           74   08-29-02   4:23p  www71E2.TMP
AAX5254   TMP       25,024   08-30-02  11:53a  AAX5254.TMP
AAX5255   TMP       25,696   08-30-02  11:53a  AAX5255.TMP
WWW60D4   TMP           74   08-30-02   1:22p  www60D4.TMP
WWW6134   TMP           74   08-30-02   1:22p  www6134.TMP
        10 file(s)        54,162 bytes

Directory of C:\WINDOWS\TEMP\D180

D181      TMP    1,788,944   09-01-02  11:29a  D181.TMP
D2F0      TMP    2,101,916   09-01-02  11:29a  D2F0.TMP
         2 file(s)     3,890,860 bytes

Total files listed:
        13 file(s)       3,945,024 bytes
         0 dir(s)    2,989,236,224 bytes free
```

Figure 5-8 The text file can be deleted after you've used it. The batch file recreates it every time it's run.

Tip Although the Disk Cleanup Wizard does an admirable job of cleaning up after Windows, it doesn't pick up your clothes, so to speak. Use Windows Explorer to look through your own files and delete old documents and images that you don't expect to use again.

Files You Must Not Delete

As mentioned earlier in this chapter, it's important not to delete system files. Other critical files include files with the DLL extension.

When you have thousands of files, you eventually end up in the unenviable state known as DLL Hell. This condition arises when you have many, many DLL files—some useful, some worthless, and you can't tell which are which. The torture becomes even more exquisite when you suspect that you don't have the particular DLL file you need despite having several DLL files (identically named) but with different sizes and dates.

The solution to DLL Hell is available at DLL Help (*http://support.microsoft.com/ servicedesks/fileversion/dllinfo.asp*), a searchable database of information about file versions that ship with particular Microsoft products. The investment of some time is well worth it if you can eliminate excess DLL files.

- Don't delete files beginning with $—such as $MFT.

- Don't delete files with the SYS, DAT, MOD, CPL, or VXD extensions.

Actually, rather than trying to memorize all the file types, you'll be safe if you follow two rules of file deletion.

- If you don't know what a file is, don't delete it.

- If you think you know what a file is but have even a little bit of a reservation about whether you need it, make a new folder called Delete Pending. Move the file into that folder. Proceed as usual. If nothing untoward happens for some reasonable period of time, go ahead and delete the file.

How to Recover a File If You Delete It

No one's perfect, right? And we imperfect people occasionally do precisely what we're not supposed to—including deleting a crucial file. If the system lets you know that an important file is corrupted or missing from Windows 98, you can usually obtain the file from the Windows 98 CD without resorting to more drastic measures.

Note The following procedure depends on you already having a Windows 98 Startup Disk. If you don't have one, you should, even if you never have to recover a lost Windows 98 file. See Chapter 12, "Maintaining a Healthy Computer," for information on how to make and update a startup disk.

If Windows 98 Will Start

Windows 98 includes a System File Checker tool that can verify the soundness of your operating system files, restore damaged ones, and extract compressed files from the Windows 98 CD.

To use System File Checker to extract a file from the Windows 98 CD, follow these steps:

1   Click Start, select Programs, Accessories, System Tools, and then click System Information.

2   On the Tools menu, click System File Checker.

3 Click Extract One File from installation disk, enter the name of the file you want to extract in the Specify The System File You Would Like To Restore text box, then click Start.

4 In the Restore From text box, type the path to the Win98 folder on the Windows 98 CD, type the destination folder in the Save File In text box if necessary, and then click OK.

5 If you want to back up the existing file before overwriting it, you can specify a location for the backed up file.

6 Click OK and then Close. Restart your computer if you're prompted to do so.

7 If you don't specify a CAB file in the Restore From box, System File Checker searches the folder and all CAB files in the folder.

If Windows 98 Won't Start

If the file is crucial enough, Windows 98 displays an error message during startup and refuses to start. In those circumstances you need to restore the problem file at the command prompt. Here are the steps to do it.

1 Insert the Windows 98 Startup disk in drive A, and start the computer.

2 When the Windows 98 Startup menu appears, choose Start Computer With CD Support.

3 Insert the Windows 98 CD in the CD drive.

4 When the A:\ prompt appears, type **ext** and press Enter. Type in the path to the CAB files. If your CD drive is normally D, it is now temporarily E, so you'd type **E:\win 98**.

5 Enter the name of the file you want to extract, then the location to extract to.

6 You're then asked to approve the options you've entered. After you enter Y, the extraction proceeds.

7 Remove the Startup disk and the CD from their respective drives and restart your computer.

Note When you start your computer with the Startup disk and CD support enabled, the system creates a virtual disk drive for startup files using the first available disk drive letter. If you have a hard disk drive C and your CD drive is D, the files are on virtual drive D and the CD drive is temporarily moved over one letter to E.

Key Points

■ What were once called directories and files are renamed folders and documents in Windows 98. Only the names have changed and both sets of names are still used by many people.

■ System files and hidden files should remain hidden for safety's sake unless you have a specific reason for viewing one.

■ Cookies are text messages sent to a Web browser by a Web server. Cookies can't damage your computer and contain only information that you have voluntarily provided.

■ File extensions tell you what program or process created the file.

■ The registry stores all the information about the computer—both hardware and software, along with user specific settings. While care must be taken when changing the registry, it's surprisingly robust and difficult to damage seriously.

■ The operation of Windows 98 eventually results in numerous stray files. Regularly seek them out and eliminate them with Disk Cleanup.

Chapter 6

Fearless Web Browsing

This chapter is all about the Internet and Web browsing. It's a big scary (virtual) world out there, whether you're an experienced globetrotter or setting sail for the first time. There's always more to learn, and this chapter is here to help.

First we'll talk about how to choose an Internet service provider (ISP), set up a connection using the Internet Connection Wizard, and connect and disconnect from the Internet using a dial-up connection. You can skip these sections if you're already connected, but you'll want to read the rest of the chapter, which is chock full of valuable information and tips on using Microsoft Internet Explorer to browse the Web.

Lingo   An *ISP* (Internet service provider) is a company that provides Internet access. Most ISPs provide Web access, one or more e-mail accounts, access to newsgroups, and possibly some storage space for a personal Web site.

Choosing an ISP

Like choosing a romantic partner, selecting an ISP can be difficult. Countless candidates offer wildly divergent drawbacks and benefits, all couched in confusing language. Fortunately, choosing an ISP doesn't have to involve years of rejection, awkward approaches, or messy breakups—although not every relationship works out and you might have to try several ISPs before you find a good match.

Types of Connections

In an ideal world, you should be able to choose an ISP based on your needs for speed, cost, and reliability. However, a fourth factor is inescapable—geography. Depending on where you live, some choices just may not be available. Digital Subscriber Line (DSL), cable, and wireless are available only in limited areas. In addition, the maximum listed speeds are often in excess of what you actually experience. See the Table 6-1 to compare types of connections.

Table 6-1   Internet Connection Types

Type of Connection	Download/Upload Speed	Requirements
ADSL (Asynchronous) runs at a different speed up and down	256 Kbps-8 Mbps download 192 Kbps-1 Mbps upload	No more than 18,000 feet from a telephone company central office (CO).
IDSL Integrated Services Digital Network (ISDN) over a DSL line	128 Kbps each way	No more than 26,000 feet from a telephone company CO.
SDSL (Synchronous DSL—speed is the same in both directions)	Maximum of 1.5 Mbps for both the upload and download	No more than 20,000 feet from the telephone company CO.
Cable	128 Kbps-8 Mbps download 128 Kbps-1 Mbps upload	Access to broadband cable service.
ISDN	64-128 Kbps each way (one channel or two)	No more than 50,000 feet from the telephone company CO.
Dial-Up	28.8-53 Kbps download 28.8-40 Kbps upload	Analog telephone line. Sometimes referred to as Plain Old Telephone Service (POTS).
Wireless	256 Kbps-1.54 Mbps	Line of sight to ISP's antennas.
Satellite	150 Kbps-3 Mbps download 33.6 Kbps - 128 Kbps upload	Line of sight to satellite (southern sky in North America).

Tip   Visit *http://www.dslreports.com* for an immense amount of information on DSL, including the providers in your area, technical data, user reviews, and ratings of providers.

Bits and Bytes   A bit is as basic a unit of data as they come in the computer world—it's a pure digital on or off (0 or 1), just like a light switch. It takes 8 bits to make up one byte, and it takes one byte to make a single character, such as the letter *a*. A kilobit (Kb) is 1024 bits, and a kilobyte (KB) is 1024 bytes. Similarly, a megabit (Mb) is one million bits, and a megabyte (MB) is either 1,048,576 bytes (2 to the 20th power) or one million bytes. Disk manufacturers typically use the one million bytes definition, whereas Windows uses the 2 to the 20th definition. Some practical implications are that a 2 MB floppy disk can store 1.44 MB in Windows, and a 100 MB Zip disk stores only 95.8 MB, as reported by Windows.

Network speeds are measured in either kilobits per second (Kbps) or megabits per second (Mbps). Hard disk drive speeds are rated in megabytes per second (MBps). We've experienced 640 Kbps DSL connections that download files at 60 kilobytes (KBps) downloads from a fast Web site, and 1.5 Mbps cable Internet connections that download at 180 KBps.

More Considerations

Given the number of providers in some areas, often offering connections that appear to be the same, consider these additional factors when choosing an ISP.

- Setup fees
- Contract length
- Hours per month
- Number of e-mail accounts
- E-mail account type

Lingo   *Post Office Protocol* (POP) accounts are the most common type of e-mail accounts. With a POP account, all mail is downloaded from the server to your local computer (although you can leave copies on the server if you want). Internet Messaging Access Protocol (IMAP) accounts store all messages on the server in one or more message folders, allowing you to access your mail from any location (though you can download messages to your computer if you want).

- Web mail support
- Free Web server space
- Nationwide dial-up access and toll-free numbers

When shopping for a dial-up ISP, ask the salesperson about the ratio of users per modem. If the ISP has many more than ten users for every one of its modems, you'll start getting busy signals during peak usage hours.

Normal dial-up modems take around 25–27 seconds to connect; V.92 dial-up modems take around 13 seconds (when used with a V.92 ISP); ISDN and dial-up DSL take a second or two, and always-on DSL and cable are always on (no connection time).

Finding an ISP

Finding the right ISP can be overwhelming. Start with local computer publications, newspapers, and computer magazines. Ask your friends about their ISPs. Try the Internet Connection Wizard, discussed later in this chapter. Still hunting? Check the Web sites below, but don't agonize too long. It's not the end of the world if you have to change later.

- *http://www.boardwatch.com*

- *http://www.cnet.com/internet/*

- *http://www.epinions.com*

- *http://www.etestinglabs.com*

- *http://www.isp.com*

If you don't have Internet access, go to a public library to do your ISP research—most provide free Internet access. If you have a laptop with an 801.11b wireless network adapter, you can also get free or low-cost Internet access at an increasing number of public places—airports, coffee shops, and so forth.

The Online Services Difference Online services such as Microsoft Network (MSN), America Online (AOL), and CompuServe are different from other ISPs, although the differences are becoming more blurred. In the past, online services were closed, proprietary systems. Today, online services still hold onto their proprietary content and software, though most allow you to use industry standard software in addition to their own software (which you still have to use for some things).

These services are easy to use, and if you're a US Postal Service customer, you've undoubtedly received many CDs and other solicitations from all of them. Make sure you know the real costs (no local number means toll charges) and how to cancel before you sign up—even for a "trial offer." (Cancellation procedures are often hard to find.)

Using the Internet Connection Wizard

The Internet Connection Wizard helps you get connected to the Internet and even find an ISP if you need to (though it only offers limited selection). If you're using an ISP that provides its own software, use that instead.

See Also *For information on manually specifying dial-up settings, see "Working with Dial-Up Connections" in Chapter 14, "Connecting from Home or On the Road."*

Creating a New Account

To use the Internet Connection Wizard to find a dial-up ISP and create a new account, follow these steps:

1 Click Start, choose Programs, Accessories, Internet Tools, and then Internet Connection Wizard.

2 Select the first option and click Next.

3 Select an ISP from the list and review its offering. When you've selected an ISP you like, click Next.

4 Follow the directions on the screen.

5 The Internet Connection Wizard connects to the ISP of your choice and assigns you a user ID and password. Follow any additional instructions to finish setting up your account.

Transferring an Existing Account

If you have an e-mail account with one of the larger ISPs and want to transfer it to a new computer, follow these steps.

1 Click Start and choose Programs, Accessories, Internet Tools, and then Internet Connection Wizard.

2 Select the second option to transfer an existing account.

3 Select your ISP from the list and then click Next. If your ISP isn't listed, use your ISP's software to set up your connection. You can also set up the connection manually by selecting My Internet Service Provider Is Not Listed and then clicking Next.

4 Fill out the information requested and then click Next. Follow any additional directions.

Connecting Through a LAN

Getting Internet access through a network connection isn't just for corporate users anymore—users of home networks and broadband Internet connections also connect to the Internet through a local area network (LAN).

Lingo   A *local area network* (LAN) is a network consisting of computers in a single location.

Although setting up the network may not be easy, using one to connect to the Internet is. If you're not already up and running on the Internet, use the following steps to get connected.

1   Click Start, choose Programs, Accessories, Internet Tools, and then Internet Connection Wizard.

2   Select the third option and click Next.

3   Choose I Connect Through A Local Area Network (LAN) and click Next.

4   Select the Manual Proxy Server check box if you need to manually configure *proxy server* settings (ask your network administrator or ISP); otherwise, leave the settings as shown in Figure 6-1 and click Next.

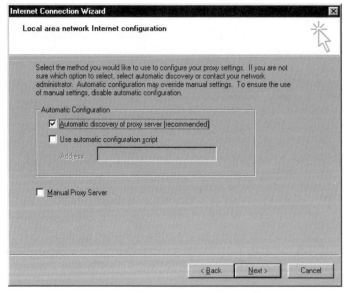

Figure 6-1 If your network or ISP has a proxy server for additional performance and security, you should make use of it.

Lingo   A *proxy server* sits between your Web browser and a real server. It intercepts all requests to the real server to see if it can fulfill the requests itself. If not, it forwards the request to the real server. A proxy server uses its cached Web pages to serve already accessed Web pages to requesting clients without requiring outside access to the Internet. Because proxy servers are closer to you than the rest of the Internet (they usually sit on your local network or on the ISP's network), getting Web pages from a proxy server is usually much faster than from other locations.

---

5   Enter the proxy server settings provided by your ISP or network administrator (if you chose the Manual Proxy Server selection) and then click Next.

6   Choose whether or not to set up an e-mail account and then click Next. To set up an e-mail account, enter your name, e-mail address, mail servers, account name, and password, as prompted by the wizard.

See Also   Refer to Chapter 13, "Building and Using a Network," for more information about how to set up a LAN.

Connecting and Disconnecting from the Internet

You can't go anywhere on the "information superhighway" without first establishing a connection to the Internet. If you're using a cable or DSL Internet connection, you're always connected, so go ahead and skip this section (although users of so-called dial-up DSL should read on).

Dial-up connections are supposed to be established automatically when you open Internet Explorer or check your e-mail, but they often aren't. Similarly, Windows theoretically disconnects from the Internet when you close your last Internet program, but in actuality rarely does, so you should also learn how to do this manually.

Connecting Automatically—the Easy Way

If your software is set up correctly, Windows connects to the Internet automatically whenever you launch an Internet application such as Microsoft Internet Explorer or Microsoft Outlook Express. If this doesn't happen and you want it to, follow these steps to remedy the situation:

1   Open Control Panel and double-click Internet Options. This is also accessible from the Tools menu in Internet Explorer.

2   Click the Connections tab, shown in Figure 6-2.

Figure 6-2 Use the Connections tab to specify how Windows should connect to the Internet.

3   Select the connection that you want Windows to dial by default and click Set Default.

4   Select the Always Dial My Default Connection option and click OK.

Note   If your ISP provides its own dialing software, use it instead of Windows built-in software.

Tip   If your computer normally connects to the Internet over a network connection but connects through a modem when disconnected from the network, select the Dial Whenever A Network Connection Is Not Present option.

Connecting Manually—Not Quite as Easy

Sometimes you need to manually establish an Internet connection. Maybe the Windows automatic connection feature decides to take a vacation, or perhaps you manually disconnected from the Internet and now want to reconnect. Although manually connecting to the Internet isn't as easy as having it done for you, it's not difficult. Use your ISP's dialer software, or follow these steps:

1   Open My Computer, double-click Dial-up Networking, and then double-click the appropriate Internet connection.

2   In the Connect To box, type your username and password (if necessary), and select the Save Password check box if you want to save yourself this hassle next time.

3   Verify that the phone number is correct and click Connect. After Windows establishes a connection, a connection icon appears in the System Tray.

See Also   *For information on manually creating dial-up connections, see the "Working with Dial-Up Connections" section of Chapter 14, "Connecting from Home or On the Road."*

Disconnecting

Closing all Internet applications should cause Windows to ask whether you want to disconnect from the Internet, but it usually doesn't. To disconnect manually, right-click the connection icon in the System Tray and choose Disconnect from the shortcut menu. To adjust when Windows automatically disconnects for you, follow these steps:

1   Open Control Panel, double-click Internet Options, and click the Connection tab

2   Select the appropriate connection, click Settings, and then click Advanced.

3   Select the Disconnect If Idle For check box, as shown in Figure 6-3, and specify how long Windows should wait after your last Internet action before automatically disconnecting.

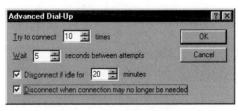

Figure 6-3 Setting an automatic disconnect time is a good idea, although most ISPs eventually disconnect if the connection remains idle for a period of time.

4   Select the Disconnect When Connection May No Longer Be Needed check box to have Windows prompt you to disconnect when you close all Internet applications.

Getting Around with Internet Explorer

Once you've established an Internet connection, it's time to start poking around on the Web. This section gets you going with Internet Explorer. It tells you how to get the latest version; familiarizes you with its interface; and also shows you how to enter Web addresses, deal with slow pages, and choose your home page. All with a sprinkling of advanced surfing tips and techniques.

Although other Web browsers are available—such as MSN Explorer (which is a customized version of Internet Explorer), Netscape Navigator, and Opera—Internet Explorer is the most popular, by far.

See Also   For information on privacy and security on the Web, including a discussion on cookies, see Security and Internet Explorer in Chapter 11, "Playing It Safe."

Get the Latest Version

Windows 98 comes with Internet Explorer 4, and Windows 98 SE includes Internet Explorer 5. Although Internet Explorer 5 is a step in the right direction, everyone should upgrade to Internet Explorer 6 (covered in this chapter) and continue to upgrade as newer versions become available. Not only does upgrading provide additional features (such as Print Preview and extra control over privacy), newer versions also provide greatly increased security from hackers and display new Web pages better than older versions.

To upgrade to the latest version of Internet Explorer, choose Windows Update from the Start menu and then select the appropriate version of Internet Explorer. You can also visit the Internet Explorer Web site (*http://www.microsoft.com/windows/ie*), where you can download the latest versions (a 6 to 17 MB download) or order the latest version on CD for a nominal cost.

See Also   The section "Updating Your Software" in Chapter 12, "Maintaining a Healthy Computer," contains more information on using Windows Update.

Getting to Know Internet Explorer

Launch Internet Explorer by double-clicking the icon on the desktop or the icon on the Quick Launch toolbar (next to the Start button). Figure 6-4 illustrates parts of the Internet Explorer interface.

- **Standard Buttons toolbar**   Contains commonly used commands, such as Back, Stop, Search, and Print. Click the small triangle to the right of Back and Forward to jump multiple pages backwards or forwards.

Tip To view more than one page at a time, open a new browser window. To do this, choose New from the File menu, then Window, or right-click a link you want to follow and choose Open In New Window.

■ **Address Bar** Displays the Uniform Resource Locator (URL) of the current Web page and is used to enter addresses.

■ **Links Toolbar** Contains shortcuts to commonly used Web sites.

■ **Explorer Logo** Animated while loading a Web page.

■ **Explorer Bar** Displays the contents of the Search, Favorites, Media, and History bars, or the hierarchy of folders on your computer.

■ **Status Bar** Displays the status of pages being loaded and also displays the URL for a link when you hover the mouse pointer over it.

■ **Security Zone** Displays the security zone of the current Web page. Privacy reports and encryption status appear to the left of the security zone.

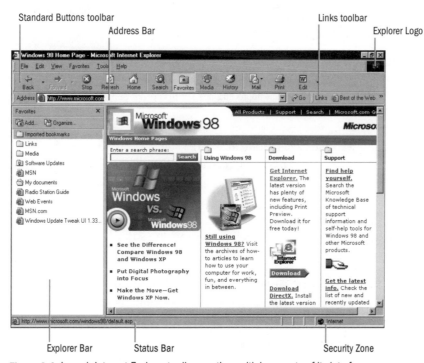

Figure 6-4 Launch Internet Explorer to discover the multiple aspects of its interface.

Entering Web Addresses

Usually you open a Web page by clicking a hyperlink on another Web page (or in an e-mail), choosing the page from your Favorites menu (discussed later), or by using a search engine. However, if you already know the address of the Web page, or think you might be able to guess it, you can also enter the address directly in the Address bar of Internet Explorer. This is usually faster than performing a search and might also be faster than browsing through numerous pages looking for the proper hyperlink or hunting through a cluttered Favorites folder.

To go to a Web page by entering its address or URL, click in the Address bar, type the URL of the page, and then press Enter or click Go.

Tip   To change the text size on a Web page, choose Text Size from the View menu and select a size, or, if your mouse has a wheel, hold down the Ctrl key and scroll to change the size.

If you don't know the exact address, you can guess based on the company's name and the kind of Web site it would have. For example, *http://www.microsoft.com* would be a good guess for Microsoft Corporation, as would *http://www.adobe.com* for Adobe.

Note   The most recent domains (*museum, coop, aero, biz, info, pro, name*) were approved in November 2000 by the Internet Corporation for Assigned Names and Numbers (ICANN). The new domains are the first top-level domains approved since 1988. *Info, biz,* and *name* are accepting registrations.

However, many Web sites that belong in another category are registered as .com just because it was and is the most popular top-level domain. For example, even though Earthlink is an Internet company, its address is *http://www.earthlink.com*.

Unleashing the Power of the Address Bar

Though it masquerades as a modest toolbar, the Address Bar has a number of hidden and powerful talents.

- Click once in the Address bar to highlight an URL, and then type the URL you want—the old URL is replaced automatically. Double-click if you have trouble selecting the entire address.

- If the URL begins with *http://*, no need to type it—Internet Explorer automatically fills this in.

- To quickly type a URL that begins with *www* and ends with *.com*, enter the center portion of the name and press Ctrl+Enter. (For example, to go to *http://www.microsoft.com*, type **Microsoft,** and then press Ctrl+Enter.)

- As you type a URL, Internet Explorer may display a drop-down list of recently viewed Web sites, as shown in Figure 6-5 (display this list by clicking the down arrow at end of the Address Bar or pressing F4). If you see the URL you're trying to type, click it or press the down arrow on the keyboard until it's selected and then press Enter.

Figure 6-5 Use the Address Bar to enter Internet addresses which may prompt the display of a drop-down list of recently viewed sites.

Note   To visit a File Transfer Protocol (FTP) site (a type of Internet location predating the Web that stores nothing but files), enter **ftp://** followed by the FTP address.

- For an address that doesn't connect, try deleting the file name from the address, or the file name and one or more levels of subfolders. For example, if *www.adatum.com /techcomm.html* returns a Page Not Found message, try plain *www.adatum.com*.

- Copy and paste addresses to and from the Address Bar by right-clicking in the Address Bar.

Note   The extension on Web file names indicates the tool used in its construction. The extension .htm or .html refers to Hypertext Markup Language. The extension .asp means the file is an Active Server Page, a file that may contain text, Hypertext Markup Language (HTML) elements, and ASP script commands

---

Dealing with Slow Pages and Reloading

Sometimes a Web page seems to take forever to load because the Web is performing slowly; other times it's just a quirk of the Web site. In any case, if a Web page is taking an inordinate amount of time to display, it's time to stop and reload—no ammo required.

- To stop a slow Web page from loading, click Stop or press Esc.
- To reload a Web page, click the Refresh button or press F5.

When you reload a Web page, Web page forms are reset unless you let Internet Explorer repost your form data (it'll prompt you). If you run into a Web page that spawns pop-up windows (a favorite gimmick among unsavory Web businesses), methodically close each window as it pops up.

Tip If pop-up ads are making you pop your cork, install one of the many ad-killer programs available. One of the best is Filtergate (*http://filtergate.com*). Entering "ad filter" in any search engine turns up many more.

Setting a Home Page

The page that appears when you start Internet Explorer is called your *home page*. As such, it acts as the starting point for your Web travels, and should therefore be either the Web site you most frequently access, or a good jumping off point to the Web sites or information you like to access (MSN, Yahoo, and others have specially designed pages that provide you with a customized home page containing headlines and links of interest). To change your home page, follow these steps.

1 Launch Internet Explorer and choose Internet Options from the Tools menu.

2 Specify what page should be your home page:

- Click Use Current to use the Web page you're currently viewing.

- To use a different page, type the URL of the Web page.

- To use the default home page (usually *http://www.msn.com*), click Use Default.

- Click Use Blank to make your home page a blank document, speeding up Internet Explorer's load time.

Keeping Track of Web Pages

Getting around with Internet Explorer is relatively easy (as you learned in the previous sections), but remembering the location of every significant Web page you've ever visited is not. This is why Internet Explorer comes with a couple of memory-enhancing features—Favorites and the History folder—as well as several techniques for saving pages to your hard disk or e-mailing pages to friends.

The following sections show you how to save references to your favorite Web pages with the Favorites feature; to use the History folder to go back to recently viewed pages; and to save, e-mail, and print pages of note.

Playing Favorites

The Favorites list is a special folder for storing shortcuts to your favorite Websites. Select the Favorites menu in Internet Explorer to see what's in your folder—Microsoft or your ISP prepopulates it with some useful and not-so-useful links.

Note   Internet Explorer's Favorites feature works just like Netscape Navigator's Bookmarks feature.

Adding to the Favorites list

To add a Web page to the Favorites list, use the following steps:

1   When the page is displayed, choose Add To Favorites from the Favorites menu.

2   Modify (or accept) the title of the Web page in the Name text box, as shown in Figure 6-6.

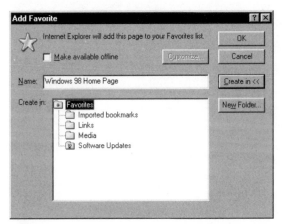

Figure 6-6   Use the Add Favorite dialog box to add Web pages to the Favorites list.

3   To store the favorite in a subfolder, click Create In, and then select the appropriate folder, or click New Folder to create one.

4   To set up the page for offline viewing, select the Make Available Offline check box. Internet Explorer downloads the page to your hard disk drive and makes it easy for you to periodically synchronize the Web page so that you can view a fresh copy while disconnected from the Internet.

5   Click OK. To return to a saved favorite, choose it from the Favorites menu.

Tip For short-term saving, create a shortcut on the desktop to a Web page by choosing Send from the File menu and then choosing Shortcut To Desktop. Or you can drag the small Internet Explorer icon at the left of the Address bar to the desktop. When you no longer need the shortcut, delete it.

Browsing While Disconnected from the Internet

Internet Explorer comes with the optional Offline Browsing Pack, which allows you to synchronize and then view Web pages while disconnected from the Internet. To use this feature, add the pages you want to view offline to your Favorites menu, right-click the pages in the Favorites menu and choose Make Available Offline from the shortcut menu. To set up a synchronization schedule or synchronize the pages, choose Synchronize from the Tools menu. To switch to offline browsing mode, choose Work Offline from the File menu.

If you can't find any of the offline browsing features, connect to the Internet and then use the following steps to install the Offline Browsing Pack:

1 Open Control Panel and then click Add/Remove Programs.

2 Select Internet Explorer and click Add/Remove.

3 Choose Add A Component and then click OK.

4 Select Offline Browsing Pack and then click Next.

Organizing the Favorites List

It doesn't take long to develop an extensive and cluttered Favorites list. To tidy things up, choose the Organize Favorites command from the Favorites menu.

■ In the Organize Favorites dialog box, you can perform all the necessary steps to organize your list.

■ Click Create Folder to create a new folder in which you can place favorites.

■ Select one or more favorites, click Move To Folder, select the folder in which you want to place them, and then click OK.

■ Select a favorite and click Rename to change the favorite's title.

■ Click and drag favorites and folders up and down to rearrange the order in which they appear (this works in the Favorites menu and Favorites bar as well).

■ Click Close when you're finished.

Importing and Exporting Favorites

To import a list of favorites or a bookmark file from another computer or Web browser or to export your favorites to a bookmark.htm file (which is simply a Web page consisting of your favorite hyperlinks), use the following steps:

1   Choose Import And Export from the File menu to open the Import/ Export Wizard, and then click Next.

2   Choose Import Favorites or Export Favorites and then click Next.

3   If you chose to import favorites, choose whether to import favorites from a file or an application, and then click Next.

- Select Import From An Application to import favorites from another Web browser. If another Web browser is not installed on your system this option is dimmed.

- Select Import From A File Or Address to import favorites from a bookmark file (a Web page with nothing but hyperlinks). Click Browse to locate the bookmark.htm file.

4   If you chose to export favorites, choose the folder from which you want to export (choose Favorites to export all favorites), and then click Next.

5   Type the file name and path of the file to which you want to save your favorites, click Next, and then click Finish.

Tip   You can also manually copy shortcuts from the Favorites folder on one computer to the Favorites folder on another computer. Just open the Favorites folders in Internet Explorer and copy away (right-click a subfolder on the Favorites menu and choose Explore to find the Favorites folder).

Paying Attention to History

The second memory booster that Internet Explorer provides is the History folder. The History folder keeps track of all the Web pages that you visit so that you can retrace your steps, if necessary.

To use the History folder, as shown in Figure 6-7, click History on the toolbar, and then use the following features in the History pane.

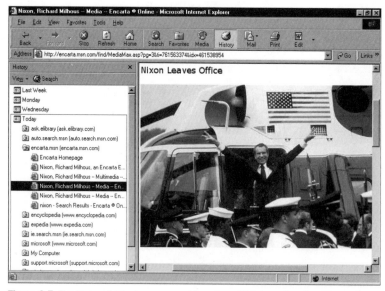

Figure 6-7 The History folder keeps an archive of your Web browsing—just like setting up audio taping in the White House. Keep this in mind.

▪ Click the time period (for example, Tuesday or Last Week) from which you want to view visited Web pages.

▪ Click a site to view the Web pages within the site that you visited.

▪ Click a page to retrieve it from the Internet (Internet Explorer only keeps a reference to it, not the actual Web page).

▪ To delete a site or page from the list (perhaps you're just a tiny bit embarrassed about all those visits to the Britney Spears Web site), right-click it and choose Delete.

▪ Click Search to hunt for a page within the History folder.

▪ To change the way pages are displayed, click View and choose the desired view:

  ● **By Date** Categorizes pages viewed by day and week.

  ● **By Site** Displays a list of sites you've visited, in alphabetical order.

  ● **By Most Visited** Displays the frequently visited pages and locations (Outlook locations can also appear here).

  ● **By Order Visited Today** Displays the pages you viewed today, in chronological order.

■ To adjust how many days are recorded in the History folder, select Internet Options from the Tools menu and then enter a number in the Day To Keep Pages In History box. Increasing the number of days allows you to look back further into the past but also permits anyone else who gains access to your computer to look deeper into your browsing habits.

■ To empty the History folder, choose Internet Options from the Tools menu and then click Clear History.

Caution   Just as you can use the History folder to jog your memory, anyone with access to your hard disk drive can use the History folder to see which Web sites you've viewed. For more information on covering your tracks (such as checking for spyware, deleting temporary files and cookies as well as clearing the Document history), see the "Cover Your Tracks" section of Chapter 11, "Playing It Safe."

Saving Web Pages

Sometimes a shortcut to a Web page just isn't enough. Perhaps the page has a lot of detailed information that you want always available, or maybe the page is transient—it might change or vanish at any time. To save a Web page to your hard disk drive, follow these steps.

1   When the page is displayed in Internet Explorer, choose Save As from the File menu.

2   Open the folder in which you want to save the Web page. Use the Save In text box and the buttons to the right of it to help find the proper folder.

3   If necessary, modify the file name to something more descriptive.

4   Choose the file type you want to save the Web page as.

● **Web Page, Complete (*.htm, *.html)**   saves the Web page in its entirety, with all pictures and other associated files saved in a subfolder.

● **Web Archive, Single File (*.mht)**   saves the Web page in its entirety as a single file, making it easier to transport and creating less clutter. Internet Explorer is the only browser that can read this file type.

- **Web Page, HTML Only (*.htm, *.html)**   saves the Web page without any associated images or associated files. Creates a small file with all proper formatting.

- **Text File (*.txt)**   saves the Web page as pure text, without any formatting or pictures. Creates the smallest but least attractive file.

5   Click Save.

E-mailing Web Pages

When you encounter a Web page that you *must* share with someone, it's easy to send the page or a link to it by e-mail.

■   To send the entire Web page as an attachment, choose Send from the File menu and then choose Page By E-mail.

■   To send a link to the Web page, choose Send from the File menu and then choose Link By E-mail. Note that because of new security features in Outlook and Outlook Express, this may not work (if you don't see the URL in the body of the mail message, as shown in Figure 6-8, use the next technique instead).

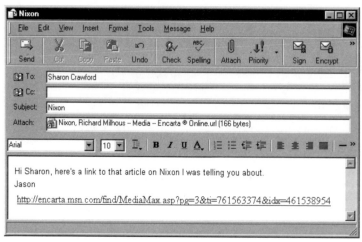

Figure 6-8 The Send Link By E-mail command creates a new mail message with a link in the body of the message and as an attachment (which some e-mail programs strip out).

■   Right-click the URL of the current Web page in the Address Bar (the entire address should automatically be selected) or right-click the desired hyperlink and choose Copy. Compose a new e-mail message, right-click on a separate line, and choose Paste.

Note   Many URLs are too long to work as hyperlinks in an e-mail program (the URL wraps to a second line which won't be part of the link), but recipients can still copy and paste the entire URL into the Address Bar of their Web browser.

Printing Web Pages

For those times when nothing less than a hard copy of a Web page will do, Internet Explorer provides three different ways to print a Web page or portion of a page—the Print toolbar button, the Print Preview command, and the Print command.

The first way to print is to click Print on the toolbar, which prints the Web page instantly.

The second way to print is to choose Print Preview from the File menu and then use the Print Preview window to view the Web page, as discussed in the following steps:

1   Click Zoom In and Zoom Out to control how much of the page you see.

2   Select As Laid Out On Screen to print the Web page *frames* as they appear on screen or select Only The Selected Frame to print a portion of the page.

Lingo   A *frame* is a Webmaster trick that allows a Web browser to display multiple Web pages within a single window so that they appear to be a single Web page. This is most frequently used to allow one part of a Web page to scroll while the rest remains stationary.

---

3   Use Next Page and Previous Page to flip through the pages.

4   Click Page Setup (the icon to the right of Print) to select the proper paper and orientation.

5   Click Print to open the Print dialog box (discussed next).

6   Click Close to exit Print Preview.

The third way to print a Web page is to choose Print from the File menu to specify exactly how you want the page to print (see Chapter 8, "Printing," for more information).

Tip   To save ink and potentially paper, select only the text or graphics you want to print, choose Print from the File menu, and then in the Print Range frame, choose Selection.

Searching on the Web

Never before has so much information been available in one (virtual) location as exists now on the World Wide Web. *Everything* is out there somewhere; the challenge is finding it. The following sections help you search more effectively by providing a quick overview of the most popular search engines. They also show you how to perform searches from the Address bar and the Search bar, and demonstrate how to perform advanced searches using Boolean logic.

A Quick Guide to the Web's Search Services

No search engine is perfect for every search. There are four types of search engines, and each has strengths and weaknesses. See Table 6-2 for descriptions of search engine types.

Table 6-2 Types of Internet Search Engines

Type	Description	Pros	Cons	Examples
Web Crawler	Automatically crawls through the Web looking for Web sites to catalog	Most exhaustive results	Results often inaccurate	http://www.google.com http://www.alltheweb.com http://www.altavista.com http://www.hotbot.com
Directory	Human tended and categorized listings of sites	Most accurate and relevant results; can be browsed by category	May come up empty for difficult topics	http://www.looksmart.com http://dmoz.org http://www.yahoo.com
Hybrid	Pairs a directory with a crawler	Focused and relevant (directory), or exhaustive results (crawler)	Less accurate (crawler), or less exhaustive (directory)	http://www.yahoo.com http://search.aol.com http://www.lycos.com http://search.msn.com http://search.netscape.com
Metasearch	Automatically searches through other search engines, displaying the top results from a number of different search services	More broad-ranging results than a crawler or directory	More shallow (not as numerous) results; occasionally redundant	http://www.mamma.com http://www.metacrawler.com http://www.search.com http://www.dogpile.com

See Also   For more information on search engines, including searching tutorials and search engine reviews, visit http://www.searchenginewatch.com.

Others Places to Look

Besides general Internet search services, numerous topic-specific search services are also available. These services may provide better quality results because they deal exclusively with a specific subject matter and often have stringent guidelines covering what kinds of information is gathered and from where. Use a specialized search service when one is available for your topic—otherwise use a general search service.

The Table 6-3 provides a sampling of special-purpose search services.

Table 6-3 Specialized Search Services

Web Site URL	Specialty
http://www.askjeeves.com	Popular questions among the general population
http://www.google.com/unclesam	U.S. Government Web sites
http://www.epinions.com	User reviews and opinions on all sorts of things—movies, electronics, appliances, and so forth
http://www.orbitz.com	Airfares, hotels, and car rentals
http://www.travelocity.com	Airfares, hotels, and car rentals
http://www.expedia.com	Airfares, hotels, and car rentals
http://groups.google.com	Newsgroup posts
http://www.pricewatch.com	Prices of computer hardware and other electronics
http://www.salescircular.com	Newspaper ad inserts (sales flyers)

Searching from the Address Bar

The quickest way to search for something on the Web is to type **find**, **go**, or **?** in the Internet Explorer Address bar, followed by your search terms. These cues instruct Internet Explorer to submit the search terms to the default search engine.

MSN Search is the default search service in Internet Explorer. To change which search service is used for Address bar searches, click Search and then click Customize in the Search bar. Select the search services you want to use for each type of search and then click Save.

Tip After finding the page you want, search for a specific word on the page by choosing Find (On This Page) from the Edit menu.

Using the Search Bar

Use the Search Bar when you want more control over the search process than is allowed by searching from the Address bar, which performs a simple search for the keywords you specify in the default search engine. The Search bar lets you control such things as the type of information for which you're searching, as well as which search engine is used.

To use the Search Bar, click the Search toolbar button and then use the following search tips.

- To perform the same search in another search engine (the first search is performed using MSN Search by default), click Next, (or click the triangle to the right of Next), and choose the search engine in which you want to search.

- If you find a particularly good Web site and you want to find more like it, choose Show Related Links from the Tools menu.

- To perform a search that you've run in the past, choose Previous Searches. (Optionally, click Clear to erase previous searches.)

- To customize the Search Bar, click Customize. Select the search services you want to use for each type of search and then click Save.

Advanced Search—Boolean Searches and Other Tips

There's an art and a science to getting the information you want out of a search engine—simply typing in some keywords might not deliver the results you're seeking. Sophisticated techniques are occasionally necessary—for these instances, we provide you with the following list.

- Enter keywords that you think are unique to your topic of interest and that you're sure appear in the Web pages you're seeking. This is an important skill that usually improves with experience.

- If the search doesn't return sufficient results, remove search terms or make them more general.

- Use the base form of words or the form that you think is most likely to be used in Web pages.

- To search for a specific phrase, enclose the phrase in quotes.

- For more advanced searches, go directly to the search service's home page and click the Advanced Search (or similar) link. Advanced Search pages often allow you to do nifty things like search only for pages created within a certain time period (though searching by time period is quirky, so don't count on it being completely accurate).

If the search service supports it, use Boolean logic to include and exclude terms. Boolean logic, developed by British mathematician George Boole, is a method of specifying information using the logical operators OR, AND, and NOT. It's extremely useful in Web searches.

- To include only pages that contain all the search terms you specify, place a plus sign or the word AND before the required words—for example, nuclear+radiation (don't include spaces after the plus or minus signs).

- To exclude pages with specific words from a search (so that only pages that don't contain the excluded words are returned), place a minus sign or the word NOT before the additional words—for example, radiation NOT nuclear NOT weapons.

- To specify words that could be present in a page (but aren't required), type the word OR before the search terms. (This is the default behavior of most search engines.)

- To form advanced queries, use parentheses just as in algebra. For a quick brush-up on Boolean algebra, search for Boolean+logic+tutorial.

Note Boolean logic works with many, but not all, search services. Some search services have specific ways that they process Boolean logic, so if using Boolean logic doesn't seem to help, go to the Help page for the search service you're using.

Downloading Files

Sooner or later, you'll need to download a file. It may be a new driver for some piece of hardware or a program that you need. Downloading files is fairly simple. Here's how to do it:

1 Find the file that you want to download and click its download link.

2 In the File Download dialog box, choose Open or Save.

- Choose Open to immediately open the file without first saving it to a permanent location. (This is handy for small programs that you want to install.) Windows saves the file to a temporary folder and immediately opens the file after it's downloaded.

- Choose Save to save the file to a permanent location. Choose this option if you're concerned that the file may contain a virus, or if you need it for future use.

Caution Files that you download from the Internet may contain viruses. This isn't a concern for files from major companies such as Adobe and Microsoft, but it is for files from unknown companies or files located on a personal Web site. If you're unsure, save the file to your hard disk drive and use a virus scanner to scan the file (usually by right-clicking the file and choosing Scan For Viruses).

---

3 If you chose to save the file to your hard disk drive, use the Save As dialog box to specify the desired location. You might find it helpful to create a folder called Downloads for saving downloaded files. This will make it easy to find downloaded files and keep the desktop tidy.

Tip   If you use a dial-up Internet connection and have trouble downloading large files because of repeated error messages or interruption of service, try using a download manager, such as Star Downloader (available at *http://stardownloader.com*)—just be aware of the fact that many shareware programs of this type provide advertisements and/or track your usage (though Star Downloader currently isn't one of them).

Install on Demand   Some programs and components attempt to install themselves automatically using the Install on Demand feature. Because installed programs have free reign to perform any actions they want on your computer (including deleting files or sending information across the Internet), accept Install on Demand programs only from software companies you trust not to have virus or spyware-ridden programs. Virtually every big company can be trusted, as can smaller companies that you're familiar with. Some examples include Microsoft with its Visual Basic Scripting Support, which installs automatically when you come across a Web page that makes use of it (such as Windows Update), and Macromedia with Flash and Shockwave, which are widely used on the Web.

Key Points

- To browse the Web, you must choose an ISP, set up your connection, and actually connect to the Internet.

- Update Internet Explorer to the latest version to ensure the best security, speed, stability, and features when you surf the Web.

- Enter a Web address (URL) in the Address bar—press Ctrl+Enter to automatically fill in the http://www. and .com.

- Use the Favorites folder to keep track of Web sites you want to revisit.

- Checking the History folder for a log of the Web sites you visited can help you jog your memory (but remember, anyone else on your computer can view your wandering as well).

- You can save, e-mail, or print Web pages that you like.

- Perform quick searches directly from the Address bar by typing **find** followed by your search terms.

- Use the Search bar and/or Boolean logic for more advanced searches.

- Exercise caution with downloaded files until you scan them for viruses.

Chapter 7

Using E-Mail and Newsgroups

Reading and writing e-mail are two of the most important activities people perform with computers. For many, e-mail is as indispensable as a telephone, if not more so. Almost all of our business communication is done with e-mail, which is convenient and efficient, but does leave us chatting up grocery store clerks with alarming regularity.

Most everything you need to use e-mail effectively is covered in the following sections, including both basic information and advanced tips honed from years of e-mail experience (in other words, don't skip this chapter, even if you're an e-mail pro). We also briefly cover newsgroups, which are useful sources of information from other users.

This chapter discusses use of Microsoft Outlook Express, version 6, which comes free with Microsoft Internet Explorer 6. (If you're still using the version that came with Microsoft Windows 98, it's time to upgrade.)

See Also See the sections entitled "Get the Latest Version" and "Using The Internet Connection Wizard" in Chapter 6, "Fearless Web Browsing," for information about updating Internet Explorer and getting connected to the Internet.

Outlook or Outlook Express? Microsoft makes two popular e-mail programs for Windows—Outlook and Outlook Express. Outlook Express is Microsoft's free e-mail program that comes with Windows and Internet Explorer. It's fast, powerful, easy to set up (if need be), and it's free. Outlook is a powerful e-mail and scheduling program that is included with Microsoft Office (though you can also buy it separately). Outlook is also the best client for Microsoft Exchange Server mail systems, which are popular in businesses.

Which should you use? If you need any of the following features and are willing to obtain a copy of Outlook, use Outlook; otherwise, use the free and slightly more efficient Outlook Express, which you'll have to use anyway if you want to work with newsgroups:

- Outlook's Calendar is a great way to manage your time, and it can be synchronized with most Personal Digital Assistants (PDAs), should you have one.
- Outlook provides powerful task (To Do) lists for keeping track of what needs to be done, and it can also be synchronized with most PDAs.
- Outlook provides complete access to all Exchange Server features (Outlook Express has only limited support).
- Outlook provides the most powerful message rules for processing incoming (and outgoing) e-mail.

Setting Up and Personalizing Outlook Express

Before using Outlook Express, you need to set it up to work with your e-mail accounts. Even if Outlook Express is already set up, read the following sections to learn how to configure it to suit your needs. You might want to import settings from other mail programs, change the way messages are sent and received, or possibly set up more than one identity so you can separate your business and personal lives. A couple minutes of extra setup time now can save you a good deal of hassle later.

Open Outlook Express by clicking Start, choosing Programs, and then choosing Outlook Express. Use the following sections to set up and personalize Outlook Express for your needs.

Importing Settings and Messages from Another Program

If you're switching to Outlook Express from another program on the same computer, the first time you run Outlook Express it asks whether you want to import settings and data. Use the wizard it provides to import the appropriate settings and data.

If Outlook Express doesn't ask if you want to import from another program, choose Import from the File menu and then choose the type of data or settings you want to import. Then use the displayed wizard to import your data or settings.

Setting Up an E-mail Account

The first time you run Outlook Express, it prompts you to set up an e-mail account, unless you did so already. Even if you already set up one e-mail account, you might still need to set up others (not many people have only one e-mail account anymore).

Use the following steps to set up an e-mail account.

1 Open Outlook Express. If the Internet Connection Wizard doesn't appear, choose Accounts from the Tools menu, click Add, and then click Mail.

2 In the first page of the Internet Connection Wizard, type your name in the Display Name text box as you want it to appear on e-mail messages you send. Then click Next.

3 In the next page, type your e-mail address in the E-mail Address text box and then click Next.

4 From the drop-down box choose the type of e-mail server (POP3, IMAP, or HTTP). In the Incoming and Outgoing Mail text boxes type the server names provided by your ISP or network administrator, as shown in Figure 7-1, and then click Next.

See Also   POP (Post Office Protocol), IMAP (Internet Message Access Protocol), and HTTP (Hypertext Transfer Protocol) mail servers are discussed in the "More Considerations" section of Chapter 6, "Fearless Web Browsing."

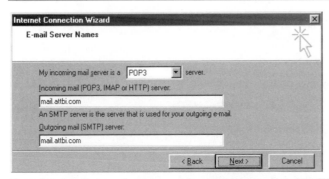

Figure 7-1 Specify the mail server names for a POP server account. (Most ISP accounts use POP servers.)

5 Type your account name and password and then select any desired or necessary options:

● Remember Password provides added convenience (and lessened security) by eliminating the need to enter your password.

● Log On Using Secure Password Authentication (SPA) provides secure password authentication. Select this only if directed by your ISP or network administrator.

6 Click Next, and then click Finish when you're done entering your settings. Click Close if the Internet Accounts dialog box is open.

7 If you set up an IMAP or HTTP (Hotmail) mail account, click Yes when prompted to download folders from the mail server.

Use the Show/Hide IMAP Folders dialog box to select which IMAP folders you want to see in Outlook Express. (You can open this dialog box at any time by opening your IMAP Inbox and choosing Show/Hide IMAP Folders from the Tools menu).

> **Tip** Be careful with what you put for your display name—don't make it too whimsical if you plan on using the account for business. If you use the same e-mail account for both personal and work purposes and you want a whimsical display name for personal correspondence, set up the account twice—each time with a different display name. You can also use the Identities feature (discussed later) to help keep your business and personal identities separate.

> **See Also** See the "Changing How Mail Is Checked for IMAP Accounts" section of this chapter for more information on working with IMAP folders.

Managing How Mail Is Sent and Received

The Outlook Express default for sending and receiving e-mail works fine; however, it might not suit your needs as well as it could. Spending a few minutes to tell Outlook Express how *you* want it to handle your e-mail can be the difference between frequently becoming annoyed by the program or loving it.

Specifying the Default E-mail Account

If you have more than one e-mail account, Outlook Express automatically sends messages using the default account unless you specify otherwise (as we describe in the "Composing Messages" section of this chapter). To change the default e-mail account, use the following steps.

1 Choose Accounts from the Tools menu.

2 Click the Mail tab, as shown in Figure 7-2.

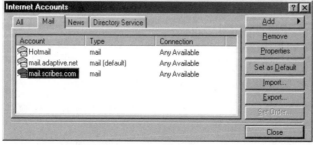

Figure 7-2 Use the Mail tab to set the default e-mail account. You can also import and export account settings to a file.

3 Select the e-mail account you want to use by default and then click Set As Default.

Leaving Messages on the Server

Users of IMAP and HTTP-based (Hotmail) e-mail accounts can gain access to their e-mail from any computer because their mail resides on the server—not their computer. Post Office Protocol (POP) server users don't have this luxury. (Most ISP e-mail accounts are POP server-based.)

You can work around this limitation of POP servers in a couple of ways. Closing your e-mail program when you're away from your main computer is one way. This prevents the e-mail program from downloading new messages and removing them from the server. While new messages are on the server, you can access them remotely using your ISP's Web mail interface, if it has one. Messages that have been removed from the server can only be accessed from the e-mail program that downloaded them.

Another workaround is to set up Outlook Express to leave a copy of your messages on the server for a little while, so that you can view them from other locations. To set up Outlook Express to do this, use these steps.

1 Choose Accounts from the Tools menu and click the Mail tab.

2 Select the proper account and click Properties.

3 Click the Advanced tab, as shown in Figure 7-3.

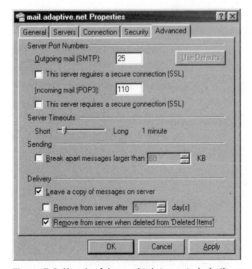

Figure 7-3 Use the Advanced tab to control whether messages are left on the server, how long Outlook Express should wait for a mail server, and whether it should break apart large messages when sending them.

4   In the Delivery frame select the Leave A Copy Of Messages On Server check box.

5   Use the Remove From Server… check boxes to control when messages are removed from the server. Click OK when you're done.

Caution   Most ISPs provide about 1.5–10 MB of mailbox space, so it's important that you remove messages from the server regularly. To keep from accidently filling your mailbox, select the Remove From Server When Deleted From 'Deleted Items' check box, and always empty your Deleted Items folder regularly.

Forcing Accounts to Use a Dial-Up or LAN Connection

Sometimes an e-mail account insists on using a specific dial-up connection—even if you're connected to the Internet through a LAN connection or another dial-up account. To fix this problem (or ensure that you don't have to) follow these steps:

1   Choose Accounts from the Tools menu and click the Mail tab.

2   Select the proper account and click Properties.

3   Click the Connection tab.

4   Clear the Always Connect To This Account Using check box. This allows Internet Explorer's Internet Connection settings to determine how to connect to the Internet, centralizing your connection settings. Click OK when you're done.

Changing When Outlook Express Sends and Receives E-mail

Outlook Express enthusiastically checks for new mail and sends messages you write—too much for many people and, of course, not enough for some. To change how often Outlook Express checks for new messages, choose Options from the Tools menu and then use the following options on the General tab.

■   **Send And Receive Messages At Startup**   Checks for new mail and sends messages you've written every time you start Outlook Express.

■   **Check For New Message Every *x* Minutes**   Sends and receives e-mail at the interval you specify.

Tip   To specify whether Outlook Express should automatically connect to the Internet to check for new messages, use the If My Computer Is Not Connected At This Time box. To control whether Outlook Express should switch dial-up accounts or hang-up automatically, use the Connection tab.

Changing How Mail Is Checked for IMAP Accounts

IMAP-based e-mail accounts contain multiple folders that are stored on the mail server. When you open a folder while online, Outlook Express downloads the *header* for each message (when offline, Outlook Express displays the list of headers it downloaded the last time you were online). Complete messages are downloaded only when you decide to read them—either in the Preview Pane or by opening the message.

Lingo A *header* is the small amount of information at the beginning of an e-mail or newsgroup message that reports such things as who sent the message, the subject, and the time the message was sent.

You can change Outlook Express's default downloading behavior, for example, to do such things as download the headers for all your IMAP folders or download new messages in their entirety when checking for new messages. To do so, you need to change your IMAP folders synchronization settings, as described below.

1 Select your IMAP server in the Folders list. (For more information, see An Overview Of The Outlook Express Interface in the Folders list.)

2 To show or hide folders in your account, click IMAP folders, select a folder, and then click Show or Hide, as shown in Figure 7-4. Click OK when you're finished.

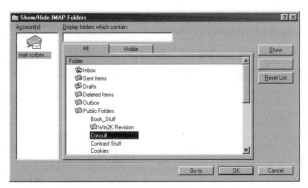

Figure 7-4 Use the Show/Hide IMAP Folders dialog box to control which folders are displayed in the Folders list.

3 Select a folder, click Settings, and then choose the synchronization setting you want.

4 To enable or disable synchronization of a folder, select or clear the check box next to the folder's synchronization setting.

5   Click Synchronize to update your IMAP folders now. (IMAP folder synchronization is also performed every time Outlook Express performs a Send/ Receive operation.)

Changing How Messages Are Sent

Before you start composing and sending e-mail using Outlook Express, make sure that it sends messages in the way you want. To do this, choose Options from the Tools menu, click the Send tab, as shown in Figure 7-5, and then use the following options.

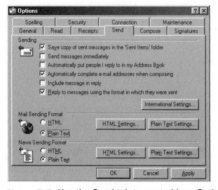

Figure 7-5 Use the Send tab to control how Outlook Express sends messages.

- **Save A Copy Of Sent Messages In The 'Sent Items' Folder**   Leave this check box selected, unless you don't want to keep a copy.

- **Send Messages Immediately**   When this check box is cleared, Outlook Express keeps messages in the Outbox until the next time it checks for new mail (set from the General tab).

- **Automatically Put People I Reply To In My Address Book**   Clear this check box if you don't want your Address Book populated with the addresses of everyone you ever reply to.

- **Automatically Complete E-mail Addresses When Composing**   Outlook Express will complete e-mail addresses while you type.

- **Include Message In Reply**   Clear this check box if you don't want the message you're replying to included with your reply.

- **Reply To Messages Using The Format In Which They Were Sent**   Outlook Express will automatically switch to HTML when replying to HTML messages (or Plain Text if you leave HTML as your default message format).

- **Mail Sending Format**   Choose HTML or Plain Text to control the default message format. (Plain Text is preferred for compatibility, speed, and security.)

Create an E-mail Signature

A *signature file*, or sig file, is a short file that's appended to the end of e-mails that you send. Typically it contains your name and contact information and sometimes a quote or saying. You can include whatever you'd like. To create a signature file and specify whether or not it's added to all outgoing e-mails, use the following steps:

1   Choose Options from the Tools menu, and click the Signatures tab, as shown in Figure 7-6.

Figure 7-6   Use the Signatures tab to manage your signature files.

2   Click New to create a new signature.

3   Type the text that you want to appear in your signature in the Edit Signature Text box, or choose the File option and specify the text or HTML file you want to use as your signature.

4   To create additional signatures, rename them, or remove them, use New, Rename, and Remove.

5   Specify when Outlook Express should automatically add signatures to messages using the check boxes at the top of the dialog box. Click OK when you're done.

> **Tip**   You can add a signature to any message by choosing Signature from the Insert menu and then selecting the proper signature. (The Insert menu is only available when you're composing a message.) To assign different signatures to different e-mail accounts, select a signature you want to use, click Advanced, select the accounts with which you want to use the signature, and then click OK.

Cover Your Bases—Enable the Automatic Spelling Checker

Even if you lost all the school spelling bees, you can always have great spelling if you tell Outlook Express to automatically check your messages for spelling errors before sending them. To do so, follow these steps:

1   Choose the Options command from the Tools menu, and click the Spelling tab.

2   Select the Always Check Spelling Before Sending check box.

3   To tell Outlook Express what kinds of words to ignore when checking for spelling errors, use the check boxes in the When Checking Spelling, Always Ignore section of the dialog box.

4   Click OK when you're done.

Note   The spelling checker is only enabled in Outlook Express if you have Microsoft Office or a third-party Outlook Express spelling checker program installed.

Maintaining Multiple Identities

The Identities feature of Outlook Express makes it easy to keep your different e-mail identities separate. Anyone who has had to maintain separate business and personal e-mail identities will immediately see the benefit of this feature. There's nothing worse than sending a risqué joke to your friends, only to find out that it also went to your coworkers and boss.

Although much of the Identities feature can be duplicated using separate e-mail accounts and Address Book folders, creating separate identities is an easy way to clearly distinguish between your separate identities, reducing the potential for mistakes.

Tip   You can share Outlook Express with multiple users using the Identities feature, though most users prefer to set up separate Windows Profiles instead. This permits each user to maintain his or her own Windows and applications settings as well.

To use the Identities feature, follow these steps.

1   Choose Identities from the File menu and then choose Add New Identity from the subsequent menu.

2   In the New Identity dialog box, type the name of the new identity in the Name text box, optionally select Require A Password to password-protect the identity, and then click OK.

3   Click No when asked if you want to switch to the new identity.

4   To control which identity is used when starting the program and when pulling information out of Outlook Express—for example, when you want to synchronize with a PDA—use the two boxes at the bottom of the Manage Identities dialog box (you can also use this box to rename the Main Identity).

5   Click Close when you're finished managing identities.

6   To switch between identities, choose Switch Identity from the File menu.

Caution   Password protecting your Identity makes it inconvenient, but not difficult, to access your locally stored e-mail from another Identity. In Windows 98, not even separate user profiles can stop another local user from gaining access to your locally stored Inbox (profiles can be secured in Windows NT, Windows 2000, and Windows XP).

Reading E-mail

Once you've set up Outlook Express the way you like, it's time to actually put it to use receiving and reading your e-mail.

An Overview of the Outlook Express Interface

Before we get into the meaty parts of using Outlook Express, it's useful to review the main Outlook Express interface, as shown in Figure 7-7, and described on the next page.

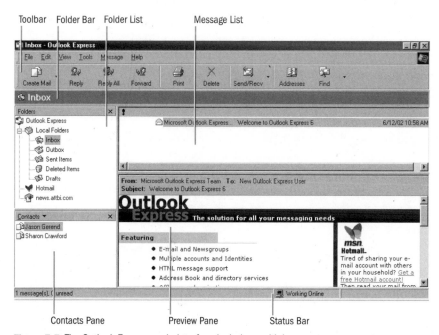

Figure 7-7 The Outlook Express main interface includes multiple panes.

Tip   To turn on or off parts of the Outlook Express interface, choose Layout from the View menu.

■ **Toolbar**   Contains frequently accessed commands such as Create Mail, Reply, and Send/Recv.

■ **Folder Bar**   Displays the title of the currently open folder. If the Folder List is hidden, clicking the folder title opens the folder list.

■ **Folder List**   Displays a list of folders accessible to Outlook Express.

■ **Message List**   Displays your e-mail or newsgroup messages.

■ **Preview Pane**   Displays the contents of the currently selected message.

■ **Contacts**   Displays the contents of the Address Book.

■ **Status Bar**   Displays the current status of Outlook Express, including Send/Receive progress, Online/Offline status, and how many unread messages are in the current folder.

■ **Views Bar**   Allows you to quickly change whether all messages are displayed, only unread messages, or only messages that you've read (this is hidden by default).

■ **Outlook Bar**   Displays key folders in the style of the Outlook Bar in Microsoft Outlook (this is hidden by default).

■ **Outlook Express Welcome Page**   Displayed by default when Outlook Express opens (but hidden in this figure). Provides an overview of your e-mail and newsgroups, with hyperlinks for common tasks. Similar to Outlook Today in Microsoft Outlook.

Tip   To make Outlook Express open your Inbox first, instead of the Outlook Express Welcome Page, choose Options from the Tools menu and then select When Starting, Go Directly To My 'Inbox' Folder.

Checking for New Messages

Although Outlook Express is set up by default to check for new mail when you open it and then every 30 minutes thereafter, you might want to manually check for new mail from time to time. To do so, Click Send/Recv on the toolbar or press F5.

To switch Outlook Express into offline mode, choose Work Offline from the File menu. Outlook Express won't try to check for new mail or download message bodies when in offline mode.

When You Can't Get Your E-mail Nobody's e-mail account works all the time—no matter how reliable his or her ISP. Therefore, it's useful to know what to do if your e-mail stops working all of a sudden. Try these procedures, in the same order:

- Check your Internet connection. Fire up your Web browser and surf a few pages. If you can't pull up any pages, your e-mail isn't going to work. Wait for your connection to come back up or contact your ISP.
- Try closing and reopening Outlook Express.
- Wait—usually the problem is your mail server snoozing on the job. Wait an hour or two and try again.
- Disable your virus scanner. Sometimes your virus scanner stops working but doesn't tell you (Norton Antivirus 2000 is especially prone to this). Disable the e-mail checking component of your virus scanner and then enable it again.
- Check your settings. Installing other programs can occasionally mess up your account settings, so double-check that they're correct, and fix them if they're not.
- Re-create the account. Sometimes, mysteriously, an e-mail account with all the correct settings won't work, but if you create another account with the same settings, the duplicate account will. Delete the redundant account after trying this.
- Contact your ISP or network administrator. If it's been longer than you can stand to be without e-mail, check your e-mail using your ISP's Web interface (if they provide one) and then give your ISP a call to see what's wrong.

Reading Messages

To read your e-mail, select the appropriate Inbox (you might have multiple Inboxes if you have Hotmail or IMAP accounts), and then select or double-click a message to view it in the preview pane or in its own window. Simple stuff, but we have a few tips for making this task more efficient:

- When viewing a message in its own window, use Previous, Next, and Delete on the message toolbar to view other messages or delete the current message without going back to the main Outlook Express window.
- To change whether a message appears read or unread, right-click the message and choose Mark As Read or Mark As Unread.
- To add a person to your address book, right-click a message from the person whom you want to add and then choose Add Sender To Address Book.

Tip Messages are marked as read after opened or viewed in the Preview Pane for 5 seconds or more. To change the time delay, choose Options from the Tools menu, click the Read tab and change the Mark Message Read After Displaying For 5 Seconds setting.

Opening and Dealing with Attachments

Attachments are simple to deal with once you understand the basics and learn how to protect yourself from viruses. (For more information, see the sidebar in this section entitled Viruses and Attachments.) To work with an attachment that you know is safe, use the following techniques.

- If you're viewing a message in the Preview pane, click the paper clip icon in the upper right corner of the message.
- Click an attachment to open it.
- Click Save Attachments to save the attachment(s) to your hard disk drive.

Note When you open an attachment, the attachment is copied to a temporary folder on your hard disk drive. If you make changes to the file, save the file in a more permanent location so that you won't lose your changes or misplace the file.

Viruses and Attachments E-mail attachments are the number one source of viruses these days, and as such, they should be treated with extreme caution. To avoid being bitten, take the following precautions:

- Don't open attachments that you didn't specifically request until verifying with the sender that they're safe.
- Use Outlook Express 6 or newer with the latest security patches.
- Always run a virus-prevention program such as Norton Antivirus and keep its virus definition files up-to-date.
- Make sure that your virus-prevention program is set up to check your incoming (and, for extra points, outgoing) e-mail.
- Don't fall for social engineering attacks—the most effective viruses are those that trick you into thinking they're innocuous. The ILOVEYOU virus is one such example, but we've also seen convincing viruses claiming to be from Microsoft containing a "patch" to protect against some new security risk. (Microsoft never sends patches through e-mail.) If the e-mail seems strange, don't open any attachments!
- If you ever receive an attachment with .exe, .bat, .vbs, .reg, or .com at the end of the file name (and Outlook Express doesn't automatically remove it), delete it (unless you specifically requested it).
- If you're suspicious of an attachment, save it to your hard disk drive and check it with your virus scanner.
- Don't take the fact that your virus scanner didn't find a virus as proof that an attachment is safe. Virus prevention companies are perpetually three or more days behind virus authors, and your computer is even more out-of-date, so it's vital that you keep your wits about you.

Tip Attachments are often sent in compressed format. To open these attachments, you need a suitable compression program such as WinZip (or Stuffit Expander if you receive files from a Macintosh user). You can download trial versions of these programs from *http://www.winzip.com* and *http://www.alladinsystems.com*.

Replying To and Forwarding Messages

Outlook Express makes it simple to reply to people who e-mail you; it also makes it easy to forward messages to other people. (You can move along to a more interesting section if you want, but peruse the e-mail etiquette section below first). These features can come in handy in numerous situations, such as when you receive a message about a project that others are involved in, when you receive a glowing message praising your skills (and you want to forward it to all your friends), or when you receive a particularly funny joke that you can't resist passing on.

To reply to or forward a message, click Reply or Forward. To reply to everyone to whom the original message was addressed, click Reply All. (Otherwise, the reply is sent to the first person listed in the To box.)

Netiquette: Replies and Forwards

Because e-mail plays such an important role in communication today, it's vital to maintain good manners, especially when replying to e-mail and forwarding it. Here are some concrete recommendations (you can find additional tips by performing an Internet search on "netiquette").

■ Reply promptly to messages, even if only to say that you don't have time to reply.

■ Don't reply in haste and repent at leisure. Compose your response, but instead of instantly clicking Send, choose Save from the File menu and let it rest for a day or two. Then decide if you still want to send the e-mail, as is.

■ Don't forward chain letters. It's rude and costs you a lot of respect in the eyes of your recipients. We know that superstitions are easy to believe, but we haven't forwarded a single chain letter. Despite this, we have not lost our jobs, been dumped by our partners, or been forced to share a cardboard box under an overpass with another person who failed to forward a chain letter.

■ Don't forward virus warnings—99.99 percent of these are hoaxes. Even if you're sure it's true, check *http://www.Symantec.com* or *http://www.mcaffee.com* for verification. If you really want to help someone avoid viruses, you'll show them the sidebar "Viruses and Attachments" earlier in this chapter, along with the section "Security Basics" in Chapter 11, "Playing It Safe."

- Don't forward jokes (clean or dirty) or pleas on behalf of endangered anemones to everyone in your Address Book. Only forward messages to people you know will appreciate them—and don't make a habit of it.

- Don't forward pyramid schemes and other scams to anyone other than the FTC. We know that multi-level marketing is the exciting new way of selling that allows you to double your income, increase your quality of life, and lose weight while you sleep, but resist the impulse to tell the world about it.

- Don't put anything in an e-mail you wouldn't want your mother to see. E-mail feels evanescent but it *never dies*.

Deleting Messages

To delete messages, select the message(s) you want to delete and then press the Delete toolbar button or the Delete key. Use the following techniques to manage messages that you've deleted:

- To recover a deleted message, open the Deleted Items folder from the folder list and drag the message back into the Inbox (or another folder). For IMAP accounts, right-click the deleted message and choose Undelete.

- To show or hide deleted messages in an IMAP folder, open the folder, choose Current View from the View menu, and then choose Show Deleted Messages.

- To empty the Deleted Items folder, right-click the Deleted Items folder and choose Empty Deleted Items Folder.

- To purge deleted messages from an IMAP folder, open the folder and choose Purge Deleted Messages from the Edit menu.

Tip   To make Outlook Express automatically empty the Deleted Items folder every time you close the program, choose Options from the Tools menu, click the Maintenance tab, and then select the Empty Messages From 'Deleted Items' Folder On Exit check box. If you use an IMAP account, select the Purge Deleted Messages When Leaving IMAP Folders check box to purge deleted messages whenever you switch to a different folder.

Printing Messages

Although most e-mail lives out its lifespan safely inside the digital world of computers, occasionally it's necessary to bring an e-mail into the Real World by printing it out. E-mailed driving directions and company memos are a couple of instances that come quickly to mind.

Printing an e-mail is no different from printing anything else. To print an e-mail, select the message that you want to print and click the Print toolbar button or choose Print from the File menu to open the Print dialog box. Then use the following procedures.

- To specify such things as which printer to use, print quality and color, select the desired printer from the Name box, and optionally click Properties.
- In the Print Range frame, specify whether to print the entire message, only a specific page range, or only the selected text or graphics (saving ink and paper).
- Specify the number of copies you want in the Number Of Copies box.
- Select the Collate check box to collate copies, keeping pages in order.

Writing and Formatting E-mail

Composing e-mail is a task with a number of nuances. For example, after writing a message, you should check for spelling errors. You might also want to make the message look a bit fancy or attach a file. These techniques, among others, are covered in the sections that follow.

Composing Messages

Composing e-mails is easy; if you need a hand with it, use the following steps.

1   Click the Create Mail toolbar button.
2   To send the message from a specific e-mail account, select the desired e-mail account in the From drop-down box.
3   In the message window, specify the recipient by using one of these techniques.

- Type the recipient's e-mail address in the To or Cc (carbon copy) fields. Separate multiple names with semicolons.
- If the recipient is already in your Address Book, type the recipient's name or nickname in the To or Cc fields.
- Click the To or Cc to select a contact from the Address Book using the Select Recipients dialog box. To select a recipient from a different Address Book or Address Book folder, choose the proper entry from the drop-down list at the top of the dialog box.
- To add secret recipients, click To, select the desired recipients, and click Bcc (blind carbon copy).

Tip   Outlook Express attempts to automatically complete the name or address of the recipient while you type. If the correct name or address appears, press Enter to use it; otherwise, keep typing until it does (or you're finished typing). Click Check to check names and make sure Outlook Express can find the proper e-mail address.

---

4   Type a short but descriptive subject for the message in the Subject field.

Caution   Don't include exclamation points, question marks, or typical advertising words such as "diet", "free", or "trial" in the Subject field of your message—your message might be mistaken for spam and deleted.

---

5   Type the e-mail in the main body of the message window.

6   To flag a message as important or unimportant, click the triangle next to the Priority button and choose the appropriate priority.

7   Click the Spelling toolbar button to check for spelling errors, if you have a spelling checker installed.

8   Click the Send button to send the e-mail. Outlook Express then delivers the message immediately, unless you've turned off that option, in which case it'll place the message in the Outbox. Messages in the Outbox are delivered the next time Outlook Express checks for new mail.

You can also opt to finish a message later by choosing Save from the File menu. To return to the message, open it from the Drafts folder.

See Also   For information on sending digitally signed or encrypted e-mails, see "Configuring Digital IDs" in Chapter 11, "Playing It Safe."

Communicating Effectively

Communicating Effectively   Many people forget everything they know about etiquette when they go online, which is a shame, because e-mail is one of the social realms in which good manners are most important. Here are some suggestions for minding your manners when writing e-mails.

- Don't write personal e-mails to someone's business e-mail account unless you know it's Okay—you could get your friend into a lot of trouble.
- Watch the tone of your e-mail carefully and never write while angry (all caps indicate THAT YOU'RE SCREAMING!).
- Sarcasm is often lost in e-mail, so use it sparingly or use smileys such as :) or J to make it clear that you're joking (though you should avoid the overuse of emoticons such as smileys in business messages—they're unprofessional).
- Mark unimportant messages with the Low Importance flag.
- Only use the High Importance flag when it's *really* important.

Fancy E-mail—How to Make Messages Pretty

Although plain-text e-mails are usually the best way to go, sometimes it's appropriate to spice up your messages a bit. For example, a birthday greeting to a friend could be jazzed up with a funny image, and a complicated business message could benefit from a bulleted list or some subheadings. (Note, though, that formatted e-mail can be extremely annoying when abused and you should only use it when necessary.)

> **See Also**   Refer to the section "Changing How Messages Are Sent" earlier in this chapter to change the default message-sending format as well as read about the merits of Plain Text.

If you want to apply fancy formatting to your messages, use the following techniques:

- Use the formatting toolbar to format your e-mail as you would a regular word processing document, with bulleted lists, bold text, and different fonts.

- If the formatting toolbar isn't visible, switch the message format to HTML by choosing Rich Text (HTML) from the Format menu.

- To write a message using *stationery*, click the triangle to the right of the Create Mail button in the main Outlook Express window, and then choose the stationery you want to use (choose Select Stationery to preview the different options).

- If you really want to send a pretty e-mail, send an online greeting card from Web sites such as *http://www.egreetings.com* or *http://www.hallmark.com*.

> **Lingo**   *Stationery* is a combination of background images with special fonts. To properly view a message written on stationery, the recipients must have an e-mail program that can display HTML messages and also must have the same font installed (which might not be the case if they're using a Mac or UNIX system).

Sending E-mail Attachments

If you want to send a file of some sort through e-mail, use the following steps:

1 Click Create Mail to create a new message, and then click the Attach button.

2 Select the file(s) you want to attach. To select multiple files, hold down the Ctrl key and click each file.

3 Click Attach. Outlook Express then attaches the file(s) to the e-mail, displaying the file names in the newly visible Attach field. To delete a file that you attached, select the file and press Delete.

Polite Attachments   Because attachments take a long time to download and can easily transmit viruses, it's important to be polite when sending them. The following list presents some guidelines to go by when sending attachments:

- Ask before sending attachments. This gives the recipient an opportunity to say no and also alerts them to expect the files so that they don't mistake the attachments for a virus.
- Use an up-to-date virus-protection program to scan the files for viruses.
- In the body of the e-mail message, briefly explain the attachments and tell the recipient how to open them if they're in an unusual file format.
- Don't send a single e-mail with more than 1.5 MB of attachments, if possible. Some e-mail accounts can't handle messages larger than this.
- Before sending pictures through e-mail, reduce their size (unless the recipient prints the images). For viewing on the computer, 640×480 or 800×600 is generally large enough.
- When sending documents, publications, and bitmap (.bmp) pictures, use a compression program such as WinZip to compress the files into one or more .zip files.

Using the Address Book

Consider the Address Book your virtual Rolodex—it's where to store all of your e-mail addresses, phone numbers, and mailing addresses.

The following sections show you how to create new contacts, create groups of contacts, and organize contacts into folders.

Tip   You can synchronize Outlook Express's Address Book with your Hotmail or MSN online Address Book by opening Outlook Express's Address Book and choosing Synchronize Now from the Tools menu.

Viewing Your Addresses

Addresses are unsurprisingly stored in the Address Book, and you can use several methods to access them:

- **The Address Book**   Click Addresses to open the main Address Book window, as shown in Figure 7-8.
- **The Contacts Pane**   Double-click a contact in the Contacts pane to create a new message addressed to the contact.
- **The Select Recipients dialog box**   Click To or Cc in a message window to select recipients from the Address Book using the Select Recipients dialog box.

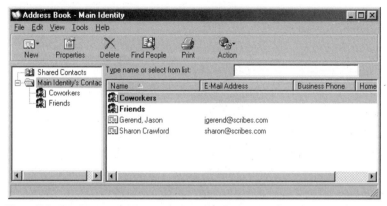

Figure 7-8 E-mail groups appear separately in the Folders And Groups pane of the Address Book window.

Note If Outlook is installed when you set up Outlook Express, Outlook Express uses Outlook's Contacts folder as its Address Book. To change this behavior, open the Address Book in Outlook Express, choose Options from the Tools menu, and then use the Options dialog box to specify whether or not to share contact information between the two applications.

Creating Contacts

You can create new contacts through any of the following methods.

- Right-click a message and choose Add Sender To Address Book.

- Drag an e-mail message to the Contacts pane.

- Click New in the Address Book, and choose New Contact.

Once you've created a new contact, you need to fill in the relevant information. This isn't rocket science, but a few things are worth noting about the process. Figure 7-9 shows an example of a filled-in contact.

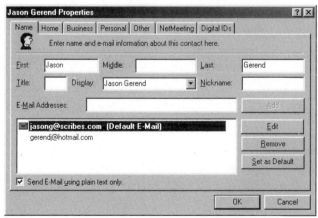

Figure 7-9 Filling out a contact is easy—just type the information you know.

- To force the contact to be filed by last name, first name, or some other method entirely, select the name as you want it to appear from the Display drop-down box, or type it in explicitly.

- Type a nickname for the contact in the Nickname field, if you want. You can then address messages using the nickname.

- To add an e-mail address, type the address in the E-mail Addresses box and then click Add.

- To specify the default e-mail address for the contact, select it and then click Set As Default.

- To force Outlook Express to send only plain-text messages to the contact, choose the Send E-mail Using Plain Text Only check box.

Creating Groups

Some users need to frequently e-mail a consistent group of people. Coworkers, buddies, family, and business clients are a few examples. You could manually specify each and every name each and every time you need to send an e-mail to these groups, but a more elegant solution is to add them all to e-mail groups. Then you can address a message to the group, and Outlook Express automatically sends it to all members of the group (if you want to hide the recipients from each other, use the Bcc field instead of the To field). To create e-mail groups, use the following procedure.

1 Open the Address Book by clicking the Addresses button.

2 Click New and then choose New Group.

3 Type a name for the group in the Group Name text box, as shown in Figure 7-10.

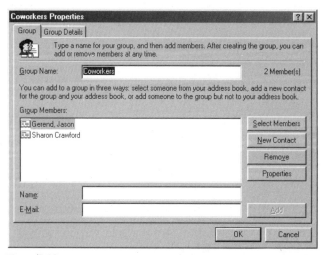

Figure 7-10 Adding contacts to an e-mail group makes it easier to send to all members of the group at once. Contacts that you add to groups can still be accessed individually.

4 Click Select Members.

5 Select the contacts you want to add to the group and then click Select. Click OK when you're done selecting members.

6 To add a person to the group without adding them to your Address Book, type the person's name and e-mail address in the Name and E-mail text boxes of the group properties dialog box and then click Add.

7 To enter additional information about the group, such as a mailing address or Web site, use the Group Details tab.

8 Click OK when you're finished creating the group.

Organizing Contacts with Folders

To organize contacts into categories, move them into separate folders. This can be helpful if you have so many contacts that it becomes difficult to find them when they're all grouped together. It can also be useful when you want to keep some contacts separate from the others—for example, personal contacts.

Caveats About Using Address Book Folders When you organize contacts into folders, consider a couple of things.

- When using the Select Recipients dialog box to address an e-mail message, only the contacts stored in the main contacts folder are listed. To select from another folder, use the drop-down list box at the top of the dialog box.

- Only contacts in the main contacts folder can be accessed from the Contacts pane of the main Outlook Express window.

To organize contacts into folders, open the Address Book and then use the following techniques.

- To create a new folder, click New, choose New Folder, type the folder name, and click OK.

- Drag contacts and e-mail groups into the new folder to move them there.

- To share contacts between all identities in Outlook Express, drag the contacts to the Shared Contacts folder.

Dealing with Large Amounts of E-mail

If you've been using e-mail for a significant length of time, chances are good that you receive a torrent of e-mail, both wanted and unwanted. This can be overwhelming unless you deploy some special tactics, such as organizing your messages into folders, changing folder views, searching for messages and auto-matically processing messages using rules. Fortunately, this is just what the fol-lowing sections discuss.

Organizing Messages into Folders

If you have an Inbox overflowing with hundreds of messages, it's time to create some additional folders. You can use these additional folders to categorize mes-sages, making it easier to find what you're looking for. You can also offload old messages into a folder you create to archive them. (This method is especially useful if you synchronize a PDA with Outlook Express, because few PDAs can store *all* of the e-mail you receive).

To create a new folder and move messages into it, use the following steps.

1 In the main Outlook Express window, right-click a folder in the Folders list and choose New Folder.

2 In the Create Folder dialog box, shown in Figure 7-11, type the name of the new folder.

Figure 7-11 Extra folders are essential when dealing with large quantities of e-mail.

3 Select the folder in which to store the new folder and then click OK.

4 To move messages into the new folder, select the messages and drag them into the folder on the Folders list.

> **Tip** To select a contiguous block of messages, select the first message, hold down the Shift key, and then select the last message. To select multiple individual mes-sages, hold down the Ctrl key and click each one.

Try This!   Sometimes you want to save a message to your hard disk drive or a floppy disk—outside the walls of Outlook Express. Perhaps this is because you want to save the message into the same folder as other files relating to the same topic or project, or maybe you want to place the message on a floppy disk to read from another computer. Whatever your reason, here's how to save a message outside of Outlook Express.

1   Select or open the message you want to save.

2   Choose Save As from the File menu.

3   In the Save Message As dialog box, select the folder in which you want to save the message.

4   Type a descriptive file name in the File Name box.

5   Choose a file type for the message, and then click Save.

    You can save your message using the following file types.

■   Mail (*.eml) is the native message format for Outlook Express (can only be opened by Outlook Express).

■   Text Files (*.txt) are plain text files, readable by any text editor.

■   Unicode Text Files (*.txt) are used for international language support, readable by most text editors.

■   HTML Files (*.htm, *.html) are Web page files, readable by any Web browser or Web page editor (including Word 2000 and later).

Finding Elusive Messages

Ever find yourself scrolling endlessly through your Inbox searching for one specific message that continues to elude you? Instead of getting frustrated, perform a search. To do so, follow these steps.

1   Click the Find button (or click the triangle next to Find and choose Message In This Folder to perform a simple search in the currently selected folder).

2   To specify where Outlook Express should begin searching, click Find, then Message, and then Browse. Select the desired folder and then click OK. Select the Include Subfolders check box to search through subfolders as well.

3 Type the text for which you want to search in one or more of the fields in the Find Message dialog box, as shown in Figure 7-12:

- *From* searches for the sender name you type.

- *To* searches for the recipient name you type (useful when you know that the message was sent to someone else and cc'd to you).

- *Subject* searches the subject field of messages for the text you type.

- *Message* searches the actual body of messages for the text you type.

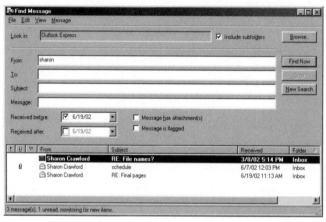

Figure 7-12 Using the Find Message window is the fastest way to find difficult to locate messages.

4 Optionally specify a date range using the Received Before and Received After boxes.

5 To search for messages that have attachments or are flagged only, select the Message Has Attachment(s) or Message Is Flagged check boxes.

6 Click Find Now to search for the message(s). If Outlook Express locates any messages, it displays them at the bottom of the window. Double-click a message to open it.

Changing Folder Views

Sometimes a change of view can make a world of difference. Maybe you want to sort messages by sender instead of by date or group messages by conversation topic (just like in a newsgroup). Changing the way Outlook Express displays a folder can make it much easier to deal with a crowded Inbox. The following techniques show you how.

- To sort messages by a different attribute, click a column heading. Click it again to switch between ascending and descending sort order.

- To change which columns are displayed, choose Columns from the View menu. Use the Columns dialog box to modify the columns and then click OK.

- To hide messages that you've read, choose Current View from the View menu, and then Hide Read Messages.

- To group messages on the same topic together (based on the subject field), choose Current View from the View menu, and then Group Messages By Conversation.

- To create a custom view, choose Current View from the View menu, choose Define Views, click New, and then specify what conditions Outlook Express should use to display or hide messages, as shown in Figure 7-13.

Tip   If you find yourself changing views often, turn on the Views Bar. To do so, choose Layout from the View menu and then select the Views Bar check box.

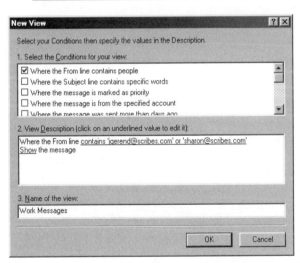

Figure 7-13 This custom view displays messages only from the specified senders, making it easy to see work-related messages.

Processing E-mail with Message Rules

Outlook Express's message rules feature is an extremely powerful tool that you can use to automatically process incoming e-mail. You can automatically sort messages into folders, forward messages, highlight messages, or even reply to messages with an e-mail you create ahead of time.

> **Note** If you find the message rules in Outlook Express aren't powerful enough, switch to Microsoft Outlook—it has more flexible and sophisticated message rules, including rules that work on IMAP accounts.

To create a message rule, use the following steps.

1   Choose Message Rules from the Tools menu, and then choose Mail.

2   Select the conditions in which Outlook Express should process incoming e-mail from the first list box, as shown in Figure 7-14.

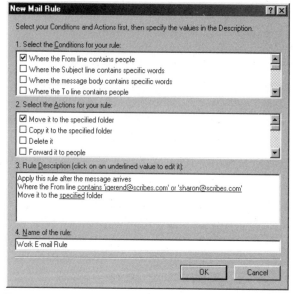

Figure 7-14 Use the New Mail Rule dialog box to create advanced message processing rules.

3   Select the actions you want to perform on messages that meet the proper conditions.

> **Tip**   Select the Stop Processing More Rules action to tell Outlook Express to stop trying to perform other rules on the same message. This can help eliminate confusing message processing behavior.

4 Click any underlined words in the Rule Description box to fill in the details of your conditions and actions.

5 Type a name for the rule in the Name Of The Rule text box and then click OK.

6 Use the Message Rules dialog box shown in Figure 7-15 to manage your message rules. (Click OK when you're done.)

● To modify an existing rule, select it and click Modify.

● To use a rule as the basis for a new rule, select it and click Copy.

● To run an existing rule on the messages already in your Inbox, select the rule and press Apply Now.

● To change the order in which rules are applied, select a rule and use Move Up and Move Down.

● To tell Outlook Express to automatically delete messages from a certain e-mail address, click the Blocked Senders tab, click Add, type the address, and click OK.

Tip   A quick way to add someone to the Blocked Senders list is to select a message from the person you want to block and choose Block Sender from the Message menu.

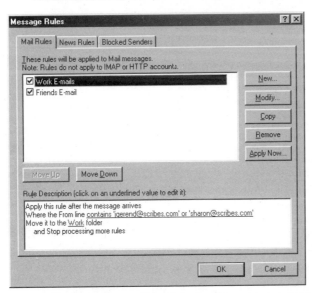

Figure 7-15 Use the Message Rules dialog box to manage your message rules.

Try This! Some examples of useful things that you can do with message rules follow.

- Move messages from a group of people into a different folder. For example, move all messages from your friends into a Friends folder.

- Automatically reply to messages with certain words in the subject or from a specific person or company. This can be handy if you receive e-mails asking the same question or if you want to automatically reply to someone telling them that their e-mails are being automatically deleted because you don't want to talk to them.

- Forward messages you receive with certain words in the subject to someone else. For example, you could forward all messages containing the name of a project you're working on to your project coworkers.

- Highlight messages that contain specific text so that you know to pay special attention to it.

Can That Spam

Most people hate *spam*—even those who work at Hormel. It clogs your Inbox, saps bandwidth from the Internet, and often signs you up to receive yet more spam. Unfortunately, there is no cure for spam, but you can take steps to reduce its affect on you and your Inbox:

> **Lingo** *Spam* is an insidious form of advertisement involving the sending of vast quantities of unsolicited e-mails to users (spamming them).

- Whenever you fill out an online form, look for a check box titled "Do Not Share My Address Information With Other Companies" or something similar, and select it.

- Get two extra e-mail accounts: use one for online orders and forms, and use the other for more public postings such as newsgroups and message boards.

- Create a message rule moving messages with typical spam keywords in the subject to a junk mail folder that you create. Periodically look through the junk mail folder and then empty it.

- When you delete spam, turn off the Preview Pane and make sure not to open the spam messages. This prevents HTML-based spam from contacting the advertiser and informing them that you have a valid e-mail address. To turn off the Preview Pane, choose Layout from the View menu and then clear the Show Preview Pane check box.

■ Don't reply to spam or follow links promising to unsubscribe you, unless you know that the company is reputable. Most of the time replying or following a link just notifies the spammer that your e-mail address is valid, causing them to send you even more spam.

Newsgroups: All the News That's Fit to Print (and Then Some)

Newsgroups are like big virtual bulletin boards. Users can post messages in a newsgroup for anyone else to read and reply to. Over 34,000 publicly accessible newsgroups (though the number you can access varies depending on your ISP) contain a virtually limitless amount of information. Some of this information is accurate, relevant, and interesting; other information is… less so. Because newsgroups consist entirely of messages posted by users, they contain both the best and worst of human experience.

You can find free and extremely useful tips on Outlook Express in the microsoft.public.windows.inetexplorer.ie6.outlookexpress newsgroup; stories of European travel in rec.travel.europe; or more than you want to see or know about every unsavory topic you can imagine in the alt. newsgroups.

Caution   Parents, take note—newsgroups are NOT a place for children to go roaming unsupervised.

The following sections cover setting up news accounts, finding a newsgroup that interests you, reading messages and synchronizing newsgroups. However, working with newsgroups is similar to working with e-mail, so we only cover topics where key differences exist (and then only briefly). For more information on performing an action such as composing a newsgroup post, see the equivalent e-mail section earlier in this chapter.

Setting Up a News Account

If your ISP didn't set up your news server account automatically, follow these steps to set it up now.

1   Choose Accounts from the Tools menu.

2   Click Add and then choose News.

3   Type the name you want to use on the newsgroups—you don't have to use your full or real name here. Click Next.

4   Type the e-mail address to which you want other newsgroup users (as well as the numerous advertisers that like to spam newsgroup users) to write. Click Next.

Caution   Disguise your real e-mail address by adding "nospam," "deleteme," "remove," or something similar somewhere in your address. This prevents automated "spambots" from collecting your e-mail address and spamming you. Just make sure that you include instructions on removing the disguise in the body of any message that you post to a newsgroup.

---

5   Type the name of your news server (as provided to you by your ISP) and then click Next. Click Finish when you're done.

Opening and Subscribing to Newsgroups

Before viewing newsgroup messages, you need to open a newsgroup. If you like the newsgroup, or suspect you might, you can subscribe to it. Subscribing to newsgroups is free and doesn't involve giving anyone your personal information—it's just a way of book marking favorite newsgroups.

Note   The first time you download the list of newsgroups takes a while, especially if you have a dial-up Internet connection. Be patient, you'll only have to do this once.

To open and subscribe to newsgroups, select your news server from the folder list, click Newsgroups, and then use the following techniques, as shown in Figure 7-16.

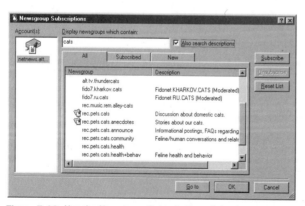

Figure 7-16 Use the Newsgroup Subscriptions dialog box to open and subscribe to newsgroups.

- To search for a newsgroup with specific text in the newsgroup name, type the text in the Display Newsgroups Which Contain text box. To include newsgroups descriptions in the search, select the Also Search Descriptions check box.

- To browse the list of newsgroups, scroll through the listings.

- To open a newsgroup, select it and click Go To.

- To subscribe to a newsgroup, double-click the newsgroup or select it and click Subscribe.

- To unsubscribe from a newsgroup, select it and click Unsubscribe. You can also right-click a subscribed newsgroup in the Folders list and choose Unsubscribe from the shortcut menu.

Tip   Perform your searches at *http://groups.google.com* for vastly better results than in Outlook Express. Once you've found a good newsgroup, you can go back to Outlook Express and subscribe to it.

Reading and Downloading Messages

After opening a newsgroup, you can view messages just like you would in e-mails in your Inbox, with a few differences.

- To download additional headers, choose Get Next 300 Headers from the Tools menu.

Tip   Broadband Internet users might want to increase the number of headers Outlook Express downloads at a time. To do so, choose Options from the Tools menu, click the Read tab, and enter a higher number (such as 1000) in the News section of the dialog box.

- To expand a *thread*, or conversation, click the plus sign next to it.

- Right-click a message and choose Mark As Read or Mark As Unread to change whether the message appears read or unread. To mark all messages in a newsgroup as read, right-click the newsgroup and choose Catch Up from the shortcut menu.

- To watch a conversation for new messages, click in the column with the glasses icon (to the left of the message) so that the glasses icon appears next to the thread. When new messages are posted in the watched thread, Outlook Express highlights the thread and newsgroup in red. To ignore a thread (perhaps because it's degenerated to personal insults), click in the column again so that it shows a red stop sign.

■ To put back together a message that has been split into multiple parts (to accommodate a large attachment), select the messages, right-click them and choose Combine And Decode. Arrange the messages into the proper order, and then click OK.

■ To download messages later, select the messages, choose Mark For Offline, and then choose whether to download the selected messages, conversation, all messages, or no messages.

Posting to a Newsgroup

Posting messages to a newsgroup is virtually identical to sending an e-mail message, so we won't hold your hand here. However, take note of a few things before posting to a newsgroup.

■ To post a reply back to the newsgroup, click Reply Group.

■ To send an e-mail reply to the author of a newsgroup post, click Reply.

■ *Lurk* for a while in a newsgroup before posting to it, so that you can get a feel for what's acceptable.

Lingo   *Lurking* in a newsgroup means reading the newsgroup for a while without posting. It doesn't involve hanging out in dark alleys.

■ Before asking a question, take five or ten minutes to browse through the newsgroup, perform a search on *http://groups.google.com*, and search for the newsgroup's FAQ at *http://www.faq.org*. Few things are more rude (or embarrassing) than asking a question that was answered just a few posts ago.

■ Don't post newsgroup messages in HTML format unless absolutely necessary. Because of their larger size, HTML messages are usually considered rude.

Synchronizing Newsgroups

To control which newsgroups are updated when you synchronize your newsgroups and how they're synchronized, use the following steps.

1 Select your news server in the Folders pane of Outlook Express.

2 Select a newsgroup, click Settings, and then choose the synchronization setting you want.

3 Select or clear the check box next to a newsgroup's synchronization setting to enable or disable synchronization of that newsgroup.

4 Click Synchronize Account to update your newsgroups.

Cleaning Up After Newsgroups

Newsgroups can take up significant hard disk space, particularly if you download lots of messages containing attachments. (We won't ask what kind of attachments they are.) To clean up after newsgroups and free up hard disk space, use the following steps.

1 Choose Options from the Tools menu.

2 Click the Maintenance tab, and click Clean Up Now.

3 Click Browse to specify a single newsgroup to clean up (otherwise Outlook Express cleans up all local files).

4 Use the Local File Clean Up dialog box, as shown in Figure 7-17, to take the appropriate cleanup action.

- *Compact* removes wasted space without throwing away any cached messages.

- *Remove Messages* deletes all downloaded message bodies, leaving just the headers (though you can download the messages later if they're still available on the server).

- *Delete* deletes all downloaded headers and message bodies, removing them from your view of the newsgroup.

- *Reset* deletes all downloaded messages and resets Outlook Express to remember which messages you've viewed, so that headers are downloaded again.

5 Click Close and then OK when you're finished.

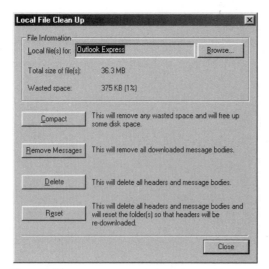

Figure 7-17 You can clean up Outlook Express's local files.

Key Points

■ To manage your e-mail accounts, choose Accounts from the Tools menu.

■ Take five minutes before using Outlook Express to configure its settings the way you want—it'll save you time in the long run.

■ E-mail attachments are the number one source of viruses, so use caution when opening them and be polite when sending them.

■ E-mail groups make it easy to quickly send messages to a large number of people.

■ If you receive a large number of e-mails, create additional folders, and organize your messages into these folders.

■ Create message rules to help process incoming e-mail, for example, moving them into folders or taking action as necessary.

■ Guard your primary e-mail address with your life; use secondary accounts when buying things online, filling out forms, and posting things in newsgroups. This reduces the amount of spam you receive.

■ Newsgroups are a tremendous source of information and opinions, both good and bad, and work much like e-mail folders.

■ Use *http://groups.google.com* to search through newsgroups for the answers to any questions you have before posting the question.

Chapter 8

Printing

Despite all the hoopla that initially surrounded the concept of a "paperless office," printing isn't going away anytime soon. Whether it's tax documents, photos, or flyers for business, people always have need for the printed page.

This chapter gets you up and running with a new (or old) printer, provides some printing tips that even the most experienced users find beneficial, and covers nuts and bolts information such as setting printing preferences, managing documents in the print queue, and using printers on a network.

See Also - *For help with printer problems, use the Windows 98 Print Troubleshooter, which is located in the Help system. You can also access the Microsoft Knowledge Base at http://support.microsoft.com.*

Installing and Removing Printers

To install a printer, plug it in and go to the Printers folder (or the printer driver's setup program) to install the printer drivers, if the printer isn't automatically detected. To remove a printer, pull its plug (gently) from the back of your computer and then access the Printers folder to remove the printer driver. (If your printer installed additional software, use the Add/Remove Programs tool instead.)

If you need help with this process, use the following two sections; otherwise, move along.

Adding a Printer

Before you can print, you need to add a printer. A number of methods for installing a printer are available, as described below..

- The best way to install a printer is to download the latest drivers from the printer manufacturer's Web site and install the drivers as directed.

- The next best method for newer printers (1999 or later) is to locate the documentation and software that came with the printer and follow the instructions.

- If the printer is a Universal Serial Bus (USB) printer, plug it in and turn it on. Windows automatically detects the printer and asks you for the appropriate drivers and printer name. Then it does the rest for you.

If you have an older printer, or you can't get a hold of printer drivers supplied by the printer's manufacturer, use the following steps to install the printer.

Tip Only install the print programs you plan on using—printer drivers often come with extra software that you don't need. The fewer programs you install, the more stable Windows 98 is.

---

1 Plug the printer into the appropriate port on your computer, load the ink cartridges or toner as directed by the printer manufacturer, and then turn on the printer.

2 Open the Printers folder by clicking Start and choosing Settings and then Printers.

3 Double-click Add Printer to start the Add Printer Wizard. Click Next in the first page of the wizard.

4 Choose Local Printer and then click Next. (Network printers are discussed in the "Using a Network Printer" section of this chapter.)

5 Select the printer manufacturer and printer model of your printer, or click Have Disk to specify the location of printer drivers that came with the printer or that you downloaded for it.

Tip If you can't find your printer's exact model, pick the closest model to it or check the printer's documentation to see if it is compatible with other printer models. If worse comes to worst, pick Generic for the Manufacturer and Generic/Text Only for the printer.

---

6 Select the appropriate printer port (LPT1 for a parallel port printer or USB01 for a USB printer) and then click Next.

7 Type a name for the printer (such as the printer's model number), choose whether or not you want it to be the default printer for your system, and then click Next.

8 Choose Yes to print a test page or No to skip this step. (You can always print something useful later as your test.) Click Finish to complete the installation.

Removing a Printer

Removing a printer is easy—just use the following methods.

- If you used printer drivers supplied by the printer's manufacturer, use the Add/Remove Programs tool to uninstall the software.

- Open the Printers folder, select the printer you want to delete, and then press Delete.

See Also See "Uninstalling Software" in Chapter 3, "Running Programs," for more information on uninstalling software.

Getting the Most from Your Printer

After decades (yes, decades) of using computer printers, we've come up with some suggestions to maximize your printing pleasure. The following sections present a lot of valuable and poorly understood information, especially about printing photos, that is useful for experienced printers and novices alike.

Basic Printing—with a Twist

Although some variance occurs in how each application prints, in general, here's how it works. (This is pretty basic, so skip ahead if you want.)

- To print something, choose Print from the File menu of your application.

- To print immediately using the default print options, click the Print toolbar button. (For some applications, this just opens the Print dialog box.)

- To select the proper margins, paper tray, and other options, choose Page Setup from the File menu.

- To preview your printout, choose Print Preview from the File menu.

Tip Print Screen on your keyboard takes a snapshot of the screen (a screenshot), and saves it to the Clipboard. Open any image editing program, such as Microsoft Paint, and choose Paste from the Edit menu to view the screenshot. Then print it as you would any other document or save it to your hard drive.

If you encounter the famous Print dialog box, as shown in Figure 8-1, use the following list to maximize your printing experience.

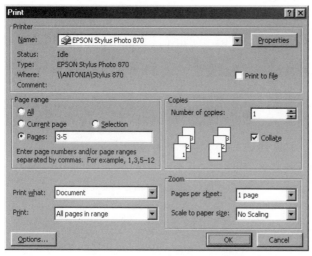

Figure 8-1 Use the Print dialog box (this one is from Microsoft Word 2000) to control how your document prints.

1   Select the desired printer from the Name box and optionally click Properties to specify such things as print quality and color.

2   In the Print Range area, specify whether to print everything, the current page, a specific page range, or only the selected text or graphics.

3   Specify the number of copies you want in the Number Of Copies box.

4   Select the Collate box to collate copies, keeping pages in order.

5   If a Zoom section is present, use it to print multiple pages per sheet of paper or to scale a document that expects a certain paper size to print on a different paper size—for example, you could shrink an 8.5-by-11-inch Letter document to print on 5.5-by-8.5-inch Half-Letter paper.

6   Click OK to print.

Tip   To save ink and paper, select only the text or graphics you want to print, choose Print from the File menu, and then, in the Print Range section, choose Selection.

Try This! Choosing the Print To File check box creates a mysterious .prn file that can be used to print a document at another computer, even if the other computer doesn't have the proper program. (It does need access to a printer that uses the same driver, however.)

To print a .prn file once you've transported it to the destination computer (through e-mail, a floppy disk, or CD-ROM), open a DOS prompt and type **copy a:\printout.prn LPT1 /b** (where a:\printout.prn is the path to the .prn file, LPT1 is the printer mapped to that port, and /b tells Windows it's a binary file).

Printing Photos

Photos are the closest reproduction to visual reality we have. As such, they're difficult to reproduce digitally. However, the quality of inkjets and digital cameras has risen to the point where they can, under the right conditions, produce results that are virtually indistinguishable from 35 mm prints. Unfortunately, getting the right conditions can be difficult, which is what the following sections are about.

Use the Right Resolution for the Print Size

The best photo printer in the world won't be able to make a satisfactory 4-by-6-inch print from a 640-by-480 image. Similarly, scanning an 8-by-10-inch photo at 300 dots per inch (dpi) is overkill if you intend to make wallet size prints.

In brief, you'll get the best results if the images that you print are 200 dpi or higher. You can get away with 160–170 dpi if you want to make larger prints and don't mind sacrificing a little quality.

Because few things are listed in dpi, we've provided a Table 8-1, which lists typical print sizes and the resolutions that are needed for each print size. We've also included the approximate dpi for each print size/resolution combination—just to give you a better feel of how dpi relates to resolution and print size—as well as the minimum camera type that yields a good printout at a given size.

Table 8-1   What Resolution to Use for a Given Print Size

Image Size (in inches)	Recommended Resolution (dpi)	Minimum Resolution (dpi)	Minimum Camera Type
2.5 × 3 (wallet)	640 × 480 (215 dpi)	320 × 240 (100 dpi)	VGA
3.5 × 5	1024 × 768 (205 dpi)	800 × 600 (160 dpi)	SVGA
4 × 6	1200 × 800 (200 dpi)	1024 × 768 (170 dpi)	1 megapixel
5 × 7	1600 × 1200 (230 dpi)	1152 × 864 minimum (165 dpi)	2 megapixels
8 × 10	2048 × 1536 (205 dpi)	1600 × 1200 minimum (160dpi)	3 megapixels

Resolution, DPI, and Print Size Digital pictures consist of tiny colored dots. These dots are called pixels when in a computer or dots when printed out. Understanding how dots, pixels, resolution, and print size interrelate is fairly difficult, so take a deep breath before continuing.

Okay, the first things to discuss are dots per inch (dpi) and pixels per inch (ppi). Dpi and ppi are measures of how many dots can be placed in a square inch of paper (dpi) or screen space (ppi) and are roughly equivalent. The higher the dpi or ppi, the less grainy the image (because the dots or pixels are more closely packed). Table 8-2 shows some common media and their associated dpi or ppi. As you can see, a modern inkjet printer can output more information per square inch than a computer monitor.

Because traditional CRT computer monitors can display only up to 100 ppi, digital images are generally set at 72 or 96 dpi, even if the images are scanned or captured at a higher dpi. Additional detail above 100 dpi won't show up on a computer screen.

Because printers and monitors are capable of different dpi outputs, you usually must adjust the dpi of an image before printing (unless the image editing software does this for you), lest you end up with a picture that is larger and grainier than the original. For example, if you scanned a 4-by-6-inch photo at 300 dpi, the image acquisition software would create a 72 dpi, 1800 × 1200 image. If you then printed the image without adjusting the dpi back up to 300 dpi, the print would be huge (16.7-by-25 inches), and grainy, because the density of the dots (dpi) was decreased. Instead, you should reset the dpi of the image back to 300 dpi, so that it would print out as a pleasing 4-by-6-inch photo.

Given a fixed number of pixels in an image, changing how many of those pixels or dots you cram into a square inch (dpi) affects the final print size and graininess of the image. In this example, changing the dpi from 300 to 72 increased the final size of the image four times—by spacing each dot out four times more. This also means that the image would be roughly four times as grainy, or put another way, the dots would be four times easier to see.

Table 8-2   Dots or Pixels per Inch for Common Mediums

Media	dpi or ppi
Cathode Ray Tube (CRT) display	50–100 ppi (depending on the screen size and resolution)
Quantum Extended Graphics Array (QXGA) (2048x1536) Liquid Crytal Display (LCD) display	123 ppi
Photo inkjet printer	Up to 250 dpi (yes, even so-called 2880 dpi models)
35 mm photograph color print	200–300 dpi
35 mm photograph black-and-white print	300–400 dpi
35 mm camera film	3000+ dpi

Use the Right Printer

If the printer you're using isn't capable of photo quality output, printing pictures is going to be an exercise in futility. Although solid specifications aren't available to guide you when you determine whether a printer can print good quality photos, look for the following characteristics.

- **Inkjet**   Inkjet printers produce the best photos (excepting dye sublimation printers)—better even than most expensive color laser printers.

- **600 dpi or better**   Although higher dpi isn't always better, inkjet printers that can't print at 600 dpi or better won't cut it.

- **Photo printers**   So-called "photo" inkjet printers usually have five different color tanks with which they print, instead of a normal inkjet's three. This can improve color reproduction. Although many "normal" inkjets can print photos better than older "photo" printers, at the same ages, photo printers usually print better pictures than normal printers, although sometimes at the expense of text quality and economy.

Use the Printer's Highest Quality Settings

To get the best pictures from your printer, you need to use the printer's highest quality settings. Click Properties in the Print dialog box, and then use the printer's software to specify the maximum quality settings (the exact procedure varies by printer driver).

Printing with the highest quality settings does take additional time and additional ink (which translates into additional money). If you don't need the best quality for all of your photos, try printing at a variety of quality settings to determine the best compromise between quality, time, and cost.

Use the Right Paper

Using the right paper is almost as important as using the right resolution for an image. Normal inkjet paper is too porous to hold the amount of ink needed to print a high-quality photo. Specially coated paper intended for high-resolution printing is better—but it won't look like a photograph taken with a traditional film camera. For that you need photo paper, either glossy or matte depending on the effect you want.

If the printer's manufacturer produces or recommends a particular brand of paper, try that first—it usually produces the best pictures. If the results aren't what you'd hoped for or if you want to try saving a buck or two, experiment with other papers to find one you like.

Use Color Management and Calibration

Ever notice how the colors in a picture look different when you print the picture? This is because every image input and output device sees and works with colors differently, and unless they can speak a common color language, what you see might not be what you get.

The first thing to do is verify that you have *color profiles* associated with your monitor and printer as well as your scanner and digital camera, if you happen to have those devices.

Lingo   A *color profile* (.icm or .icc) is a file that contains information about how a particular device deals with colors. Associating a color profile with a device helps Windows keep colors consistent onscreen and off.

To verify that your printer has a color profile associated with it, right-click the printer in the Printers folder, choose Properties, and then click the Color Management tab. If you don't see any color profiles listed, install updated printer drivers from the printer manufacturer—they usually come with the correct color profile. To check on your monitor, right-click a blank space on the desktop, choose Properties from the shortcut menu, click the Settings tab, click Advanced, and then click the Color Management tab.

If you're still unsatisfied with your color accuracy, look into a software solution, or if you can afford it or must have accurate colors, purchase a hardware color profiling and calibration solution.

Use an Online Printer or Service Bureau

The highest quality method of printing a photograph is using an online photo printing company or a service bureau. These companies use professional photo printers, which typically deliver much better output than consumer printers. Professional printers also use photograph-style paper and yield archival quality prints, which don't deteriorate as rapidly as inkjet prints (which might only last five to ten years before colors begin to fade, unless printed with special archival grade paper and inks).

Caution   Garden variety copy shops typically are no better—in fact are sometimes worse—than your consumer level inkjet printer. If the shop uses a color laser printer, you're probably better off printing at home.

Another not-so-obvious factor is cost—printing photos using an online printing company is often cheaper than printing on a consumer printer. When using your own printer, you need to factor in the cost of photographic paper, inkjet cartridges, and wear and tear on the printer. Online printers charge a flat fee—typically U.S.$.49 for a 4-by-6-inch photo, which is usually as good as or better than the cost of printing on your own printer.

To print a photo with an online printer, you need to upload the photos at the highest resolution and quality possible. The company then prints your photos and mails them to you. To use a service bureau, bring the pictures to the company on a Zip disk or CD. Some popular online photo printing companies include *http://www.shutterfly.com* and *http://www.ofoto.com*, and there are many others. Just search for "online photo prints."

Saving Money

It all started with King Gillette, who famously gave away razors to sell blades. The economics of printing can be deceptive. Printers are cheap; ink cartridges are expensive. Cheap printers can cost more to operate in the long run because their ink cartridges cost more and hold less ink.

To maximize your cost savings, use the following recommendations.

- If you print mostly text documents, set the default print settings to black and white.

- If most of the time you don't need high quality printouts, set the default print settings to the lowest quality setting.

- When making a lot of copies of a text document, print once and then make photocopies of the printout. Printing on an inkjet printer usually costs more than a copy shop charges for copies.

- If you print lots of text, buy a laser printer—they're faster than inkjets, offer great text quality, and offer the cheapest text output. Just keep in mind that inexpensive laser printers can't print color, and even expensive laser printers aren't as good as inkjets when it comes to photographs.

- Look closely at the cost savings of recycled or refilled ink cartridges before using them—they can clog print heads more quickly than new cartridges. However, this usually happens only after a large amount of printing, so the cost savings might offset the decreased life of the printer.

- Buy ink cartridges online or buy third-party cartridges, which are usually cheaper than those made by the printer manufacturer and higher quality than recycled or refilled cartridges.

- Flip over printed pages that you no longer need and print drafts on the blank side.

Changing How Documents Print by Default

By setting the default printer settings to suit the type of printing you do most often, you can minimize the number of times you have to adjust them. If you usually print text documents for your own use, set the defaults to Black, Economy (or similar). If you usually print photos, set the defaults to Color, High Quality (or similar). You'll still need to adjust the print settings when you want to print at a higher or lower quality setting than your defaults, but at least this happens less than if you use the printer driver's standard settings.

Printer drivers vary from printer to printer, so you should consult your printer's documentation for help on specific settings, but here's how to get started.

1   Open the Printers folder by clicking Start, choosing Settings, and then Printers.

2   Right-click the printer and choose Properties from the shortcut menu.

> **Tip**   To change the default printer, right-click the printer in the Printers folder that you want to use by default and then choose Set As Default from the shortcut menu.

3   Use the tabs in the dialog box to adjust the printer's settings. The available tabs will vary from printer to printer.

Managing the Print Queue

Most of the time you don't need to worry about the print queue. You press Print in an application, and a few moments later your printer starts printing the document.

The document might not print so quickly if you print to a network printer or print multiple documents at the same time. In these instances, your documents are placed at the end of the print queue, behind any documents already waiting to print. Once again, you won't usually need to pay any additional attention to the printing process—you just have to wait a bit longer.

However, if ten big documents are waiting to print and you need to print directions to an appointment for which you're late, it's time to dig into the print queue and reorder which documents print first. On a different occasion, perhaps you need to stop a large document from printing because you found a mistake. To perform these tasks and others, use the following steps.

1 Open the print queue by double-clicking the printer icon in the system tray or by clicking Start, choosing Settings, and then Printers and then double-clicking the printer to which you're printing.

> **Note** If you are printing to a network printer, the only actions you can perform are pausing or canceling your own documents.

2 Select a document from the window, as shown in Figure 8-2, and then take the appropriate action.

- To move the document to the head of the line, drag it under the currently printing document. (You can't preempt a document that's already started to print.)

- To pause a document, right-click it and choose Pause Printing.

- To cancel a document, right-click it and choose Cancel Printing.

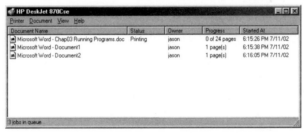

Figure 8-2 The print queue displays the documents waiting to print.

3 To pause the printer, temporarily stopping all documents, choose Pause Printing from the Printer menu. Choose Pause Printing again to resume printing.

4 To cancel all documents in the print queue, choose Purge Print Documents from the Printer menu.

Dealing with Print Jobs That Refuse to Die Ever hit print on a 50-page docu-ment, only to realize that you've forgotten to include page numbers? Even though you *can* stop the document from printing by right-clicking it in the print queue and then selecting Cancel Printing (or, if you're using Word and you're quick, double-clicking the little printer icon in Word's Status Bar), this doesn't work all the time. In our experience, more often than not Windows keeps right on printing or starts spewing page after page of gibberish.

To deal with this dire situation, turn off your printer. Amazingly enough, this almost always stops the currently printing document. (If it doesn't, try pulling the printer's power plug.) Attempt to cancel the document in the print queue again and then turn the printer back on and hit Page Eject if there's a stuck page.

Although this method usually works, in some instances the printer just picks up where it left off—spewing countless pages of garbage. (We're really not insulting your documents.) To remedy this, delete the spooled document from the Windows spool folder. To do so, open the c:\windows\spool\printers folder and delete any files that you find or if you don't want to disturb documents waiting patiently in the print queue, delete only the .spl and .shd files associated with the stuck documents. (Compare the Modified times for the print job in Windows Explorer and the print queue.)

Installing and Using a Network Printer

Once installed properly, using a network printer is no different from using a locally connected printer—you just have to walk farther. However, first you need to install the printer, which is what the next section is about. You might also want to share a locally connected printer with other users on your network or capture a printer port so that programs developed for Windows 3.*x* can print to your network printer. All of these tasks are covered in the next sections, so if you need to perform any of them, read on.

Adding a Network Printer

To use a network printer, you must first install it on your system. To use printer drivers provided by the printer manufacturer instead of those provided with Windows 98, install the drivers according to the manufacturer's directions.

If the setup program doesn't properly set up the printer to work over the network, follow these steps.

1   Right-click the printer in the Printers folder and then choose Properties from the shortcut menu.

2   Click the Details tab and check that the printer's network location is listed in the Print To The Following Port box, as shown in Figure 8-3.

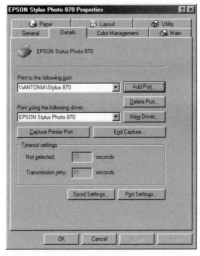

Figure 8-3 Most printer drivers choke if the printer is located on the network instead of plugged into the back of the computer. To remedy this, point the printer to the correct network location instead of the local printer port.

3   If the correct network location isn't listed, click Add Port.

4   Choose Network and then type the printer's network path or click Browse, select the printer, and then click OK.

5   Click OK in each dialog box, until you're back in the Printers folder.

If the above procedure doesn't work, or if you want to use printer drivers included with Windows 98, use the following steps.

1   Open the Printers folder by clicking Start and choosing Settings and then Printers.

2   Select the nonfunctional printer driver, press Delete, and then click No when asked if Windows should remove unneeded files (unless you want to use Windows 98's built-in drivers, in which case click Yes).

3   Double-click the Add Printer icon to start the Add Printer Wizard. Click Next in the first page of the wizard.

4   Choose Network Printer and then click Next.

5   Click Browse to locate the network printer or type the network path in the Network Path Or Queue Name box.

Tip   If you're using a Windows XP computer on your network and you turn on the Internet Connection Firewall feature, you cannot share files or printers with the computer. To fix this, turn off the firewall on the network adapter connected to your local network, or open up User Datagram Protocol (UDP) and Transmission Control Protocol (TCP) ports 135-139, as well as TCP and UDP port 445. This procedure is discussed in Microsoft Knowledge Base Article Q298804 at *http://support.microsoft.com*.

---

6   If you want to print to the network printer from MS-DOS or Windows 3.*x* programs that aren't network aware, select the Yes option; otherwise, choose No. Click Next to move on.

7   If you chose Yes in step 5, click Capture Printer Port, select a printer port (LPT2, for example), and then click OK. Click Next.

8   Type a name for the printer, choose whether to use the printer by default, and then click Finish. If prompted, direct Windows to the location of the latest printer drivers.

Caution   Windows 98 can only connect to network printers whose share names are shorter than 13 characters, including spaces.

Sharing a Printer on a Network

Printer sharing is one of the reasons networks first became popular. Sharing one or more printers on a network saves money and usually allows everyone access to a better printer (and in any case, not everyone needs to print at the same time).

To share a printer on the network, you first need to locally install the printer on your Windows 98 computer. (You could install it on another computer, but then you wouldn't need this procedure would you?) You must also ensure that your network is set up properly. (For more information on networks, see Chapter 13, "Building and Using A Network"). Once these tasks are completed, use the following steps to share a locally connected printer with other users of your network.

1   Double-click the Network tool in Control Panel and click File And Print Sharing.

2   Select the I Want To Be Able To Allow Others To Print To My Printer(s) check box, and then click OK.

3   Click OK to save the network changes and then click Yes to restart your computer.

4   Open the Printers folder by clicking Start, and choosing Settings and then Printers.

5   Right-click the printer and choose Sharing from the shortcut menu.

6   Choose Shared As, as shown in Figure 8-4.

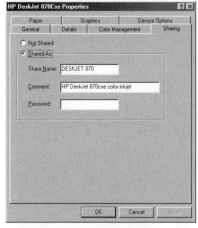

Figure 8-4 Use the Sharing tab to control whether a printer is shared on the network and how it will appear to network users.

7   Type a share name for the printer. The share name is the name network users see for the printer and should be 12 characters or less.

> **Note**   If you are using Windows 3.x or MS-DOS clients on the network, the share name must be eight characters or less and can't contain any spaces.

8   Type a description of the printer in the Comment text box.

9   To force network users to supply a password to print, type a password in the Password box. Click OK when you're done. If you entered a password you will be prompted to confirm it.

Capturing Printer Ports for Pre-Windows 95 Programs

If you want to print to the network printer from MS-DOS programs or
Windows 3.x programs that aren't network aware, use the following steps.

1   Open the Printers folder by clicking Start, and choosing Settings and
then Printers.

2   Click the Details tab, and make a note of the path listed in the Print To
The Following Port drop-down box.

3   Click Capture Printer Port and select a printer port (LPT2, for example).

4   Use the Path text box to select the path you noted in step 3.

5   To reconnect the printer port to the printer each time you log on the
computer, select Reconnect At Logon.

6   Click OK in each dialog box, until you're back in the Printers folder. To
print to the network printer from a DOS or Windows 3.x program,
select the printer or specify the printer port you captured.

Key Points

- To install a printer, use the latest printer drivers and setup instructions
provided by the printer manufacturer whenever possible.

- Photos print best if the photos are set at roughly 200 dpi in an image
editing program, though you can fudge a little if you want a bigger
printout.

- When printing photos, set the printer to its highest dpi setting, which
should be no less than 600 dpi.

- For the best photos, use the paper recommended by your printer
manufacturer.

- Online photo printers or local service bureaus provide the best quality
prints, often at prices that are less than printing at home.

- To add a network printer, install the printer drivers provided by the
printer manufacturer when possible, but be aware that you might need
to then reinstall the printer using the Add Printer Wizard.

- To print to a network printer from an MS-DOS or non-network aware
Windows 3.x program, capture a printer port and redirect it to the network printer.

Chapter 9

Conquering Computer Hardware

The history of computer operating systems is also the history of hardware struggles. Some say hardware advances spur advances in software. Some say it's the other way around. Whatever the truth, when software and hardware get together, it often results in some discord. The purpose of this chapter is to smooth some of those rough edges and get everyone happily working in harmony.

Hardware and Windows 98

Microsoft goes to considerable trouble to maintain a hardware compatibility list (HCL) of all the hardware devices in the known world that work with any particular Microsoft operating system.

Any device on the Microsoft Windows 98 HCL has been thoroughly evaluated and Microsoft attests that it will work with Windows 98. Yes, many devices not on the HCL also work with Windows 98—at least most of the time. Be assured that if you run into a hardware problem with a non-HCL part, the manufacturer will send you to Microsoft and Microsoft will send you to the HCL.

So why not start out with the HCL in the beginning? You can find it at *http://www.microsoft.com/hwdq/hcl/*.

Using the Device Manager

The Device Manager is your link to all things hardware. To open the Device Manager, right-click My Computer and select Properties. Then click the Device Manager tab. Lots of information is available in Device Manager—once you know how to find it.

The default view groups the hardware devices by type. Click the plus sign next to CDROM, for example, to see the type of CD-ROM in the computer, as shown in Figure 9-1.

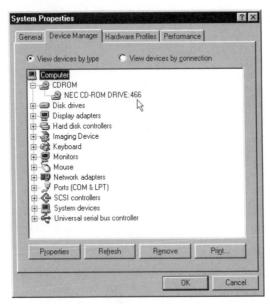

Figure 9-1 The Device Manager provides information about the hardware that makes up the computer.

Much of the data found in Device Manager is informational. That is, you can see many details but the opportunities for change are limited to just a few areas.

Tip   To get to the Device Manager quickly, hold down the Alt key and double-click My Computer, then click the Device Manager tab.

Views of Devices

In addition to viewing devices by type, you can select the option to View Devices By Connection. As you can see in Figure 9-2, this gives a whole different perspective to the hardware. In the default view (View Devices By Type), many items are grouped under System devices. In View Devices By Connection, some of those same devices are shown to be connected as Plug and Play devices, whereas others are connected through the more pedestrian PCI (Peripheral Component Interconnect) *bus*.

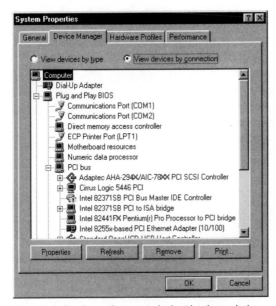

Figure 9-2 Here's another way to look at hardware devices.

Lingo   A *bus* is a set of electrical conductors used to transfer data. It's essentially a shared highway connecting different parts of a computer. A PCI bus allows up to ten expansion cards to be installed in the computer—each one becoming, in effect, part of the bus and each one controlling a device. Most computers, however, only have space for three or four expansion cards. A computer with a *Plug and Play* BIOS allows the installation of many devices without any special configuring on your part. *Basic input/output system (BIOS)* is the software that runs when you start the computer; it tests hardware and starts the operating system.

For even more information on things like interrupts and memory allocations, highlight Computer in Device Manager and click Properties. The only time you're likely to need this information is when you have an intractable hardware problem and a support technician asks for it.

Device Settings

Different types of devices are adjusted in different ways. The following list tells you where to look to change settings. The Device Manager view is by device type.

Table 9-1   Device Settings

Hardware Device	Settings Location
Hard drives and adapters	Device Manager, under Disk drives.
Video cards, display adapters	Device Manager, under Display adapters or Display in Control Panel. (See "Display Hardware and Settings" later in this chapter.)
Cameras, scanners	Device Manager, under Imaging Devices Or Scanners and Cameras in Control Panel. (See "Installing a Scanner" or "Connecting a Digital Camera" later in this chapter.)
Data and fax modems	Device Manager, under Modem or Modems in Control Panel. (See "Configuring Modems" later in this chapter.)
Mouse devices	Device Manager, under Mouse or Mouse in Control Panel. (See "Changing a Mouse" later in this chapter.)
Multimedia devices	Device Manager, under Sound, Video And Game Controllers or Multimedia in Control Panel.
Network cards	Device Manager, under Network Adapters or Network Adapter Properties (on the Configuration tab) under Network in Control Panel.
System devices	Device Manager, under System Devices.

See Also   *For more information about networks and network cards, see the section "Building a Network" in Chapter 13, "Building and Using a Network."*

Try This!   If your CD-ROM drive starts automatically when a CD is inserted (or it doesn't and you want it to), you can change the behavior in Device Manager.

1   Click the plus sign next to CDROM and click your CD-ROM drive.

2   Click Properties and then click the Settings tab.

3   In the Options frame, click the Auto Insert Notification check box. Windows 98 automatically starts a CD-ROM when it's inserted in the drive. Clear the check box and the automatic start is disabled.

Even when the box is not checked, you can still open Windows Explorer to view the contents of a CD.

Getting and Using Drivers

It might come to pass that you acquire a camera or scanner or some other hardware that won't successfully install on Windows 98. You've tried Add New Hardware in Control Panel, and you've run the software that came with the device without success. So now it's time to find a newer or better *driver*.

Lingo A *driver* is a bit of software that tells Windows 98 how to communicate with a specific piece of hardware.

Drivers are obtained, primarily, online. You need to find the Web site for the manufacturer of the reluctant device. This won't be difficult—just go to a search engine like *http://www.google.com* or *http://search.msn.com* and search by the name of the company. Virtually all hardware manufacturers have Web sites, and the vast majority of them have drivers and updates you can download.

Be sure to read and follow the instructions on how to install your new driver. Some drivers require you to remove the old driver first.

Adding a USB Port

Newer computers already have a universal serial bus (USB) port installed because more and more devices, such as printers, scanners, mice, and modems are manufactured with a USB port option. A single USB port can be used to connect up to 127 USB devices to a single computer. Undoubtedly, USB will eventually replace serial and parallel ports because USB is faster and supports Plug and Play as well as *hot-plugging*.

Lingo Just about every device that plugs into a serial or parallel port requires that you turn off the computer, plug in the device, and then restart the computer. Devices that can be *hot-plugged* can be connected or disconnected while the computer is on with only a momentary pause while the operating system recognizes the change.

If you have (or plan to have) hardware that can take advantage of a USB port and there's no USB port on your computer, you can add one easily. Order yourself a USB PCI card and install it using these steps.

1   Shut down Windows 98, then power off your computer.

2   Unplug enough cables from the back of the computer to allow the case to be opened. Make notes of what went where—even if you think you'll remember because there's a good chance you won't.

3   Open the case, find an empty PCI slot, and insert the card.

4   Close the computer case and plug in all the wires, cables, and cords.

5   Turn on your computer.

When Windows 98 starts, the Add New Hardware Wizard searches for a driver for the USB card. You'll need to provide your Windows 98 CD. After the driver is found and installed, you must reboot *again*. However, that's it.

Installing a Scanner

The easiest type of scanner to install is one that has a USB connection. Just connect the USB cable to the scanner at one end and to the USB port on the computer at the other. Windows 98 immediately advises that it has detected new hardware and what it is. (No need to turn your computer off.) The Add New Hardware Wizard launches.

You will probably have to supply the Windows 98 CD. If your scanner is a new one, Windows 98 might be able to recognize it and still not have a driver for it. In that case, you'll need to provide the CD or floppy disk that came with the scanner.

If your scanner is not USB-enabled, open Add New Hardware from Control Panel. After the Plug-and-Play detection step, choose No, The Device Isn't On The List (assuming it isn't), and click Next. You can try letting Windows search for the hardware or select your hardware from the list under the Imaging Device category. Once it's installed, the Scanners And Cameras icon is displayed in Control Panel.

Scanners and
Cameras

Opening Scanners And Cameras in Control Panel displays a list of installed devices. In most cases devices that weren't turned on when you started the computer won't be included. Turn the new device on and then restart Windows 98. If you want to add a device that Windows 98 did not detect, click Add. Selecting a device and clicking Properties allows you to perform simple troubleshooting tests.

Of course, if no scanner or camera has been detected, you won't have this icon in Control Panel to begin with.

Note While Windows 98 built-in drivers offer basic functionality for a variety of scanners and cameras, you should try installing the software supplied with the device. In many cases it offers better control over the device than Windows 98 can provide on its own.

Connecting a Digital Camera

As with a scanner, a digital camera connects most easily when it's connected through a USB port. Just plug it in and the Add New Hardware Wizard springs into action, as shown in Figure 9-3, and starts installing it.

Figure 9-3 The USB port makes many devices act like Plug and Play, even if they're not.

The wizard asks for a driver location. If you have the original software that came with the camera, use it here. Windows 98 searches and comes up with a driver.

The camera is installed as if it were an additional disk drive, as shown in Figure 9-4, and it is just like a removable hard drive except your memory card (or stick) stores only photographs. Click the new camera object to view the current content of the camera.

Figure 9-4 Your camera is installed as another disk drive (F in this case).

Downloading Photos to Your Disk Drive

Once your camera is installed and connected, the pictures display when you click the icon in My Computer. Select the ones you want to transfer to the computer and drag them to the new location.

Managing Digital Photos

In Windows 98, you can view photos in Microsoft Internet Explorer or with an imaging program. However, there's very little you can do to the pictures using Windows-only tools. Microsoft Paint comes with Windows 98, and although it offers a few functions, it's not up to doing any real photo editing.

If you're going to be using your digital camera with regularity, invest in some photo editing software. These products range from Roxio PhotoSuite at less than U.S.$30 to Adobe PhotoShop at well in excess of U.S.$500.

I am partial to Microsoft Picture It! because it's inexpensive and easy to use — especially if you're not a graphics professional and talk about histograms and color depth just gives you a headache. With good photo manipulating software, you can resize pictures, crop them, correct (within limits) for low light, and so forth.

Sending Pictures by E-mail

You don't need to do a thing to a photo to attach it to an e-mail message. However, most digital camera pictures are taken using high resolution, so each picture file is large. In that case, it's a kindness to resize a picture before sending it off. If your pictures are taken using a lower resolution and the files are not large, then you can probably figure out that you don't need to make them smaller.

To attach a photo to a message in Microsoft Outlook Express, open the photo-containing folder and drag the picture file into the message.

Configuring Modems

Installing and configuring a modem is fairly simple (almost as simple as it should be). When you first install Windows 98, it *should* detect the modem automatically. You'll only need to deal with the following steps if the modem isn't detected or if you change modems later.

Installing a Modem

Before starting any modem procedure, make sure the modem is plugged in and turned on (if it's an external modem) and that the telephone wire is plugged into the modem and into the wall receptacle (internal and external modems). To install a modem where none has been before, follow these steps.

1   Click Start and select Settings and then Control Panel.

2   Double-click Modems to start the Install New Modem Wizard.

3   You can let Windows 98 search for the modem, or you can select your
         modem directly.

         Let Windows try first—it's the easiest way. If Windows 98 has dif-
         ficulty, you can always specify your particular modem on a second go-
         round. Windows searches your communications ports and tries to find
         a modem. When it finds one, you'll see a Verify Modem dialog box. If
         the modem shown isn't correct or the designation seems too generic,
         click Change and continue with the next step.

4   If Windows 98 fails to find the modem (or if you click Change in the
         Verify dialog box), click Next to select a specific modem. Figure 9-5
         shows the window where you select a manufacturer in the left list box
         and the particular model in the right list box. If your modem isn't listed
         and you have an installation disk that came with it, click Have Disk.

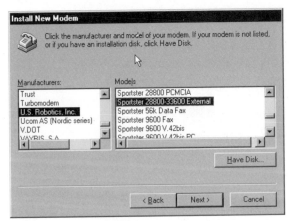

Figure 9-5 If Windows 98 can't locate your modem, you can manually install it by selecting the
manufacturer and model.

5   Keep clicking OK, Next, or Finish until the installation is complete.

Removing a Modem

When it comes time to remove a modem, don't just unplug it and plug in the
new one. (You can do that, but you leave software on the computer that might
be confusing later.) So, to remove traces of the old modem, follow these steps.

1   Click Start and select Settings and then Control Panel.

2   Double-click Modems. On the General tab, highlight the modem name.

3   Click Remove, and it's done.

Replacing a Modem

When the time comes to replace your modem, delete the old modem using the procedure described in the previous section, and then shut down Windows 98 and turn off your computer. Unplug the old modem and plug in the new one. Make sure the modem is turned on (if it's external) and that all connections— including the one to the phone line—are made, and then follow the steps described in the earlier section entitled "Installing a Modem."

Modem Settings

To find the hardware-type settings for your modem, open Control Panel and double-click Modems. Select your modem (if it isn't selected already) and click Properties. The following appear on the General tab:

- The full name of the modem

- A drop-down list box showing the port to which the modem is connected

- A slider for setting the volume of the modem speaker

- A drop-down list box for setting the maximum speed

These settings (except for volume, which is strictly a matter of preference) rarely need to change because they originate from what Windows 98 knows about your specific modem. More hardware settings are on the Connection tab, as shown in Figure 9-6.

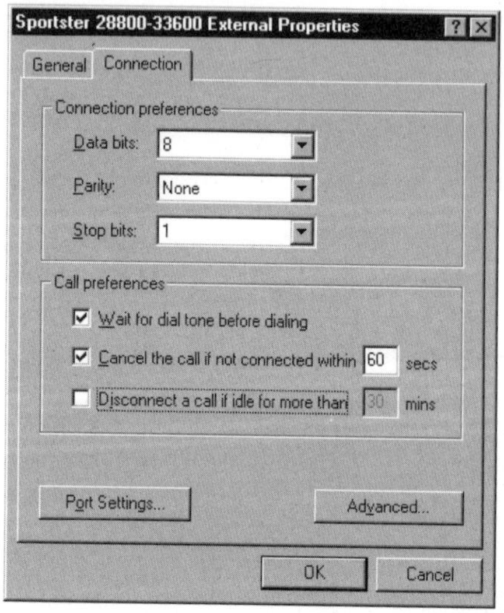

Figure 9-6 The Connection tab shows hardware settings for a modem connection.

Again, unless you have a good reason for changing the Connection Preferences, leave them alone. The Call Preferences can be changed if you find the default ones unsuitable. In particular, you can set a time to disconnect a call if the line is idle for an extended time. Although many online services disconnect an inactive line, they can take quite a long time to do it.

Dialing Properties

Windows 98 allows for the configuring of multiple dialing locations, so if you travel with your computer, you can make calls from your branch office or a hotel, without making complex changes every time you change locations.

Double-click Modems in Control Panel, select Dialing Properties on the General tab and fill out the information for your location. Click New to supply additional locations. When you change physical locations, you need only tell Windows 98 where you are and all your necessary dialing information is put into place, as shown in Figure 9-7.

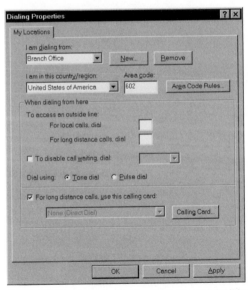

Figure 9-7 If you travel with your computer, you don't have to redo your communications settings.

Modem Troubleshooting

Most of the time, when a modem is uncooperative, it's for obvious reasons.

- It's not plugged into a phone line.

- The modem's turned off or it's not plugged into an active electrical socket (external modems).

- One or more programs have confused the settings.

After you check the first two items, double-click Modems in Control Panel. On the Diagnostics page, highlight the port your modem is connected to and click More Info. The resulting page, as shown in Figure 9-8, tells you if the system recognizes the modem and describes it in terms of speed, interrupt, memory address, and the modem's response to various internal commands.

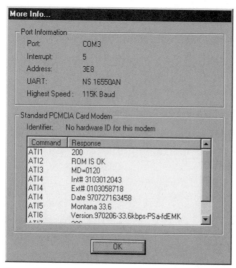

Figure 9-8 On More Info, you verify that the system finds the modem and that it is responding correctly.

If you receive a message that the system can't communicate with the modem, then the modem is either not plugged into a usable port, not turned on, or defective.

Note   *ATI2* is a check of the modem's *read-only memory* (*ROM*); if the response isn't "OK," the modem might be defective.

If your modem isn't recognized, go to the General tab of Modem properties and click Remove. After the modem is removed, reboot your system. Then reinstall the modem following the steps earlier in this chapter in the section called "Installing a Modem."

Configuring ISDN

Windows 98 provides built-in support for Integrated Services Digital Network (ISDN). Before configuring ISDN on a computer running Windows 98, you need the following:

- Installed internal or external ISDN adapter.

- ISDN telephone line service at the location where you will use Dial-Up networking to connect to the Internet.

- ISDN telephone line service at the remote location to which you want to connect, usually either your Internet service provider (ISP) or a remote access server.

You should use Point-to-Point Protocol (PPP) with ISDN for connections to the Internet. This protocol is the one typically used to access the Internet over dial-up connections. To use PPP, you must have a PPP account with your ISP. If you currently have a Serial Line Internet Protocol (SLIP) account, you should ask your ISP to change the account to PPP.

After you have installed your ISDN adapter and received notice from your telephone company that your ISDN service has been installed, you can configure Windows 98. To install your ISDN device, follow these steps:

1 In Control Panel, double-click Network.

2 Click Add, click Adapter, and then click Add.

3 Select the appropriate manufacturer and model and then click OK. If the ISDN adapter is Plug and Play–compatible, Windows 98 installs the required driver files automatically.

4 Follow the directions on the screen. The wizard requests the switch protocol, which the phone company provides. The wizard also needs telephone numbers and Service Profile Identifier (SPID) numbers, which come from your ISDN provider.

Making DSL (Digital Subscriber Line) and Cable Connections

If you live where you can get a digital subscriber line (DSL)—a city or suburb—it's a great solution if you want to use the Web but find dial-up connections grindingly slow. DSL is similar to ISDN in that both operate over existing telephone lines and both require that you not be too far from a central telephone office (for DSL, 15,000 to 18,000 feet).

In the United States, the most common form of DSL is asymmetric DSL (ADSL), which just means that the speed downloading (browsing Web pages and receiving mail at your end) is faster than uploading (sending mail). Typical downloading speed for residential ADSL is from 1 to 1.5 Mbps, and while that's not instantaneous, it's still pretty darn fast.

Caution   Both DSL and cable connections are always on, so there's no waiting around for a connection to be made. However, being permanently connected to the Internet makes your computer more vulnerable to outside attack, so you need some basic protection. See Chapter 11, "Playing It Safe," for information on firewalls.

If you have a cable television connection, you might be able to access the Internet in the same way. Cable companies that offer Internet service set aside a channel for the two-way exchange of data between computers at the main office and your computer at home. However, the local cable operator must first upgrade its network with digital and fiber-optic technology, which some cable companies haven't yet done. You don't necessarily have to subscribe to cable TV, but many of the cable companies offer a discount to existing customers, making the connection a bargain.

Cable connections are, on average, as fast as DSL connections. The downside to cable is that it's essentially a party line. If enough people sign up for the service, you could run into congestion.

Tip   Both *http://www.cable-modem.net* and *http://www.dslreports.com* have service search pages where you enter your zip code and find what's available in your area. They are excellent sources of information on both DSL and cable connections.

There are plenty of complicated ways to get DSL or cable service working—but here's the easiest approach. Once you've decided what service you want, let the supplying company provide the modem and whatever is needed to connect to your home. All you have to buy is a network interface card (NIC), a cable/DSL router, and enough Ethernet cable to connect your network card to the router and the router to the modem.

Display Hardware and Settings

The performance of the video system is critical to all versions of Windows. A slow video system makes your whole computer seem painfully slow—regardless of the processor or amount of RAM on your motherboard.

Tip   If your video card has one megabyte of memory or less, you should upgrade if you possibly can. However, you must also consider whether your monitor can handle the increase in resolution and colors. No matter how powerful the video card, it can't deliver more than the monitor can handle.

You might have to deal with three video-related chores at some point in your Windows career: changing a video card, changing a video driver, or, most commonly, optimizing the appearance of the video system that you already have. All three are addressed in the sections below.

Changing a Video Card

Installing a new video card is one of the easiest computer chores—providing you're willing to open the computer case. Here are the steps.

1 Open the box with the new video card, make sure everything is there, and read the instructions.

2 With the computer turned off, unplug the monitor cable from the computer and then open the case.

3 Remove the screw holding in the video card (the one the monitor was plugged into). Save the screw.

4 Use a gentle rocking motion to remove the video card from the slot.

5 Put the new video card in the same slot—again using the same gentle rocking motion. Make sure the card is firmly seated in the slot.

6 Replace the screw holding the card in place. Close the computer case, reattach the monitor cable, and restart the computer.

7 After the initial boot process, Windows 98 starts. The system detects the new hardware and installs it.

Changing a Video Driver

Often the manufacturer of a video card releases new drivers some time after the card was manufactured. This might be to take advantage of a feature in a new operating system or to fix a bug that wasn't apparent at the time the card was manufactured.

To install a new video driver, just follow these steps.

1 Double-click Display in Control Panel.

2 Click the Settings tab and then the Advanced button. This opens even more settings. Click the Adapter tab.

3 The Adapter page, as shown in Figure 9-9, shows the name of the video card and something about its features.

4 Click Change. The Update Device Driver Wizard launches and searches for updated drivers.

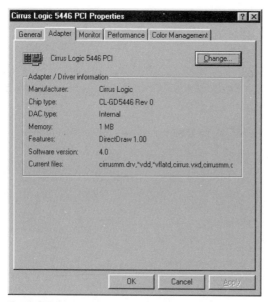

Figure 9-9 The Adapter page describes the characteristics of the video card.

You can be specific about where the new driver is located, as shown in Figure 9-10, or you can let the wizard search all the locations if you want.

Figure 9-10 The system should search various places for the new video driver.

Clear the Floppy Disk Drives option if you don't have the driver on floppy disk. Likewise, if you want the system to search the CD-ROM drive, make sure there's actually a CD in the drive. It won't do any harm if there's not, but you'll receive error messages that slow the process.

Optimizing Video Settings

The video settings you can make are limited only by the capacity of your video card and monitor. Some settings—such as especially high resolutions on small monitors—are unappealing, not least of all because they make icons practically invisible. Feel free to experiment; you can't do any harm (except as noted below).

To modify your video settings, open Display properties by double-clicking Display in Control Panel. You can also right-click a blank spot on the desktop and select Properties from the shortcut menu. Then click the Settings tab.

Changing Resolutions

Displays are described in terms of their resolution—the number of dots on the screen and the number of colors that can be displayed at the same time. The hardware you have determines the resolutions you can choose using the slider under Screen Area, as shown in Figure 9-11.

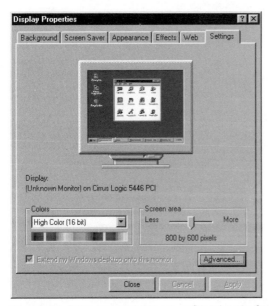

Figure 9-11 Colors and resolution are configured on the Settings tab.

You can't make your monitor and video card display more than is built into them. Notice that as you move the slider toward higher resolutions, the number of colors displayed in the Colors drop-down list box changes. As resolution numbers go up, color numbers have to go down because they're both competing for the same video memory. Resolution choices are based on what you like to look at—constrained by the capabilities of your monitor and video card.

Making Advanced Changes

Also on the Setting page is a button labeled Advanced. Click this button to access additional pages for video configuration. Different types of video cards have different effects on these pages. You might have other pages in addition to the ones described below. Consult the documentation for your video card and monitor for information on how to use these additional pages.

General   If you're using a particularly high resolution, the desktop elements can appear tiny. Try selecting Large Fonts from the Font Size drop-down list to see if that works better for you. (On the Display Properties Effects tab, you can also choose Use Large Icons.) This way you can preserve the higher resolution and have objects on the desktop that are legible.

The default setting in the Compatibility frame is to be prompted whenever you make new color settings. Whereas it's true that some programs require a reboot after colors and resolution have changed, most do not. If you don't have a problem program and you change color settings frequently, choose Apply The New Color Settings Without Restarting.

Likewise, if you change display settings often, put a check mark next to Show Settings Icon On Task Bar. This places a miniature Display icon in the system tray. Click the icon and you can change your display on the spot.

Monitor   If you replace your monitor, you usually only need to plug it in and start Windows 98 to have it detected and correctly installed. If the monitor isn't correctly detected, this is the spot where you provide the right information. Click Change and then supply the name of the manufacturer and the model. In some cases the Update Device Driver Wizard may run.

There's no reason to change settings if everything is functioning well. Sometimes Device Manager reports "Unknown Monitor" and yet the monitor appears to work perfectly well.

Several options relating to power management and Plug and Play are also on the Monitor tab. These are probably set correctly. However, if you have display problems such as a flashing screen after the monitor returns from Suspend mode, right-click each option, select What's This, and read the description. Try checking or unchecking these options to see if your problem has been solved. If you don't have a problem, leave the settings in their default state.

Performance   The Performance tab lets you adjust graphics hardware acceleration. Again, if your display is working fine, leave the Hardware Acceleration set to Full. If your mouse pointer disappears frequently, try moving the slider down one notch.

Color Management   Windows 98 includes many color profiles, and you can choose one or many. Click Add and select a profile. Add as many as you like. Highlight one and click Set As Default.

Changing a Mouse

Usually, you can change the pointing device on your computer by simply turning the computer off, unplugging the old mouse, plugging in the new mouse, and then rebooting your computer.

Sometimes you'll see a window informing you that Windows 98 has found new hardware and is installing it, but more often than not, the new mouse simply works. However, if your mouse needs a new (or different) driver, you can install it manually by following these steps (described in terms of keyboard commands because you can't use your mouse if the mouse isn't functional).

1   Use the Tab key to move the highlight to the My Computer icon. Press Alt+Enter to open the System Properties dialog box.

2   Press the Tab key to move the focus to the Device Manager page.

3   Press the Tab key twice to move the focus to the list of devices and then use the down arrow to move focus to the Mouse.

4   Press the right arrow to display the devices under Mouse. Then press the down arrow to highlight the device.

5   Press the Tab key once to move the focus to Properties and then press Enter. This opens the mouse properties dialog box.

6   Use the Tab and arrow keys to move focus to the Driver page. On the Driver page, keep tabbing until Update Driver is selected and then press Enter. The Update Device Driver Wizard starts.

From here on you can let the wizard do the work. Use the default settings except when you get to the dialog box where you specify the location for the new driver. You can check more than one box if you want to search in multiple locations.

Working with Game Controllers

Driving games and flight simulators just aren't the same without a steering wheel or flight stick (although so-called "first-person shooters" are still ruled by the mouse and keyboard). Similarly, fighting and sports games are usually best played with a gamepad. Though we won't help you in selecting a game controller except to say that USB controllers are the easiest to configure, the following steps will help you get going with your controller. (Try Epinions for reviews: *http://www.epinions.com.*)

1 Make sure that your soundcard is working properly, especially if your game controller uses the joystick port (which is usually on the sound card).

2 Download the latest drivers for your controller and install them using the directions provided by the manufacturer. If you can't locate new drivers, go ahead and use the ones that came with the device. You might have to restart Windows after installing the drivers.

3 In Control Panel, double-click the Game Controllers.

4 Verify that your game controller is listed and that the status is OK.

5 If your device isn't listed, click Add, select your device from the list, and then click OK.

> **Tip** If you have trouble getting a game controller to work, try removing it, then double-check or update your sound card drivers. Restart Windows, and open Control Panel. Use Game Controller to add the controller again.

6 Select your controller and click Properties. Calibrate or test your controller using the device manufacturer's software and then click OK.

7 If you have multiple game controllers, switch between them using one of the following methods. (Most games can only recognize a single controller at a time.)

- Select the game controller you don't want to use at the moment and click Remove. Then click Add, select the controller you do want to use, and then click OK. If all controllers use the joystick port, this is the only solution (other than buying a joystick port splitter).

- If more than one controller is hooked up at a time and your game insists on using the wrong one, click the Controller IDs tab, as shown in Figure 9-12, and then click Change. Select the controller you don't want to use (ID 1) and increase its ID to 3 or higher. Then select the controller you *do* want to use, change its ID to 1, and then click OK.

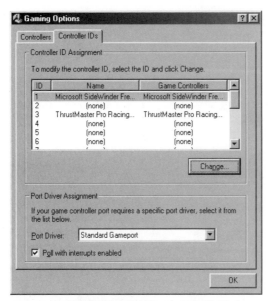

Figure 9-12 Use the Controller IDs tab to shuffle IDs between your controllers. (Most games can only use the controller with ID 1.)

Hardware Profiles

Hardware Profiles are used to set up multiple hardware configurations. This is especially useful for laptops with docking stations or workstations with removable storage media. Hardware Profiles are automatically created for laptops when the system is docked or undocked.

Creating a Hardware Profile

To create a hardware profile, follow these steps.

1   Right-click My Computer and select Properties. Click the Hardware Profiles tab.

2   Click the name of the hardware profile on which you want to base the new hardware profile, and then click Copy.

3   Enter a name for the new hardware profile in the To text box and click Ok.

4   Click the Device Manager tab to change which hardware is enabled or disabled in this profile. Click the plus sign next to the hardware type and then double-click the hardware.

5   In the Device Usage frame, click to clear or add the check mark in the Disable In This Hardware Profile check box. You might be prompted to reboot your computer. If so, reboot.

Deleting a Hardware Profile

If you find you no longer need a profile, you can delete it easily.

1 Right-click My Computer, select Properties, and then click the Hardware Profiles tab.

2 Click the name of the hardware profile you want to delete, and click Delete.

3 Again, if you're prompted to reboot the computer, do so.

Key Points

■ When considering adding hardware to you computer, consult the Hardware Compatibility List (HCL) first.

■ Drivers are pieces of software that allow Windows 98 to communicate with a particular piece of hardware.

■ Drivers and updates for hardware usually can be downloaded from the manufacturer's Web site.

■ If your computer lacks a USB port, adding one is both easy and inexpensive, and it eases hardware installation in many cases.

■ Now becoming widely available, DSL and cable Internet connections are much faster than dial-up connections, and can greatly enhance the online experience.

Chapter 10

Making Use of Control Panel Tools

In every version of Microsoft Windows, Control Panel has been mission central. As you've no doubt already learned, Windows offers two or three ways to do just about everything. However, when you can't remember *any* of them, just go to Control Panel. All the settings for Windows are grouped there by subject, which is sometimes the best way to search.

Training a Mouse

If you've never examined the settings available for your mouse, you're going to be pleasantly surprised at the ways you can make the mouse easier and more comfortable to use. Double-click Mouse in Control Panel to see the Mouse Properties dialog box, as shown in Figure 10-1.

Tip   Dead mouse? It happens. If your mouse doesn't work, check that the cable is inserted tightly into the back of the computer. These cables have a way of slowly loosening over time. You might have to restart your computer once you reseat the cable. Sick mouse? Dirt easily gets into the mechanism, and the surface on which the mouse rolls contributes grease and other miscellaneous detritus to the inside workings of the mouse. Open up the mouse and clean the mouse ball and contact points with alcohol on a cotton swab.

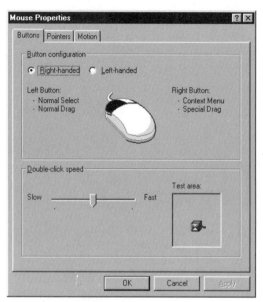

Figure 10-1   Changes to mouse behavior are made in the Mouse Properties dialog box.

Buttons Tab

The Buttons and Motion tabs of the Mouse Properties dialog box are where you can make basic adjustments to the way the mouse behaves.

Button Configuration

Left-handed folks already know that the advantages of being a southpaw in tennis and baseball do not translate to the computer mouse. If you're left-handed and you keep your mouse on the left side of the keyboard, select Left-Handed to switch the functions of the right and left mouse buttons, so your index finger naturally rests on the primary button (the one that selects and drags). However, many mice are shaped incorrectly for a leftie, so either buy one that is hand-neutral or do what you've had to do all your life—adjust.

Double-Click Speed

Double-clicking was probably a pretty tricky maneuver to learn when you first started using a mouse. If you double-click too slowly, the icon you're trying to open remains stubbornly closed.

The difference in elapsed time between a double-click and two single clicks is well under a second. A setting that's off by just a fraction of a second can waste your time and be quite frustrating, so adjust the slider to reflect your double-click speed. If you need more time between clicks, move the slider to the left. Move the slider to the right to allow less time between clicks. Each time you adjust the slider, test your double-click interval by double-clicking the jack-in-the-box in the Test area.

Tip   The object is to set the slider so it matches your own natural double-clicking speed. Don't try to adjust your normal timing; make Windows 98 adjust to you.

Motion Tab

If you find you have to move your mouse quite a distance to get a small result on the screen or you move the mouse just a little and the pointer jumps halfway across the screen, adjust the speed on the Motion tab.

Under Pointer Speed, move the slider one notch toward Fast or Slow. Click Apply to see the effect. Be sure to click Apply after every change.

On smaller screens, particularly those on laptops, the pointer can be hard to see. To make the pointer more visible, select the option to Show Pointer Trails. Then use the slider to adjust the length of the pointer trail, as shown in Figure 10-2. You can see the results immediately after moving the slider without having to use Apply.

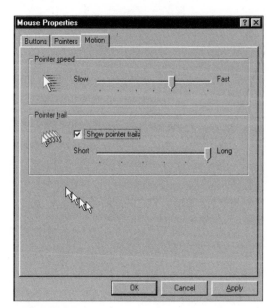

Figure 10-2 Mouse trails can help you locate the pointer on a small or poorly lit screen.

Pointers Tab

Playing with mouse pointers is still another way to fritter away hours of precious time. Click the Pointers tab to view the available choices. If the selection in the Scheme drop-down list box is meager, it means not all the pointers have been installed. If that's the case, find your Windows 98 CD, put it in the CD drive, and follow these steps.

1   Open Control Panel and double-click Add/Remove Programs.

2   Click the Windows Setup tab. The next dialog box shows what parts of Windows 98 are installed, as shown in Figure 10-3. This might take a few seconds.

Figure 10-3 The Windows Setup tab displays installed Windows components. Dimmed check boxes indicate not all components in the category are installed.

3   Select Accessories and click Details.

4   Scroll down and select the check box for Mouse Pointers.

5   Click OK twice and the pointers are installed.

Return to the Mouse tool in Control Panel and you'll see that the pointer options have been somewhat enriched. However, the true key to idling away the hours is to make a Scheme of your own devising. Here's how you do it.

1   In the Pointers tab of the Mouse Properties dialog box highlight a pointer type and click Browse.

2   Select the pointer you want and click Open.

3   Repeat for other pointer types.

Not different enough? The pointers used with Desktop Themes should fill the bill. To use cursors from the themes, follow these steps.

1   Double-click Mouse in Control Panel. Click the Pointers tab.

2   Highlight the pointer you want to change. Click Browse.

3   Navigate to the Program Files folder on your disk drive. Double-click
the Plus! folder and then the Themes folder.

4   Browse your way through the pointers. Select one and it appears in the
Preview pane, as shown in Figure 10-4.

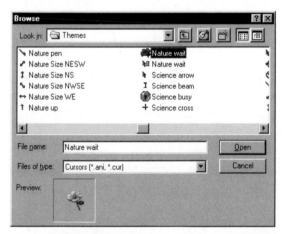

Figure 10-4 When you select a pointer file the pointer appears in the Preview pane.

5   When you find the pointer you want to use, click Open.

6   Once you have all the pointers showing on the Pointers tab, click Save
As and save your selections in a scheme of your choice.

> **Tip**   Bear in mind that pointers are more than just decoration. The pointers for Pre-
> cision Select and Text Select in particular can make your work difficult if they are too
> far from the defaults. Selecting an exact spot on a screen is really tough if you're
> using an animated cursor. On the other hand, pointers indicating Wait or Busy can be
> as whimsical as you want.

> **See Also**   If desktop themes are installed, a Desktop Themes icon is in Control
> Panel. If you don't have the icon, go to the section entitled "Changing the Desktop
> Display" in Chapter 2, "Covering the Desktop," for instructions on installing themes.

Using Keyboard Options

You can gain more control over your keyboard's behavior by adjusting its Keyboard properties. Double-click Keyboard in Control Panel to open the Keyboard
Properties dialog box, which has two tabs, Speed and Language.

Speed Tab

The Speed tab appears to offer three independent options, but the first two are
closely related. The Repeat Delay is the amount of time you can hold down a

key before it begins to repeat. Move the slider to the left to lengthen the time that passes before the repeat function kicks in. The difference between the Long and Short setting is only about a second.

The Repeat Rate determines how fast a key repeats once it starts. Fast means that a key held down long enough to start repeating zips across the screen at a headlong rate. Use the test area after making a change.

Keyboard Shortcuts

For obvious reasons, touch typists like to keep their fingers on the keyboard. Every time you reach for the mouse, it's an interruption. Fortunately, certain key combinations can replicate just about anything a mouse can do. Memorize the ones you need to use frequently.

If, like me, you're not a touch typist, you'll need this information when you return to the computer one day and find your mouse has suddenly succumbed. Keyboard shortcuts, shown in Table 10-1, allow you to reinstall a mouse driver or shut down properly so you can plug in a new one.

Table 10-1   Keyboard Shortcuts

Key	Action
F1	Opens Help.
F2	Edits the name of selected file or folder.
F3	Opens Find.
F4	Opens the selected drop-down list. Press again to close.
F5	Refreshes the active window.
Tab or F6	Changes the focus within a dialog box or window. F6 is somewhat picky about what dialog boxes it chooses to work in.
F10 or Alt	Moves the focus to the menu bar. Use the left and right arrow keys to move the focus between menus. Use the down arrow to open the menu.
Backspace	Moves up one level in the folder hierarchy.
Right arrow	Expands the highlighted folder. If the folder is already expanded, go to the sub-folder.
Left arrow	Collapses the selected folder. If it's already collapsed, move up one level in the folder hierarchy.
Alt+Tab	Moves between open applications. Hold down Alt, and each press of Tab changes the focus to the next application.
Alt+Shift+Tab	Moves the focus through the open items in the opposite direction from Alt+Tab.
Ctrl+Esc	Opens the Start menu.
Alt+F4	Closes the current application. If no application is open, activates the Shut Down window.

Table 10-1 Keyboard Shortcuts *(continued)*

Key	Action
Alt+Spacebar	Opens the Control Menu (same as clicking the icon at the extreme upper-left corner of the application or folder window).
PrintScreen	Copies the current screen to the Clipboard; from there it can be pasted into Paint or another graphics application.
Alt+PrintScreen	Copies the active window to the Clipboard.

Note Some shortcuts won't work if Sticky Keys is turned on under Accessibility Options. See the next section, "Improving Accessibility."

Improving Accessibility

Computers are a ubiquitous part of everyday life. Anything that makes the computer harder to use makes out lives harder. For a long time, Microsoft has included a whole package of tools with its operating systems that make the computer—as it stands and without additional hardware—more usable for those of us with less than perfect sight, hearing, or dexterity.

Double-click Accessibility Options in Control Panel to open the properties dialog box, as shown in Figure 10-5.

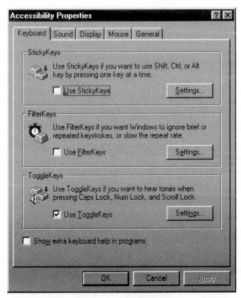

Figure 10-5 Accessibility Options include a wide range of aids for sight, hearing, and mobility.

Visibility Enhancements

To make the content of the screen easier to see, you might configure elements to be larger or to use a color scheme with more contrast. To do so, follow these steps.

1   Click the Display tab and select Use High Contrast.

2   Then click the Settings button. Under High Contrast Color Scheme, choose an option and click OK.

3   On the Display tab, click Apply. Continue trying color schemes until you find one you like.

To turn the High Contrast setting on and off from the keyboard, select the Keyboard Shortcut check box on the settings page, as shown in Figure 10-6.

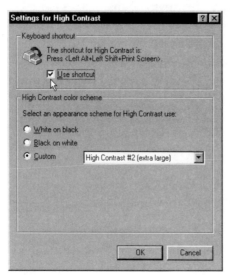

Figure 10-6 Check the Use Shortcut checkbox to be able to toggle between high-contrast settings and the regular display.

Sound Help

Many of the warnings emitted by the computer come as sounds. If you're not likely to notice beeps and bells, click the Sound tab in the Accessibility Properties dialog box. SoundSentry changes the auditory signals in Windows to visual ones. Click Settings to select exactly how you want the visual cues to display.

ShowSounds tells any programs that are capable of it to display text messages when a sound is made.

Hand Aid

By default, the keyboard and mouse are set to the requirements of some mythical average user. Because none of us is average, the ability to change these settings is also built in. The "Training a Mouse" and "Using Keyboard Options" sections earlier in this chapter address some adjustments that you can make. If those settings don't go far enough or don't cover what you need, the Accessibility Options probably will. On the Keyboard tab of Accessibility Options, consider these choices.

StickyKeys

If it becomes problematic when you're called on to press multiple keys to execute a command—Ctrl+Alt+Del is an example—turn on StickyKeys. With StickyKeys enabled, you can press Control, Alt, or Shift and the key remains active until you press a key other than Ctrl, Alt, or Shift. Click Settings to enable a keyboard shortcut for turning StickyKeys on and off and to set other options.

FilterKeys

If your fingers don't move as swiftly as that so-called average user mentioned earlier, FilterKeys can help. When you enable FilterKeys, Windows ignores the inadvertent keyboard touch and the accidental repeat. In other words, it makes your keyboard a little less sensitive. Click Settings to set the options.

ToggleKeys

ToggleKeys is a useful feature for anyone who doesn't touch type. All we hunt-and-peck folks have had the experience of looking up at the screen and discovering that we've been typing for some time with the Caps Lock key on and our text looks like this: oN tUESDAY, mR. jOHNSON FLEW TO THE u.s. vIRGIN iSLANDS.

Enable ToggleKeys and the computer sounds a warning beep when Caps Lock, Num Lock, or Scroll Lock is pressed. Click Settings to enable a keyboard shortcut for ToggleKeys.

MouseKeys

To dump the mouse entirely, click the Mouse tab in Accessibility Properties. Enable the option to use MouseKeys and all the maneuvering of the pointer can be done using the numeric keypad on your keyboard. Click Settings to configure how MouseKeys work.

Note   If you have a mouse on the computer, it won't be disabled when MouseKeys is turned on. You can still use the mouse when you want to.

General Accessibility Options

Click the General tab to make some overall settings to Accessibility Options. The essential one is under Automatic Reset. The default setting is for accessibility options to be turned off after five minutes of inactivity. If you want the options you've set to be on all the time, clear the check box.

Also on the General tab are options for notifications and an option to enable an input device other than a keyboard and mouse.

Multimedia Means Audio and Video

Years ago, when the first Macintosh user figured out how to produce rude sounds from a computer, PC users were positively pea-green with envy—but not for long. Soon the PC could produce an equally appalling array of noises. Now the technology has gone much further, and your PC can also play music and videos, which can be as pleasant as you want them to be.

Using Sound

To make basic sound settings, double-click Sounds in Control Panel. The Sounds Properties dialog box Events window, as shown in Figure 10-7, lists everything on your system that can be associated with a sound. Most are Windows events. For example, opening a program produces a sound, as can maximizing or minimizing a window. As you add programs to your system, some of them add sound files that are associated with the events.

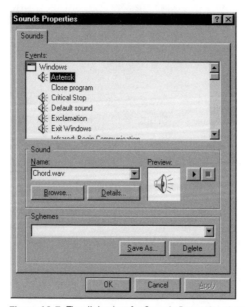

Figure 10-7 The dialog box for Sounds Properties shows what sounds are associated with what events.

If there's a Speaker icon next to the event, a sound is associated with it. Highlight the event—the name of the sound file appears in the Name drop-down list box—and click the button next to the Preview window to hear it. (If your speakers have an On/Off switch, make sure they're turned on.)

Several sound schemes are included with Windows 98, and you can choose one of them from the Schemes drop-down list box.

If sound schemes don't appear in the Schemes drop-down list box, you can install them. Go to the Add/Remove Programs icon in Control Panel. Under the Windows Setup click Multimedia and then click Details. Select Multimedia Sound Schemes—Sample Sounds, too, if you like. Make sure your Windows 98 CD is in the CD drive and click OK twice.

Customizing a Sound Scheme

All the sound schemes that come with Windows are nice enough but none is perfect. There are either too many sounds, not enough, the wrong sounds attached to various events, or whatever. To make as many customized sound schemes as you like, follow these steps.

1   Double-click Sounds in Control Panel.

2   Starting at the top of the Events list, select an event to attach a sound to.

3   Select a file from the Name drop-down list box. To make sure it's the one you want, click Preview to hear it.

4   Select (None) in the Name drop-down list box for events that you want to keep silent.

5   Repeat steps 3–5 until you've completed the list.

6   Select Save As to save this particular assortment of sounds under a suitable name. (The new scheme appears in the Schemes drop-down list box.)

Acquiring New Sound Files

Thousands of sound files are available on the Web. A search for *sound files* turns up many, many entries. Bear in mind that WAV files tend to be large. Also, your search might turn up many sounds that are rude and crude and just as many that are amusing.

Making Your Own Sound Files

With an audio input device on your computer (a microphone or a CD player, for example), you can use the Sound Recorder to make a WAV file that can then be associated with a Windows event.

Here's how to make a WAV file with the sound recorder.

1   Click Start, select Programs, Accessories, Entertainment, and then Sound Recorder.

2   Select New from the Sound Recorder's File menu.

3   To begin recording, click the Record button with the dark red dot (lower right-hand corner).

4   Start the CD or start speaking into the microphone.

5   Click the Stop button with the black square to stop recording.

6   Choose Save from the File menu to save the sound clip.

Figure 10-8 shows the Sound Recorder recording from a CD.

Figure 10-8 Record sound clips using input from a CD or a microphone.

Windows 98 stores sound files in the Windows\Media folder. You'll probably want to move any additional sound files you acquire to that folder because a single location makes it easy to set up and change sound schemes.

Special Effects and Editing

Use the Effects menu in Sound Recorder to change some sound qualities—for example, to add an echo or decrease the speed. The sound can also be edited using the menu controls.

Tip   You can only edit an *uncompressed* sound file. If you don't see the green line in Sound Recorder, the file is compressed and you can't edit it unless you change the sound quality. You can change the sound quality when you save the file by clicking Change at the bottom of the Save As dialog box.

Using Media Player

Microsoft Windows Media Player has evolved from a relatively trivial Windows program into a genuinely useful tool. This is all the result of the growth of streaming audio and video over the Internet—plus the explosion in the use of MP3 technology for music distribution.

Tip   When you upgrade your Microsoft Internet Explorer to version 6.4, Media Player also upgrades to version 6. Nevertheless, you can (and should) go a step further and upgrade to Media Player 7.1. Select Windows Update from the Start menu and download the necessary file.

To start Media Player manually, click Start, Programs, then Accessories, followed by Entertainment, and then at last Windows Media Player. Even when first launched, as shown in Figure 10-9, it's pretty impressive.

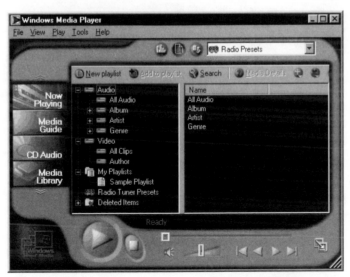

Figure 10-9 Big improvements have been made in Windows Media Player—version 6 is to version 7 as a canoe is to the Starship Enterprise.

Until version 7 of Media Player, Real Network's Real Jukebox was *the* application for organizing CD tracks into personalized play lists. Now it's more like a draw—and for just about everything else, Media Player prevails. It's especially good at compressing and decompressing streaming audio over the Internet. Generally, you don't have to go looking for Media Player when it's needed. Click on a music or video link on the Internet (or locally) and Media Player opens and plays the video or music without prompting from you.

Finding audio and video on the Internet is not a problem. Click Media Guide and follow links displayed there. You'll quickly find more video and music than you can imagine.

Media Player 7 can play the file types listed in Table 10-2.

Table 10-2   Media Player 7 File Types

Source	File Name Extensions
Microsoft media formats	AVI, ASK, ASX, WAV, WMA, WM, WMV, WAX, WVX
UNIX formats	AU, SND
MPEG	MPG, MPEG, M1V, MP2, MP2V, MP3, MPA, MPE, M3U
MIDI	MID, MIDI, MI
Apple QuickTime, Macintosh	QT, AIF, AIFC, AIFF, MOV
RealAudio, RealVideo	RAM, RA, RM, RMM
Other formats	AVI, WAV, IVF, CDA

Caution   The crucial file format that Media Player *doesn't* recognize is RMJ, which is the default Real Jukebox format. So, if you've collected a music list in RMJ format you cannot easily import the files for use in Media Player.

As a rule, Media Player is smart enough to adjust itself to circumstances. If data delivery slows, Media Player looks to the server for a data format that can keep the show from being interrupted, even if the quality is somewhat lessened.

The last few years have seen an exponential increase in the quality of audio and video playback. Unfortunately, that's accompanied by just as big an increase in the quantity of streaming audio and video being used on the Internet. As a result, you can run into some really annoying glitches, skips, and unexplained halts when trying to view and/or listen to streaming content.

Increasing the buffer range can be helpful in resolving issues when Windows Media Player stops responding. If network slowdowns are common, sometimes increasing the buffer size can keep things flowing. Click the Tools menu then select Options and then the Performance tab. In Media Player version 6, choose Options from the View menu, click the Advanced tab, and click Change. The larger the buffer, the longer it takes for your file to begin playing, but a larger buffer can definitely help to eliminate stops or stutters.

Try This! If you're using a proxy server, adjusting the settings can sometimes resolve problems with streaming media. Proxy settings in Media Player are configured to use browser proxy settings by default. When the No Proxy option is enabled, Media Player doesn't use the Internet Explorer proxy settings for playback. To change the default settings, follow these steps.

1. Choose Options from the Tools menu and then click the Network tab.

2. In Proxy Settings, highlight HTTP Browser and click Configure.

3. In the Configure Protocol dialog box, select Do Not Use A Proxy Server.

4. Click OK twice. Close Media Player and restart. In version 6 these settings are in the same dialog box as the Buffer setting.

By default, the Windows Media Player starts playing as soon as you put a music CD in the drive. To overrule this automatic play feature for a particular CD, hold down the Shift key while you insert the CD. To turn the automatic play feature off completely (or back on), right-click the My Computer icon and select Properties. On the Device Manager tab, double-click CD-ROM, select your CD-ROM drive's name, and click Properties. On the Settings tab, click Auto Insert Notification. When this option is selected, music CDs play automatically.

A Word About Licensing We're writers, so it's in our own best interest to support copyright laws—and we do. However, some of the protection schemes for recorded music can tie even a law-abiding consumer in knots. When you buy a CD and copy all (or some) of the songs to your hard disk, Windows Media Player 7 turns on a feature called Content Protection when you make the copies. This means you can't do illegal things with your music—but it also prevents you from copying those files to a new computer.

This summer I copied many, many CD tracks to my disk drive. Sometimes I like to listen to music using headphones, sometimes using speakers, and it's not always convenient to switch between the two. So I had the brilliant idea that I could plug headphones into another computer in my office and listen to the music over the network. Nothing doing. Because the files were recorded with Content Protection turned on, they could be accessed only on the computer where they were recorded.

If, like me, you are not engaged in music piracy, you can turn off Content Protection when copying CDs by following these steps.

1   Select Options from the Tool Menu.

2   Click the Copy Music tab.

3   Clear the Protect Content check box. (This option isn't present in version 6 so you don't have to worry about it.)

After you do steps 1–3, select Options from the Tool menu and click the CD Audio tab. Clear the box for Enable Personal Rights Management.

And don't think you can avoid this hassle by using Real Jukebox. They have exactly the same feature except it's phrased as a "security feature which protects your recordings from unauthorized use." Alas, it protects your recordings from you, too.

Key Points

- Control Panel is a central location where all settings are grouped by category.

- Don't try to change your movements to match the default settings. Make adjustments to the mouse and keyboard performance that fit your way of working.

- Accessibility Options add additional ways to make the computer fit *you* and not the reverse.

- Upgrade your version of Media Player to 7.1 to take advantage of streaming audio and video on the Internet.

Chapter 11

Playing It Safe

People have called the Internet the world's biggest small town because of how easy it is to communicate and form virtual communities. Unfortunately, another aspect of small towns also applies—the lack of privacy. Combine this with the distinctly urban security problem of hackers constantly searching for systems to break into, and you've got a couple of good reasons to feel uneasy.

Fortunately, you can take steps to protect your safety and privacy. You can also cover your Web surfing tracks from other users of your computer, as well as restrict your kids' access to the Web. This chapter covers these measures and others and is essential for all users—from novices to Web-surfing pros.

Stopping Hackers and Viruses

Hackers and viruses are the two biggest external dangers for computer users. Hackers might break into your computer from across the Internet or physically steal your computer. They might do this to obtain information from you, such as business secrets or financial information, or simply to wreak havoc. Viruses are more common and indiscriminate—they usually just delete things and spread themselves to people listed in your e-mail address book.

Either way, hackers and viruses are hazards to avoid at all costs. To protect yourself, use the following precautions.

■ **Install antivirus software and keep it updated**   No computer that has any connection with the outside world should be without up-to-date antivirus software. Newer programs update themselves automatically if you have a permanent Internet connection, but even older versions work fine with the latest *virus definition files*. Two popular antivirus programs are Norton Antivirus (*http://www.syman-tec.com*) and McAfee VirusScan (*http://www.mcafee.com*).

Lingo   A *virus definition file* is what antivirus programs use to recognize viruses. Because new viruses are written every day, it's important to keep your virus definition file up-to-date.

Tip   If a virus damages Microsoft Windows, you can call Microsoft's toll-free virus support number: 1-866-PCSAFETY.

- **Keep your software up-to-date**   Microsoft and other companies frequently release software patches to fix newly discovered security holes. For more information, see Chapter 12, "Maintaining a Healthy Computer."

- **Block dangerous e-mail attachment types**   To prevent Microsoft Outlook Express from opening attachment types that are potentially dangerous (such as programs and scripts), choose Options from the Tools menu, click the Security tab, and then select the Do Not Allow Attachments To Be Saved Or Opened That Could Potentially Be A Virus check box.

- **Use a firewall**   Using a persistent Internet connection such as cable or Digital Subscriber Line (DSL) without a firewall is like leaving your front door unlocked. If you have nothing of value and you don't mind being vandalized, then don't worry about it. Otherwise, purchase some sort of firewall device such as a cable/DSL router or a personal firewall such as ZoneAlarm. (Because dial-up modems are disconnected so much of the time, they are less vulnerable to hackers.)

- **Disable file and print sharing on exposed network connections**   If your Internet connection comes straight into your computer through a network card or DSL adapter without first going through a firewall, Internet sharing device, or computer, disable File And Print Sharing on the network card connected to the Internet. Leaving it enabled is like leaving your front door wide open.

See Also   For more information on firewalls, sharing an Internet connection, and File And Print Sharing, see Chapter 13, "Building and Using a Network."

- **Control how Microsoft Internet Explorer downloads scripts**   To view Microsoft Internet Explorer security settings, choose Internet

Options from the Tools menu and then click the Security tab. Internet Explorer security updates often tweak these settings (they'll say Custom), but if you're unsure you can reset them to Medium or High security by clicking Default Level then adjusting the displayed slider.

■ **Maintain physical security**   An industrial strength firewall won't do a bit of good if a hacker can simply walk up to your computer and access it (or take it). To keep your physical security tight, observe the following practices.

● Don't leave your computers unattended in vulnerable places.

● Use laptop locks with your laptop when in public.

● Use a screensaver password and possibly a Basic Input/Output System (BIOS) password when leaving your computer unattended around people you don't trust. To set a BIOS password, refer to your computer or motherboard documentation.

● Keep your network cables and devices in safe places—if someone can connect a computer to your personal network, it's much easier to hack your network.

● Be extra careful with wireless networks—they require special attention to security (as discussed in Chapter 13, "Building and Using a Network").

Tip   If you can't ensure a safe physical environment for your computer, use Windows 2000 or Windows XP—their security features are much more robust than those of Windows 98.

■ **Make frequent backups**   Performing regular backups reduces the impact of viruses and hackers—if your computer gets wiped clean, at least you can restore from a backup.

Note   If your life exposes you to venomous acquaintances, you owe it to yourself to take every reasonable security precaution. You should also consider upgrading to Windows XP, setting a logon password, and using NT file system (NTFS) and potentially the Encrypting File System (EFS).

Maintaining Your Privacy

Maybe you don't think much about privacy, figuring that you don't have anything to hide, or maybe you want absolute privacy—for example, you prefer an unlisted phone number and always pay with cash. Either way, the following sections are essential reading for anyone who uses the Internet. They cover such topics as choosing good passwords, how to be careful with your personal information, and how to prevent cookies and forms from revealing more than you want.

Use Good Passwords

The best locks and security systems aren't much good if you leave a key under your doormat and the security code on a sticky note next to the alarm keypad. Similarly, if a hacker obtains your password, no amount of security precautions can deter him or her.

Unfortunately, just about everything requires a password these days—from your e-mail account to the gardening Web site to which you belong. Combine this with modern computers that make cracking typical passwords as easy as cutting through butter with a hot knife, and you've got a messy situation.

Although this dilemma has no easy solution, you can take some steps to maximize the security of your passwords and minimize the headaches you endure trying to remember them all.

- **Reuse a small number of simple passwords for less sensitive sites**   It's easier to remember your complex, important passwords if you use a small number of relatively simple passwords for less sensitive Web sites and accounts. (Web sites that don't store information such as your credit card number or bank account info.) Try to stick with a limited number of usernames as well—knowing a password doesn't do any good if you can't remember the username.

- **Don't reuse passwords for important things**   Using different passwords prevents somebody taking one password that they obtained or cracked and using it to access all of your sensitive information and accounts. Use unique passwords for important e-mail accounts, online investing and banking sites.

- **Check for a secure connection before entering an important password**   Secure connections encrypt communication, making it difficult for hackers to intercept your password. To spot a secure connection, look for the following characteristics.

  - The Web address begins with https:// (the *s* stands for secure).

  - A lock (or key) icon appears on the status bar.

- **Don't reuse portions of old passwords**   A determined hacker with a portion of an old password uses it as a seed for cracking your existing password, making it much easier to crack.

- **Use passwords that are seven characters or longer**   The longer the password, the more time it takes for a password-cracking tool to crack it. If a site or program doesn't lock out the account after a string of failed attempts (as do most financial Web sites), use a longer password—twelve characters or longer.

- **Don't use any part of your logon name**   Many hackers use bits of your logon name as seeds for cracking your password, speeding up the process.

- **Choose passwords that contain special characters**   Including uppercase and lowercase letters, numbers, and punctuation in your passwords exponentially increases the amount of computer time hackers need to crack your passwords. (These are referred to as complex passwords.)

- **Don't use dictionary words for passwords**   Many password-cracking tools use dictionaries to speed up cracking—even long passwords that contain dictionary words can be quickly cracked. (This applies to all languages.)

- **Use acronyms for phrases that are meaningful only to you**   The best passwords use special characters to create an acronym for some phrase. The phrase should be meaningful and easy to remember for you but difficult for anyone else to understand or remember. For example, "Me, Joe, and Irene flew to Nashville in 02" could be written as M,J,&If2Ni02!—an extremely difficult password to crack.

- **Change your passwords regularly**   Change your password often, or whenever you see suspicious activity in your accounts.

- **Don't allow AutoComplete to remember important passwords**   AutoComplete (discussed later in this chapter) makes it easy for anyone with access to your Windows user account to access password protected Web sites for which AutoComplete saved your password. Don't let AutoComplete save your password for any important Web site.

- **Never write passwords down**   A great password is useless if you write it on a sticky note attached to your monitor, under your keyboard, or in a desk drawer.

A Secure Way to Write Down Passwords Writing your passwords on a piece of paper is extremely insecure. Anyone who happens upon the paper instantly learns all of your most closely guarded secrets.

If you have a lot of passwords that you're afraid of forgetting, instead of writing them on a piece of paper (which is compromised as soon as it's found), create a password-protected file in your word processor. In Microsoft Word, use the following procedure.

1 Create a document in Microsoft Word and enter all of your username and passwords in it.

2 Choose Save As from the file menu, click Tools, and then choose General Options or Security Options, depending on whether you're using Word 2000 or Word 2002.

3 Type a 13 to 15 character password that meets the recommendations we make above in the Password To Open text box. It's vital that this password be *exceptionally* secure (because a hacker who found this file would have unlimited time to crack it) and something that you can remember without writing it down.

4 Insert a floppy disk and save the file with a misleading name such as Loveletters.doc or Novelideas.doc.

Label the floppy with a misleading label such as "Life Goals" and hide it somewhere away from your computer. Better yet, store it in a safe or safe deposit box if you have one.

Tip If you don't have a word processor that can password protect files, use an encryption program such as Pretty Good Privacy (PGP).

Be Careful When Giving Out Personal Info

If you want to avoid spam and junk mail, guard your personal information carefully. To do so, use the following recommendations.

- **Read privacy policies** Before you provide any personally identifiable information to a Web site, make sure to read its *privacy policy.* (There's usually a link to it at the bottom of a form.) Look for TRUSTe (*http://www.truste.org*) or BBBonline (*http://www.bbbonline.org*) seals, which indicate good privacy policies. Internet Explorer 6 has some automatic mechanisms for handling privacy policies for sites that use cookies, as discussed in the next section.

Lingo   *Privacy policies* state what a company does with the information you provide them. Some companies state that they only use the information you provide to
fulfill your order. Others state that they take your personally identifiable information
and sell it to advertisers, who then spam you (though they don't usually word it that
way). It's also worth noting that many companies sell previously private information to
the highest bidder when they go bankrupt.

- **Only fill out the required fields, or give fake info**   When register-
  ing for a Web site or filling out a Web form, only supply the required
  information. If you're not taking delivery of a product, use a fake name
  and address, and use an e-mail account in which you don't mind
  receiving spam.

- **Be careful with online profiles**   If you want to be listed in e-mail
  directories such as Bigfoot (*http://www.bigfoot.com*), choose the
  option to screen your e-mail address so that people who want to reach
  you must do so through the e-mail directory. (This prevents advertisers
  from obtaining your e-mail address.) If you are a member of an online
  community, see if they have a similar capability. If not, be aware that
  whatever e-mail address you list will probably receive a lot of spam, so
  use your junk mail account, as discussed in Chapter 7, "Using E-mail
  and Newsgroups."

Tip   To be removed from online directories, look yourself up at each directory and
click a Change/Remove Listing link (or a similar link). Three directories to check are
http://www.bigfoot.com, *http://people.yahoo.com*, and *http://www.anywho.com*.

- **Spam-proof your e-mail account when posting to**
  newsgroups   Newsgroups are one of the primary locations advertisers find victims to spam—see Chapter 7 for more information.

- **Be cautious in chat rooms and on IM**   Although sometimes spam-
  mers troll chat rooms, worse things can happen here. Stalkers make
  spam look pretty good—so be careful to whom you give any personal
  information.

Lingo   *IM* is short for *Instant Messaging*—personal chat programs such as
Windows Messenger, America Online (AOL) Instant Messenger, and ICQ.

■ **Only send credit card info over secure connections**   Only enter credit card information into secure Web forms (discussed in the "Safe Shopping" section of this chapter). If you need to send credit card information through e-mail, encrypt the e-mail as discussed in the "E-mail Security" section of this chapter. Never give someone your credit card number over IM.

■ **Closely guard your social security number**   Web stores don't need your social security number, although you might need to provide it to your bank or online investment company.

Avoid Cookie Monsters

Cookies are small text files used by Web sites to store settings and information on your computer. Web stores use cookies to manage your shopping cart; others use cookies to store travel itineraries or country and language preferences.

Cookies can't do anything except record information that you provide to them. They can't, for example, read other files on your computer or infect you with a virus. However, a rising trend among online advertisers is to use *third-party cookies* to track which Web sites you visit. They use this information to measure ad effectiveness and present you with targeted ads.

Lingo   *Third-party cookies* are cookies that send information to a different Web site than the one you're viewing. (A cookie that sends information back to the Web site you're viewing is called a first-party cookie.) Advertisers usually use third-party cookies to track Web surfing patterns.

Some cookies store personally identifiable information, such as your name and e-mail address, but only when you provide them to the Web site. While the Web site might do any number of things with your information, no other Web site can access the cookie and read your information from it.

If privacy and cookies are important to you, use the next sections to control how Internet Explorer automatically handles cookies, views privacy reports, and overrides automatic cookie handling on a site-by-site basis.

Setting Your Privacy Settings and Restricting the Use of Cookies

It used to be that if you were concerned about cookies, you blocked them entirely. Although effective, blocking all cookies essentially blocks all online shopping, among other things. Microsoft Internet Explorer 6 alleviates this problem by reading *P3P* policies (when available on a Website) and automatically comparing theses privacy policies with your privacy preferences. When the two don't match, Internet Explorer blocks or restricts the Web site's ability to use cookies.

Lingo   *Platform for Privacy Preferences (P3P)* policies are condensed privacy policies formatted in a way that Web browsers can read and make privacy decisions about.

Internet Explorer 6 comes with its automatic privacy and cookie-handling features set to a medium privacy setting. If you find these settings too loose or restrictive, use the following procedure to adjust them.

1   In Internet Explorer, choose Internet Options from the Tools menu.

2   Click the Privacy tab, as shown in Figure 11-1, and then use the slider to determine when Internet Explorer should accept cookies and when it should block them:

- Block All Cookies: Completely disables the use of cookies. Most Web stores are unusable at this level.

- High: Blocks all cookies that don't have a privacy policy that Internet Explorer can read (a compact privacy policy) and blocks all cookies that use personally identifiable information (such as your name or e-mail address) without your explicit consent. This is a good setting for people who want the most privacy that's reasonable. However, some Web stores and financial sites won't work properly until you manually override these settings (as discussed in the next section).

- Medium High: Blocks third-party cookies that don't have a compact privacy policy or that use your personally identifying information without your explicit approval and blocks first-party cookies that use your personally identifying information without implicit approval.

- Medium: Blocks third-party cookies that don't have a compact privacy policy or that use your personally identifying information without your implicit approval. Restricts first-party cookies that use your personally identifying information without implicit approval, but deletes them when you close Internet Explorer. This is the default setting.

- Low: Restricts third-party cookies that don't have a compact privacy policy or that use your personal identifying information without your implicit approval, but deletes them when you close Internet Explorer. All other cookies are accepted.

- Accept All Cookies: Accepts all cookies.

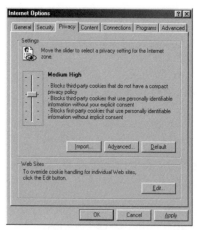

Figure 11-1   Use the Privacy tab to control how strict Internet Explorer should be when automatically handling cookies and your privacy.

Tip   To manually specify how Internet Explorer should deal with cookies, click Advanced, select the Override Automatic Cookie Handling check box, and then choose whether Internet Explorer should accept, block, or prompt you about first- and third-party cookies.

---

3   To add to or edit the list of Web sites that are explicitly allowed or denied the use of cookies, click Edit at the bottom of the Privacy tab. You can also change the cookie handling settings for a Web site as you view it, as discussed in the next section.

4   Click OK when you're finished.

Dealing with Cookies and Privacy Reports While You Surf

Once you've set your privacy and cookie-handling settings (as discussed in the previous section) Internet Explorer handles cookies automatically. When you come across a Web page for which Internet Explorer restricts the usage of cookies, a small warning icon appears on the Status bar. You can continue to browse the Web site as usual, although the functionality of the site might be diminished.

To view the privacy and cookie settings for a Web site and optionally override automatic cookie handling, use the following procedure.

1   Choose Privacy Report from the View menu or double-click the Privacy Report icon on the Status Bar.

2   To view the privacy report for all Web sites that make up the Web page you're currently viewing (many Web pages contain content, such as ads, from multiple Web sites), choose All Web Sites from the Show drop-down box, as shown in Figure 11-2. To view only Web sites for which Internet Explorer restricted cookies, choose Restricted Web Sites.

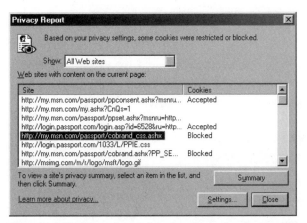

Figure 11-2 The Privacy Report dialog box shows all content in a Web page, as well as which sites contain cookies that were accepted or blocked.

3 To read the privacy policy of a Web site, select the site from the list and click Summary.

4 To change how Internet Explorer handles cookies from a site in the list, right-click it and choose from the options described in the following sections. You might do this to enable cookies on a Web store from which you want to make an order but that Internet Explorer blocked.

5 Click Close when you're finished.

Tip If you frequently override automatic cookie handling to allow cookies for sites that were restricted, adjust your privacy settings to a more relaxed setting. This saves you time and also protects your privacy more than simply accepting all cookies from restricted sites.

Using AutoComplete with Web Forms

AutoComplete is a feature of Internet Explorer that makes it easier to fill out forms on the Web. When you type a user name and password on a Web site, Internet Explorer asks if it should save them. If you click yes, next time you can simply recall the saved user name and password instead of retyping it. Auto-Complete can also record what you type in Web forms and the Address Bar, making it quicker to get to Web addresses you often use and to fill in forms with information that you frequently type, such as your address.

The following sections show you how to fill out forms with AutoComplete, change what types of forms AutoComplete pays attention to, and clear stored passwords and form entries.

Filling Out Forms with AutoComplete

AutoComplete works almost entirely in the background. When you type a Web address in the Address Bar, AutoComplete displays a list of Web sites that match what you've typed so far. To jump to one of the Universal Resource Locators (URLs), select it from the list.

When you type a user name and password on a Web page, AutoComplete displays a dialog box asking if it should save the password, as shown in Figure 11-3. Click Yes to remember the password; otherwise, click No.

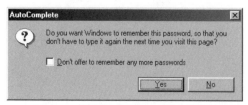

Figure 11-3 To prevent AutoComplete from remembering passwords, select the check box.

Caution   Never let AutoComplete record the user name and password for sensitive Web sites such as an online investing or banking Web sites. Anybody who can log on with your user account can access any password-protected Web site for which AutoComplete has saved your password, so use it carefully.

To retrieve a saved user name and password, place the cursor in a form with saved information, click the down arrow key on the keyboard, and then select the appropriate username from the list. Alternatively, begin typing your username and then select the full username from the list. If you have AutoComplete enabled for all Web forms, you can retrieve AutoComplete information for other types of forms using the same techniques.

To delete a stored AutoComplete entry, use the arrow keys on the keyboard to select the entry from the list that appears in a form and then press Delete.

Changing What AutoComplete Records

By default, AutoComplete is enabled for the Address Bar and any Web site that asks for a user name and password. You can also enable AutoComplete for garden-variety Web page forms; such as those that ask for your e-mail address and other contact information.

To change what AutoComplete records, or to disable it entirely, choose Internet Options from the Tools menu, click the Content tab and then click AutoComplete. Select or clear the following check boxes.

- ▪ **Web addresses**   AutoComplete for the Address Bar
- ▪ **Forms**   AutoComplete for Web forms

- **Usernames And Passwords On Forms**   AutoComplete for password protected Web sites

- **Prompt me to save passwords**   Controls whether Internet Explorer prompts you to save passwords

To clear all stored AutoComplete entries, use the Clear Forms and Clear Passwords buttons at the bottom of the dialog box.

To clear the Address Bar history, use the Clear History button on the General tab of the Internet Options dialog box, as discussed in the "Cover Your Tracks" section of this chapter.

Using the Microsoft Profile Assistant

The Microsoft Profile Assistant is an infrequently used feature that obviates the need to fill out some Web forms—when a Web site makes use of it (which isn't often). To use the Microsoft Profile Assistant, choose Internet Options from the Tools menu, click the Content tab, click My Profile, and then select a contact with your address information from the Outlook Express Address Book. After this, if a Web site needs your address information—perhaps to complete an order, it can obtain your address from your profile —after asking if it's okay, of course.

The Microsoft Profile Assistant isn't used by many Web sites, so enabling it doesn't convey many advantages, and it can present a privacy risk if a hacker finds a way to pull information from the profile assistant without asking. If you want to enable or disable the feature, here's how.

1   Choose Internet Options from the Tools menu in Internet Explorer.

2   Click the Content tab.

3   Click the My Profile tab to select a profile to use.

4   To disable the Microsoft Profile Assistant, click the Advanced tab and then clear the Enable Profile Assistant check box in the Security section of the tab.

Use an Anonymous Surfing Tool

If you want to be as secure and private as possible while surfing the Web, use an anonymous surfing tool. These products shield you from the Web sites that you view, preventing them from obtaining any information about you. Some also provide the ability to post newsgroup messages or send e-mail anonymously.

For a list of anonymous surfing tools, also called third-party proxies, see *http://www.privacy.net/proxy*. Two such products are Anonymizer (*http://www.anonymizer.com*), which also provides a free online snoop test, and AnonyMouse (*http://@nonymouse.com*).

Check Your Credit Report Frequently

Identity theft is increasingly common. To find out whether someone is using your identity to obtain credit cards and the like, obtain a copy of your credit report. If you see any incorrect information, contact each of the three credit agencies and notify them of the mistake.

To obtain a copy of your credit report, contact any (or all) of the three credit reporting agencies, or use a site such as Qspace (*http://www.qspace.com*), which provides reports from all three.

- **Equifax** *http://www.equifax.com*
- **Experian** *http://www.experian.com*
- **TransUnion** *http://www.transunion.com*

E-mail Security

For most people, e-mail is plenty secure. Unless someone gets a hold of your e-mail password or opens Outlook Express on your machine, no one can access your e-mail. (Not many hackers go through the trouble of hacking or intercepting someone's e-mail to read about their last trip to Florida or how their mother wishes they'd write more often.)

If for some reason you send e-mails that are of great interest to other people, such as confidential business ideas or plans, encrypt your e-mails. If you need to assure your recipients that e-mails you send truly are written by you and not someone pretending to be you (it's ridiculously easy to impersonate someone by e-mail), digitally sign your e-mails.

To use e-mail encryption and digital signatures, read on.

Get a Digital ID

To send digitally signed e-mails or to receive encrypted e-mails, you need your own digital ID. (To send digitally encrypted e-mails, you only need to have the recipient's digital ID.) Digital IDs, also called certificates, are small pieces of software obtained from a *certificate authority* such as Versign or Thawte that verify your identity.

To get a digital ID, choose Options from the Tools menu in Outlook Express, click the Security tab, and then click Get Digital ID to visit a Web site with a list of companies that sell or give away Digital IDs. Follow the instructions on the Web site of the certificate authority you choose to install your new digital ID.

To install your digital ID on another computer, request an additional certificate from your certificate authority and install it on your other computer. (Additional certificates are free—they make use of the same digital ID.)

Lingo A *certificate authority* is a company that distributes certificates. When using encryption or digital signatures, Outlook Express relies on certificates from trusted certificate authorities that verify the identity of certificate holders.

Reading Digitally Signed or Encrypted E-mail

Digitally signed or encrypted e-mails behave the same as normal e-mails, except that a small red ribbon icon appears next to digitally signed messages, and a small blue padlock icon appears next to encrypted e-mails. (You might also see some text explaining digital security—scroll through this text and click Continue to view your message.)

See Also For more information on reading e-mail, see Chapter 7, "Using E-mail and Newsgroups."

Note To receive encrypted e-mail, the sender must have your digital ID, which is sent with digitally signed messages.

When you receive a digitally signed message, Outlook Express automatically adds the digital ID of the sender to your Address Book entry for the sender. Once you have someone's digital ID, you can send him or her encrypted e-mail. (Microsoft Outlook users should right-click the sender's e-mail address, choose Add To Contacts, click Save And Close, and update the existing contact with the new information.)

Note Outlook Express only saves digital IDs that it receives if the default e-mail address for the sender is the same as the e-mail address used on the Digital ID.

PGP Provides Pretty Good Privacy As Well Pretty Good Privacy (PGP) is a product that provides another way to send digitally signed and encrypted files. Originally a freeware program, PGP is now owned by PGP Corporation (*http://www.pgp.com*) and incorporated into various retail products. A free version for personal use is also available (check *http://www.pgpi.com*).

PGP offers the following advantages over using X.509 certificates (which we call digital IDs) and Outlook Express built-in security functionality:

■ You don't need to obtain a digital ID from a certificate authority.

■ You have complete control over your private keys so that no one (including the government) can obtain your private keys without actually hacking your computer or cracking your key.

Of course, it also comes with the following quirks, which can either be viewed as advantages or disadvantages.

■ Many find the PGP software more confusing and less elegant to use than Outlook Express's built-in digital signature and encryption features.

■ PGP certificates, used by PGP to digitally sign and encrypt files, can be created by anyone, and don't inherently guarantee the identity of the certificate holder (unlike digital IDs from trusted certificate authorities). Instead, each PGP user can digitally sign another's certificate, indicating that *they* trust the identity of the certificate holder. If someone you know and trust has signed someone else's certificate, you can probably trust it. (PGP has some methods of making it easier to establish whether you can trust a certificate, but this is the essence of the methods.) Thus, PGP's web-of-trust method is more relative than that of digital IDs.

■ If you want to use PGP for commercial purposes, you must purchase it at *http://www.pgp.com*.

Sending Digitally Signed or Encrypted E-mail

To send a digitally signed or encrypted e-mail using Outlook Express, compose a message and then click Sign and/or Encrypt from the toolbar.

To send an encrypted e-mail to someone, you need to already have the digital ID (public key) associated with his or her contact information. To verify that you have the correct digital ID, open his or her contact information in the Address Book and click the Digital IDs tab.

If most of the e-mails you send are digitally signed and/or encrypted, configure Outlook Express to send messages this way by default. To do so, use the following steps.

1 In Outlook Express, choose Options from the Tools menu and then click the Security tab.

2 Select the Encrypt Contents And Attachments For All Outgoing Messages and/or Digitally Sign All Outgoing Messages check boxes.

3 Click OK when you're finished.

Once recipients have your digital ID (public key), you can send encrypted e-mail to them. (If you send encrypted e-mail to people who don't have your digital ID, they won't have any way of decrypting it.)

Tip Even if you specify that Outlook Express should digitally sign and/or encrypt all outgoing messages, you can still send a normal message by clicking the Sign and/or Encrypt toolbar buttons to turn off these features before sending the message.

Safe Shopping

To be a safe and savvy Internet shopper, you need to acquire some different "street-smarts" than those you use in the real world. You probably wouldn't buy a Seiko watch from a guy selling them out of his briefcase for U.S.$50 each. It's a similarly bad idea to pay U.S.$2,000 via money order for that new laptop you bought on eBay from an unrated seller.

Here are some tips for becoming a savvy Internet shopper.

- **Research businesses before buying from them** Legitimate businesses should list their street address and at least one phone number. If you're unfamiliar with a business, research consumer opinion at *http://www.bizrate.com, http://www.nextag.com, http://www.bbb.org,* and *http://groups.google.com*. If you're wary, call the business and ask them some questions or find somewhere else to shop.

- **Buy from U.S. companies** We're not being nationalistic—when you buy from companies located in America, federal and state laws protect you.

- **Find out the return policy** Are there any restocking fees? How many days do you have to return the merchandise? Is return shipping paid? Does the merchant refund your money or provide store credit?

- **Check shipping fees, taxes, and actual costs** The actual cost can sometimes be significantly different from what you think you're paying. Sometimes prices listed are after rebates; sometimes a "free" book or magazine costs U.S.$15 to ship. (Yeah, right; and there's this lovely bridge we'd like to sell you...)

Tip When you send in rebates, photocopy everything and set a reminder for yourself to check on the rebate if you haven't received it within the time listed.

- **Always pay by credit card**   Credit cards might have their evil temptations for some, but they offer the most protection against fraud and slippery businesses. Never use a debit card on line (and be really careful with debit cards off line as well).

- **Don't let retailers you don't trust save your card information**   When placing an order, most Web stores ask if they can save your card information for future orders. Until you've verified the reputation of the company, just say no.

- **Use virtual credit cards**   Some banks such as Citibank (*http:// www.citi.com*) offer the ability to generate one-time use credit card numbers. Web stores can make a single charge to the virtual credit card before it becomes invalid, preventing them from making future charges.

- **Make sure the connection is secure**   Before you enter your credit card number in a form, check for a secure connection. A secure connection has the following characteristics:

  - The Web address begins with https://. The *s* stands for secure.

  - A lock (or key) icon appears on the status bar.

- **Make sure that the URL is correct**   Hackers can sometimes redirect visitors from a legitimate Web site to a fake Web site that they use to collect your credit card information. Check the URL of the Web site in the address bar and make sure it matches the Web site you want. (Look especially for addresses that might start correctly but contain another complete URL in the address.)

- **Opt out of any mailings**   Clear any check boxes that indicate it's okay for the company to send you ads or share your name with other companies.

- **Save or print copies of your orders**   Save or print the order confirmation page for your records (see Chapter 6, "Fearless Web Browsing").

- **Review your credit card statements**   Compare your order confirmation with the amount the store actually charged, as it appears on your statement. If a store ships your order in multiple shipments, it might use multiple charges. Add them up to verify that you haven't been overcharged.

■ **Use common sense** If something smells fishy, or if a product or service sounds too good to be true, it probably is. Do some research on the newsgroups (use *http://groups.google.com*) to see if other people have experience with the product or store.

Making Safe Auction and Private-Party Purchases Buying things in Internet auctions or from private parties is inherently riskier than buying from well established Web stores. This is somewhat unavoidable; however, you can take some specific steps to reduce your risk.

■ Examine seller ratings, when available.

■ Thoroughly read the item description and ask sellers any tough questions before you bid (such as, does the thing work?).

■ Use electronic payment methods that provide fraud protection (such as virtual credit cards) when possible. Paypal (*http://www.paypal.com*) is very popular, but not without risk. Using eBay Payments allows you to pay by credit card without giving your card number to the seller, which is safer.

■ Use an escrow service for expensive purchases (escrow fees start at around U.S.$22).

■ Research selling prices before bidding—go to *http://www.pricewatch.com*, *http://www.nextag.com*, and *http://groups.google.com*, for example.

■ When selling (or purchasing) items, use shipping methods that include tracking and delivery confirmation, and ship to the buyer's confirmed address (when applicable). If you have a camera, take a picture of the item before shipping it.

Cover Your Tracks

Poking around in other people's History folder and viewing which Web sites they've visited is as big a privacy violation as reading their e-mail—unfortunately it's significantly easier to do and can even be done accidentally. Because of this (and other techniques), you should learn how to cover your tracks—both on line and off.

Before we show you how to cover your tracks, we need to state something very clearly. *Never* browse to a Web site at work that might get you in trouble. Even if you cover your tracks perfectly, proxy servers can easily track which sites users view, leaving you with no recourse but to brush up your resume.

With that out of the way, here's how to wipe clean the most obvious traces that you've left on a computer:

- **Clear the History folder**   To do so in Internet Explorer, choose Options from the Tools menu, and then click Clear History on the General tab, as shown in Figure 11-4.

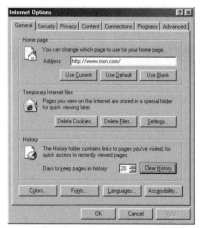

Figure 11-4 The Internet Options dialog box is where you can clear out most of your tracks.

- **Delete temporary Internet files**   Internet Explorer caches Web pages you've recently viewed for faster loading. However, they can also be used to see what pages you've visited. To empty Internet Explorer's cache, click Delete Files on the General tab in the Internet Options dialog box, select the Delete All Offline Content check box (if you have Web pages set up for offline viewing), and click OK. To make Internet Explorer empty its cache every time you close it, click the Advanced tab and then select the Empty Temporary Internet Files Folder When Browser Is Closed check box in the Security section.

- **Deal with cookies**   To delete all cookies, on the General tab, click Delete Cookies in the Internet Options dialog box. To selectively delete cookies you don't want lingering around, open the Cookies folder—usually found in either C:\Windows\Cookies or C:\Windows\ Profiles\username\Cookies (where *username* is your logged on name)—and delete the cookies you don't want.

- **Clear your document history**   Windows records your most recently accessed documents in the Documents folder on the Start menu. To clear this list, right-click a blank part of the Taskbar, choose Properties, click the Start Menu Programs tab, and then click Clear.

- **Clear AutoComplete**   Click AutoComplete on the Content tab of the Internet Options dialog box to delete AutoComplete entries for forms and/or passwords, as discussed earlier in this chapter.

- **Clean up Outlook Express newsgroups**   When you view a newsgroup in Outlook Express, it creates a local cache file with the name of the newsgroup in the file name. If you visit a newsgroup in Outlook Express but don't subscribe to it, Outlook Express leaves a telltale file on your hard drive, telling a savvy snoop that you've viewed the newsgroup. To delete these files, use the following steps.

    - In Outlook Express, choose Options from the Tools menu.

    - Click the Maintenance tab and click Store Folder.

    - Select the entire folder path (it's usually pretty long), right-click it, and then choose Copy from the shortcut menu (or write the path down).

    - Click Cancel in the Store Location dialog box, and then click Cancel in the Options dialog box.

    - Open Windows Explorer, right-click in the Address Bar, choose Paste from the shortcut menu, and then press Enter.

    - Select any cache files that you don't want lingering and then press Delete.

- **Empty the Recycle Bin**   Everything that you delete goes into the Recycle Bin, which can make for some juicy dumpster diving, especially if you've just cleaned up your cookies or Outlook Express cache files. To cover your tracks, make sure to empty the Recycle Bin.

Caution   Even performing these steps doesn't eliminate all traces of your information. When selling a computer that was previously used to store sensitive information, format the hard disk drive, reinstall Windows, and then copy unimportant files onto the hard disk drive until the disk is full, or use a data wiping program before reformatting. (This makes it more difficult for data recovery software to pull juicy bits of information off of the hard disk drive.)

Caution   Other programs such as Windows Media Player and Microsoft Word might also keep a history of recently opened files. Clear this history list (the method varies by program) or open a bunch of innocuous files to overwrite any entries in the history list you want to hide. (Windows Media Player users need the Windows Media Bonus Pack to clear the Media Player history.)

Restricting Access to Objectionable Content

Letting kids loose on the Internet without any supervision or content control is like dropping them off at the curb in Las Vegas with your credit card and telling them to have a good time.

Unfortunately, this dilemma has no easy fix. All parents must make their own decisions about Internet usage and their children. Numerous resources are available to help in making those decisions, including the following Web sites.

- *http://cyberangels.org*
- *http://GetNetWise.org*
- *http://www.SafeKids.com*
- *http://www.SafeTeens.com*

We believe that the best approach is to use the Internet with your kids. This not only allows you to prevent them from going to Web sites that you deem objectionable but also gives you an opportunity to make the Internet one big lesson about life. Use ads as a launching point for a discussion on consumerism; use spurious search results leading to adult sites as an opening to talk about sex and your morals. Write and read e-mail with your children to show them how to deal with spam and other individuals. (You probably don't want your kids following links that subscribe them to more spam or send them to objectionable Web sites.) Then give them an appropriate level of privacy.

If you want to allow your children access to the Internet while you're not sitting right beside them, consider the following suggestions for helping them stay out of trouble.

- Place the computer in a common area where you can keep an eye on their activities.

- Teach them how to use the Internet in a productive and safe manner, and set clear rules about what is unacceptable or off-limits.

- Let them know that you'll be monitoring what Web sites they view. Use the History folder to do so, although be aware that savvy kids can selectively delete sites from the History folder.

- Pay special attention to their use of chat rooms and instant messaging programs. These tools can be great for communicating with friends, but unscrupulous individuals also use them to take advantage of children.

- Evaluate content-filtering software. They all have their limitations, such as blocking educational Web sites or Web sites critical of the software (a sneaky but common practice), but they can help keep kids safe while you're busy. Some online services such as Microsoft Network (MSN) 8 and AOL provide content filtering as well.

Internet Explorer's Content Advisor—Better Than Nothing Internet Explorer comes with the Content Advisor feature, which allows you to control access to Web sites based on content ratings of the Web sites. Because most Web sites aren't rated, you have the choice of either blocking most of the Web, or letting them in. However, you can add your kids' favorite Web sites to an approved list, making it a passable and free solution for times when you can't actively monitor your children but want to give them some access to the Internet.

To use the Content Advisor, choose Internet Options from the Tools menu, click the Content tab, and then click Enable in the Content Advisor section. Use the Content Advisor dialog box to control what you prevent your children from viewing.

Key Points

- Hackers and viruses are real and substantial risks for all Internet users but can be minimized with proper techniques.

- Always use an antivirus program and keep its definition files up-to-date.

- Keep Windows and your other programs updated with the latest security patches.

- If you use a broadband Internet connection, use a firewall.

- Reuse a small number of passwords for Web sites that don't store sensitive information; use unique and complex passwords for everything else.

- Never write down passwords.

- Only provide information to Web sites when necessary and opt out of receiving mailings when possible.

- Be careful when shopping online. Research businesses and products before buying. Use common sense and never use debit cards.

- A smart snoop has many means to learn what sites you've viewed, so learn how to empty your History folder, delete temporary Internet files, and cover the rest of your tracks.

- While at work, never surf sites that would get you in trouble.

- The Internet is a wild and dangerous place for kids to roam without supervision. There are no perfect solutions to this problem, so do your research as a parent and take an active and caring role in your kids' Internet use.

Chapter 12

Maintaining a Healthy Computer

In an ideal world, you'd never have to perform maintenance. Cars wouldn't ever need oil changes, new tires, or windshield fluid refills; houses would never need new roofs or a visit from Roto-Rooter; and your computer would always work perfectly. Unfortunately, Microsoft Windows 98 users live in a world far separated from this utopian vision, making it necessary for all users to perform routine (and not-so-routine) system maintenance.

This chapter delves into all aspects of system maintenance, including housecleaning, optimizing system performance, backing up your system, and recovering from disasters. If you use Windows 98, you need this chapter.

Keeping Your Software Updated

Updating your software with the latest service packs and patches ensures that it runs with as few problems as possible. As mentioned in Chapter 11, "Playing It Safe," updating your software also increases the security of your system.

Use Windows Update (covered in Chapter 1, "Making Windows Work for You") to download and install patches, security fixes, and new Windows features.

Caution   To maximize the stability of your computer, read about each update before installing it and install only updates that apply to you.

Update your antivirus program's virus definition files every two weeks at a minimum, or sooner if you know there's a new virus you're not protected from yet. Update other programs as needed—whenever the software developers release important patches.

Some programs have built-in update mechanisms—go ahead and use those if available; otherwise, go to the software manufacturer's Web site and download any patches that apply to your software and the way you use it. Microsoft Office users can use Office Update (*http://office.microsoft.com/ProductUpdates*) to update Office. Office Update works almost identically to Windows Update, so you'll feel right at home.

See Also   For information on updating your antivirus program, see Chapter 11, "Playing It Safe." For more information on updating device drivers, see Chapter 9, "Conquering Computer Hardware."

Housecleaning

Even if your home is a mess, your computer doesn't need to be that way. Windows 98 makes it easy to perform routine housekeeping activities such as defragmenting disks, checking disks for errors, and cleaning up unneeded files. You can use the Maintenance Wizard to perform these tasks, or you can use the Drive Converter to convert a hard disk drive from the old file allocation table (FAT) file system to the newer FAT32 file system. Both tasks are covered in the next sections.

Scheduling Chores with the Maintenance Wizard

Windows 98 comes with a handy utility called the Maintenance Wizard, which automates the following tasks.

- Defragmenting disks
- Checking your disks for errors
- Deleting unnecessary files

Tip   To manually perform these tasks, use the Disk Defragmenter, ScanDisk, and Disk Cleanup tools, located in the System Tools folder on the Start menu.

What Is File Fragmentation? When saving files on a disk drive, Windows places the files next to each other, filling up the free space like books on a shelf. New files are written to the first chunk of free space, which is next to all the contiguous files.

When a file is deleted, some free space is opened up leaving a gap, just like pulling a book out of a bookshelf. The next time a file is written to the disk, Windows attempts to stuff the file into the first bit of free space, which now happens to be in-between some other files. If the hole isn't big enough, Windows might put the file in the next chunk of free space big enough for the file, or Windows might split the file into two or more fragments and place some in the first bit of free space and the rest in the next spot. As a disk becomes more and more full, the amount of fragmentation increases because there aren't enough large chunks of free space left.

Fragmented files are not in danger of any sort and behave just like any other file. However, fragmented files load significantly slower than nonfragmented files because Windows has to search two or more locations of the disk just to retrieve the single, fragmented file. Heavily fragmented files can contain hundreds of fragments, greatly increasing the amount of time it takes to read the file.

Using the Maintenance Wizard obviates the need to perform these house-cleaning tasks manually. To use the Maintenance Wizard, follow these steps.

1 Click Start and choose Programs, Accessories, System Tools, and finally Maintenance Wizard.

2 Choose Express to accept the default settings or Custom to adjust the settings to best fit your needs. Click Next to continue.

3 Select the best time to run the Maintenance Wizard and then click Next.

4 Clear the check boxes next to any nonessential program that runs at startup, as shown in Figure 12-1, and then click Next. (This screen only appears if you select Custom, instead of Express, and you have shortcuts listed in your Startup folder.)

Figure 12-1 Clear the check boxes to reduce the amount of time Windows takes to start.

5   Use the Speed Up Programs section (available in Custom mode) to control how and when your hard disk is defragmented, and then click Next.

- Click Reschedule to change when disks are defragmented. Weekly is sufficient for most people, although people who perform video editing or lots of image editing might want to defragment every other day.

- Click Settings to control which disk to defragment and whether to accelerate program starts.

6   Use the Scan Hard Disk For Errors section (available in Custom mode) to control how and when Windows checks your hard disk for errors and then click Next.

7   Use the Delete Unnecessary Files section (available in Custom mode) to control which unnecessary files are deleted (such as Temporary Internet Files) and when. Click Next to continue.

8   Review your settings and then click Finish.

The Task Scheduler: The Brawn Behind the Maintenance Wizard

The Maintenance Wizard is really just a snazzy tool for scheduling maintenance tasks with the Task Scheduler. When you run the Maintenance Wizard, it creates three customized tasks in the Scheduled Tasks folder—one task each for Disk Defragmenter, ScanDisk, and the Disk Cleanup Wizard. The Task Scheduler then runs each task according to the schedule you specified. It also runs any other tasks you create.

To change how and when the Task Scheduler runs your maintenance programs, either run the Maintenance Wizard again or double-click the Task Scheduler icon in the System Tray. (You can also access the Task Scheduler from the Start menu—click Scheduled Tasks in the System Tools folder.) Right-click the task you want to modify and choose Properties from the shortcut menu.

Converting Your Hard Drive to FAT32

If you upgraded to Windows 98 from Windows 95, chances are good that you're still using the archaic FAT16 file system. If your hard disk drive is bigger than 512 megabytes (MB), converting it to FAT32 file system saves you considerable hard disk space (up to 720 MB megabytes for a 2-GB disk drive), and makes your computer a bit faster. It's also the only way to create partitions larger than 2 GB.

Caution   Converting a hard disk drive to FAT32 is safe but not immune to problems. You should always have a backup of your important data, but it's doubly important before performing an action like this.

Although converting drives is easy, there are some caveats:

- Windows 95 disk utilities might not like FAT32—double-check or upgrade them to a Windows 98 or Windows Millennium Edition (Me) version.
- Most disk compression programs (including Windows DriveSpace) don't work with FAT32. Uncompress a disk before converting it.
- Windows NT can't recognize FAT32 partitions, so if you're running a dual-boot computer, don't convert your drive(s).
- If your computer has a hibernation power saving mode, converting the drive to FAT32 might disable this mode.
- There's no going back—the only way to get back to the FAT file system is by reformatting your hard disk drive.

To convert your hard disk to the FAT32 file system, uninstall any programs that protect the Master Boot Record (MBR), such as Norton For Your Eyes Only, and then use the following steps.

1   Choose Programs, then Accessories, System Tools, and finally Drive Converter (FAT32).

2   For more information about the conversion, compatibility issues, and other information click Details, otherwise click Next.

3   Select the drive that you want to convert and then click Next.

4   Follow the instructions in the rest of the wizard, which restarts your computer and converts the drive. This process might take as long as a couple hours, during which time you can't use the computer.

Disk Compression—Get a New Drive Instead   Windows 98 comes with the ability to compress your hard disk drive using the DriveSpace program, but we're not going to tell you how to use it or any third-party disk compression programs. Here's why.

- They slow down your computer.
- They increase the likelihood of losing data.
- They make it harder to recover a nonworking system.
- They only work on hard disk drives formatted with the antiquated FAT file system—the newer FAT32 file system can't be compressed.

If you need more hard disk space, go out and buy a new hard disk drive. Not only will a new hard disk drive add space, but it'll probably be much faster and more reliable than whatever you have now.

Optimizing System Performance

The following sections cover optimizing and upgrading various aspects of a computer's overall performance—memory management, disk speed, Windows load times, processing power, and display speed. It also covers special aspects that affect video editing. These sections are relevant for all types of users, covering both basic and advanced tweaking topics.

Improving Memory Management

Windows 98 is both good and bad when it comes to memory management. On the plus side, Windows 98 itself doesn't need much RAM to run—about 12 MB for the operating system. (Windows XP uses upwards of three times that amount.) The flipside is that Windows 98 isn't particularly smart about how it allocates the memory that it has.

The following sections provide you with advice on how to maximize the effectiveness of memory in Windows 98.

Got Enough RAM?

You can only eek so much performance out of a Ford Pinto. Similarly, running Windows 98 on a computer with 8 MB of RAM is going to be excruciating, no matter what you do.

Although Windows 98 will run on 16 MB of RAM, it won't be pretty. We consider 32 MB the minimum, 48–64 MB necessary for adequate performance, and 128 MB needed for maximum performance for most users. However, users who do a lot of image editing, graphics work, or video editing should consider 256 MB.

If you have less than 64 MB of RAM, investigate adding more. Different systems take different types of RAM, so refer to your computer or motherboard manual or the manufacturer's Web site. Some systems, especially laptops, might require too much effort and expense to upgrade—so check out some new systems before you upgrade.

Note   Windows 98 doesn't make good use of more than 256 MB of RAM, and adding more than 512 MB of RAM can make a system highly unstable. If you have more than 512 MB of RAM in your system, either remove some or disable the additional RAM. To do so, click Start, choose Run, type **msconfig** in the Open box, click OK, click Advanced, select the Limit Memory To check box, and then type **512** in the box provided.

Disable Unwanted Services and Programs   Most computers have a myriad of programs and services running unobtrusively in the background, consuming valuable system memory. Some of these are easy to spot—they have icons in the

System Tray. Others leave little trace. To clean out unwanted programs and services that are consuming RAM and slowing down the boot time of your system, refer to the following sections.

Eliminate Unneeded System Tray Programs   Many programs like to clutter the System Tray (and computer memory) with background programs. Closing these programs frees up memory and might also give your CPU a little relief.

To close a program in the System Tray, right-click the program's icon in the System Tray and choose Exit or Disable from the shortcut menu. You can also open the program and look for a Load At Startup or similarly named setting.

Remove Unneeded Network Components   Network components all consume memory and increase the amount of time Windows takes to load. If this isn't enough reason to run only the network components that you actually use, consider that running multiple protocols increases the amount of network traffic generated because each communication is sent through all protocols.

See Also   For more information on setting up and using networks, see Chapter 13, "Building and Using a Network."

To disable unwanted protocols, services, and clients, use the following steps.

Note   If your computer doesn't have a network connection, remove all protocols and services except any Dial-Up adapters and TCP/IP for the dial-up adapter.

---

1   In Control Panel, double-click the Network icon.

2   Select any unneeded network components and click Remove. Table 12-1 lists some common components that you might encounter.

3   Click OK and then restart the computer.

Table 12-1   Common Network Components

Network Component	Component Type	Purpose
Client for Microsoft Networks	Client	Communicating with other Microsoft Windows computers on a local network
Client for NetWare Networks	Client	Communicating with Novell NetWare servers
Ethernet Adapter (The name and listing will vary by vendor.)	Adapter	Communicating on a network or over a Digital Subscriber Line (DSL) or cable Internet connection
Dial-up Network Adapter	Adapter	Connecting to a remote network (such as the Internet) through a telephone line

Table 12-1   Common Network Components   *(continued)*

Network Component	Component Type	Purpose
Transmission Control Protocol/ Internet Protocol (TCP/IP)	Protocol	Communicating on a TCP/IP network, such as the Internet or any modern network
NetBIOS Extended User Interface (NetBEUI)	Protocol	Communicating on an old Windows For Workgroups
Internetwork Packet Exchange/ Sequenced Packet Exchange (IPX/ SPX)-CompatibleProtocol	Protocol	Communicating with a Novell Netware server
Fast Infrared Protocol	Protocol	Communicating with other devices over an infrared connection

Empty the Config.sys and Autoexec.bat Files   The Config.sys and Autoexec.bat files are two files used by MS-DOS to start devices and memory-resident (background) programs. Windows 98 can use these files, but it is much better to run legacy MS-DOS drivers and memory-resident programs from an MS-DOS command prompt or using MS-DOS Mode, both of which are discussed in Chapter 3, "Running Programs."

Disabling these files can improve the stability of your system, free up memory, and reduce the time Windows 98 takes to load. To disable these files, use the following steps.

1   In Windows Explorer, locate the Autoexec.bat and Config.sys files in the root directory of the C:\ drive. (Autoexec.bat might be listed simply as Autoexec, and the Config.sys file might be completely absent.)

2   Rename each file to something like Autoexec.bak and Config.bak.

3   Restart your system and make sure everything works properly.

If your system doesn't work properly, selectively disable parts of these files using the following steps.

1   Rename the files back to their original names.

2   Click Start and then choose Run.

3   Type **sysedit** in the Open box and click OK.

4   Click the C:\Autoexec.bat window and disable a line in the file by typing **REM** in front of it, as shown in Figure 12-2.

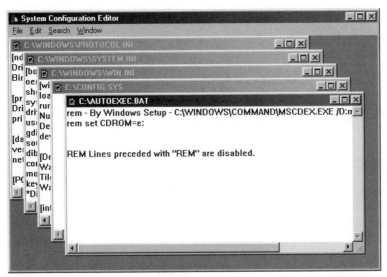

Figure 12-2 Use the System Configuration Editor (sysedit) to edit the Autoexec.bat and Config.sys files.

5   Save the file, restart the computer, and test its functionality. If it works properly, repeat steps 2 through 4, disabling another line until the system no longer functions properly. Leave the offending line enabled (by erasing *REM* in front of the line). Do this for both the Autoexec.bat and Config.sys files.

Tip   The System Configuration Editor (Msconfig.exe) provides a more elegant way to temporarily disable lines in the Autoexec.bat and Config.sys files. However, behind the scenes msconfig replaces the Autoexec.bat and Config.sys files with placeholders and redirects Windows to use its Autoexec.tsh and Config.tsh files. Although this works great for troubleshooting, it's inappropriate for long-term use. Undo any changes you made to these files with msconfig and redo them in sysedit.

Disable Unneeded Startup Programs   Many programs like to (unnecessarily) launch background tasks when Windows starts, consuming memory and increasing the amount of time Windows takes to start. To disable programs that start automatically with Windows, use the following steps.

1   Disable as many System Tray programs as possible (see the previous section).

2   Click Start, Programs, and then Startup. Any items listed here are automatically run when Windows starts. Right-click programs that you don't want to load and choose Delete from the shortcut menu. (If you experience problems, you can restore the file from the Recycle Bin.)

3 To stop hidden programs from running, click Start, and then choose Run.

4 Type **msconfig** in the Open text box and click OK.

5 Click the Startup tab and clear the check boxes next to any unwanted programs, as shown in Figure 12-3. Click OK when you're finished.

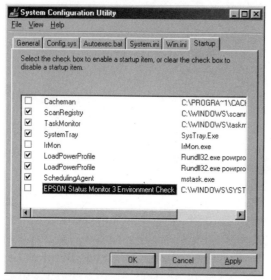

Figure 12-3 Use the System Configuration Utility (Msconfig.exe) to prevent hidden programs from running at startup.

Tip   To be thorough, while in the System Configuration Utility click the Win.ini tab, expand the [Windows] section, and then clear the Load= and Run= check boxes.

Disable Compression Drivers   If your hard disk isn't compressed, disable disk compression to free up a little more memory (unless you use compressed Zip disks or other removable media). To do so, use the following steps.

Caution   Don't perform this procedure if you are using any compressed drives. To uncompress a drive, click Start, choose Programs, then Accessories, System Tools, and finally DriveSpace. Select a compressed drive and choose Uncompress from the File menu. If you're using only FAT32 drives don't worry about this—they don't support compression anyway.

---

1 In Windows Explorer, choose Folder Options from the View menu.

2 Click the View tab, select Show All Files from the Hidden Files section, and then click OK.

3 Locate the Dblspace.bin file, which should be in the *root directory* of your drive C:\ drive and rename it Dblspace_bak.bin—or something similar. If your system has trouble booting or you encounter a compressed drive that you want to access, rename the file back to its original name and reboot.

Lingo The *root directory* is the topmost folder of a drive's folder hierarchy—it's what contains all files and folders on that drive.

Adjust Virtual Memory Settings—Or Not When determining whether to mess around with virtual memory settings (in some instances you actually should tweak the settings), use the following guidelines.

- If you have a single hard disk drive, leave virtual memory settings alone.

- If you have more than one hard disk drive, place the swap file on the most often used partition of the least often used hard disk drive. Pick the faster hard disk drive if it's a close call.

- Make sure that the hard disk on which the swap file is stored has a minimum of 256–512 MB of free space.

- If you use Adobe Photoshop or another image editing program that maintains its own scratch disk files (basically a swap file exclusively for Photoshop), create a permanent, fixed-size swap file that's twice the size of the installed RAM (and a minimum of 64 MB). Ideally, the swap file should be on the system drive (C:\), and the Photoshop scratch disk on a different disk drive (as long as it's not a slow disk drive such as a Zip or network drive). This prevents Windows virtual memory from competing with Photoshop's scratch disk files for hard disk space.

- If Windows 98 often slows down drastically for no apparent reason while the hard disk goes crazy, try creating a permanent swap file with the settings shown in Table 12-2 (the minimum and maximum sizes are the same).

Table 12-2 Manual Virtual Memory Sizing

Installed RAM	Virtual Memory Size (Minimum and Maximum)
16 MB	96 MB (get more RAM)
32 MB	128 MB
64 MB	196 MB
128 MB	256 MB
256 MB	260 MB
384 MB	390 MB
512 MB	520 MB

What Is Virtual Memory?   Virtual memory is hard disk space (called a swap file) that acts as an overflow for programs and data that don't fit in RAM. Because hard disk drives are several orders of magnitude slower than RAM modules, it's important that virtual memory be used only for infrequently needed data. If a computer has significantly less RAM than necessary to do a specific task, the system slows to a crawl as it waits for data to load from the hard disk drive.

For example, to edit a 40 MB image file on a computer with 32 MB of RAM (of which only 8 MB might be available), Windows must constantly swap data in and out of virtual memory. This is because all 40 MB of the image is needed in memory at the same time to edit or display it, and only 8 MB is available. (Most image editing programs need a minimum of three times more available RAM than the size of an image.) Needless to say, Windows would be brought to its knees, and you with it.

If you decide to modify virtual memory settings, use the following steps.

1   Double-double-click the System icon in the Control Panel.

2   Click the Performance tab, and click Virtual Memory.

3   Select the Let Me Specify My Own Virtual Memory Settings option and then select the disk drive on which you want to place the swap file.

4   To create a fixed-size swap file, type the size of the swap file in the Minimum and Maximum boxes.

5   Click OK when you're done. Click Yes, Close, and then Yes to restart the computer.

Streamline Display Settings   You can free up some additional memory by streamlining display settings. To do so, double-click the Display icon in Control Panel and then take the following actions:

■   **Disable Active Desktop**   The Active Desktop is a big memory hog. To disable it, click the Web tab and clear the View My Active Desktop As A Web Page check box.

■   **Eliminate big wallpaper images**   Choosing a solid color or a pattern instead of a desktop image saves a significant amount of memory. To peel your computer's wallpaper, click the Background tab, and then choose None in the Wallpaper frame (if you're using a Theme, use the Windows Default theme). For more information, see Chapter 2, "Covering the Desktop."

Improving Disk Speed

You can do a few notable things to make sure that your hard disk is running at top speed. First, defragment your hard disk drive (as discussed earlier in this chapter). Then use the following sections to ensure your hard disk drive is living up to its full potential.

Tip   Hard disk drives are much faster and more reliable than floppy disks and Zip disks. For the best performance and reliability, save your work to a local hard disk drive. Then copy files to floppy, Zip disk, or CD when you need to carry them around.

Enable Direct Memory Access (DMA)

If your hard disk supports Direct Memory Access (DMA), you should enable it. Doing so provides a big performance boost.

Caution   Enabling DMA on a computer that doesn't support it *might* cause trouble. Most hard disks manufactured in the last five years or so support DMA, but if you want to be sure, check your manual.

To enable DMA, use the following steps.

1   In Control Panel, double-click the System icon, and click the Device Manager tab.

2   Under the Disk Drives branch, select your hard disk drive and then click Properties.

3   Click the Settings tab, and select the DMA check box.

4   Click OK (you may be prompted with a warning) and then restart your computer.

5   After restarting, double-check to make sure the check box stays selected—if not, check with your computer manufacturer for updated drivers that enable DMA access in Windows 98.

Adjust the File System Properties

Windows 98 usually configures your hard disk cache for optimal performance automatically, but you should double-check just to be sure. To do so, use the following steps.

1   In Control Panel, double-click the System icon.

2   Click the Performance tab, and click File System.

3 In the Typical Role Of This Computer box, use the following settings:

- Network Server: if your computer has more than 32 MB of RAM.

- Desktop Computer: if the system has less than 32 MB of RAM.

- Mobile Or Docking System: if the computer has a very small amount of RAM (16 MB).

4 Drag the Read-Ahead Optimization slider all the way to the right (Full).

5 Click the CD-ROM tab, and drag the Supplemental Cache Size slider all the way to the right (Large) and choose Quad Speed Or Higher from the Optimize Access Pattern For drop-down box.

Tip If your CD-ROM drive is slower than 4X, it's past time for an upgrade (unless you rarely use your CD drive or only use it for listening to music CDs). Watch your local computer stores for sales—they often have 50X CD-ROM drives dirt-cheap.

Leave the Disk Cache Alone A disk cache speeds up hard disk access by caching recently accessed data in RAM, which is much faster than the fastest hard disk drive. It's basically the opposite of virtual memory—it's virtual hard disk space.

Like virtual memory, everyone and their grandmother seems to have an idea of the best way to tune the Windows disk cache. Once again, we're going to tell you to just leave it alone.

With that said, if you want to play with the cache settings, we're not going to stop you. Probably the easiest way to fiddle with these settings is using Cacheman from Outertech Software, which you can download at *http://www.outertech.com*. Just don't expect much of a difference.

Buy a New Hard Disk

This might seem obvious, but another way of improving disk speed is to replace your hard disk with a new one. Hard disk drive speeds and capacities have been increasing tremendously over the last five years, and even a top-of-the-line drive from two years ago can't match the speed of an average drive from today—at half the cost.

When buying a new drive, look for rotational speed as the big indicator of overall speed (a 7,200 rpm drive is generally the fastest.) Also, depending on the age of your computer, you might need to update your computer's Basic Input Output System (BIOS) to use hard disk drives bigger than 2.11 GB (for some systems built in 1996), 8 GB, 32 GB, or 137 GB. A good Web site to check out when doing research on hard disk drives is Storage Review, at *http://www.storagereview.com*.

Keep in mind that although adding a hard disk drive to your computer is relatively simple (provided that you have a spare drive bay, an extra Integrated Drive Electronics [IDE] channel, and a screwdriver), replacing your existing hard disk drive is not. Replacing a disk drive means transferring some or all of your data and programs over to the new disk drive. To transfer data from one hard disk drive to another, hook up both drives and use a disk imaging or drive transfer program or perform a simple copy operation. Only a disk imaging or drive transfer program can move Windows—otherwise, you'll have to install Windows from scratch on the new drive.

Tip   Keep a close eye on cost when evaluating potential upgrades. With new computers cheaper than ever, spending a lot of money upgrading an old system just doesn't make sense.

Making Windows Load Faster

The amount of time Windows takes to load is one of the most noticeable performance aspects of a computer. To speed up Windows load times, perform these actions:

- **Disable floppy disk polling**   Windows automatically checks for new floppy disk drives every time you start your computer, which takes a couple seconds. To stop this, in Control Panel, click System, click the Performance tab, click File System, click Floppy Disk, and then clear the Search For New Floppy Disk Drives Each Time Your Computer Starts check box.

- **(Carefully) clean out the root directory**   The root directory (C:\) can often become cluttered with various unneeded files. To speed up Windows boot times, move or delete unnecessary files from the root directory. You can safely delete .chk and .tmp files; leave any other files you're unsure of.

  Caution   If you delete a vital system file from the root directory, such as Command.com, Io.sys, or Msdos.sys, Windows won't boot. Only delete files that you know are safe to delete (leave the System.1st and Videorom.bin files alone as well).

- **Disable the splash screen at bootup**   If you have Tweak UI (available by searching at *http://support.microsoft.com* for Windows 98 tweak ui), you can stop Windows from displaying its logo during startup, saving one or two seconds. To do so, in Control Panel, click the Tweak UI icon, click the Boot tab, and clear the Display Splash Screen While Booting check box.

Tip   Removing unused .dll (Dynamic Link Libraries) from the Windows\System folder can also reduce boot times, though with some risk. Clean System Directory, a freeware program available for download at *http://downloads-zdnet.com.com/*, makes this tricky business easier, if you know what you're doing.

Making the Most of Your Processor

Although the only way to obtain more processing power is by upgrading your CPU or buying a new computer, you can make the most of your existing processor by taking the following actions.

- Turn off background spelling and grammar checking in application programs.

- Work in "normal" views instead of Page Layout views.

- Run one program at a time to provide the most processing power to the program in which you're working.

- Disable fancy screensavers (especially OpenGL screensavers).

Improving Display Speed

You can adjust a number of display settings to improve the "snappiness," or general speed of the Windows interface. To do so, use the following tasks.

- **Disable display effects**   In Control Panel, double-click the Display icon, click the Effects tab, and then clear some (or all) of the check boxes in the Visual Effects frame.

- **Disable themes**   Windows Themes, an optionally installed component of Windows, might look pretty, but they slow down your computer a bit. If you're using Themes, either uninstall them or use the Windows Default theme (see Chapter 2, "Covering the Desktop," for more information).

- **Lower your color depth**   To improve the snappiness of Windows on computers with older display cards, double-click the Display icon in Control Panel, and then use the Settings tab to lower number of colors displayed. High Color (16 bit) is a good compromise between quality and speed, though modern display cards such as the nVidia TNT/ Geforce lines, ATI Rage Pro, and Radeon can safely stick to True Color (24 bit) or 32 bit color (if supported).

- **Disable Web Content in Windows Explorer and My Computer**
  By default Windows 98 displays a pretty, but fairly useless, banner in

Windows Explorer (and My Computer) listing some summary info about the selected folder or drive. This banner takes up screen space, and also slows down browsing folders.

To disable Web views, use the following steps.

● Choose Folder Options from the View menu in Windows Explorer.

● On the General tab select Custom, and then click Settings.

● Select the Use Windows Classic Desktop and Only For Folders Where I Select "As Web Page" options, as shown in Figure 12-4, and then click OK.

Figure 12-4 Use the Custom Settings dialog box to disable Web views in Windows Explorer.

More Info   To maximize the performance of games, see the Running High-Performance Games section of Chapter 3, "Running Programs."

Take 2: Video Editing Requires Different Settings

Nonlinear (computer-based) video editing is a storage-intensive task and requires some special optimization steps. This is because capturing and playing back high-quality video requires the hard disk drive to unfailingly read and write the video stream at 3.5 megabytes per second (MBps) for digital video (DV), or 4 to 6 MBps for captured analog video. Any time the transfer rate dips below the minimum, glitches in the video and audio occur. To prevent this from happening, take the following actions.

■ **Use a dedicated video drive**   Using a separate video drive exclusively for video capture and editing helps eliminate dropped frames and glitches which can be caused by sharing a drive with Windows and your capture program.

■ **Keep the Windows swap file off the video drive**   Leave the Windows swap file on the system drive. If possible, place the swap file on the outside of the disk using a third-party disk defragmenting program such as Norton Utilities.

■ **Set up your drives properly**   The video drive should be on its own IDE channel or slaved to your operating system drive. Do NOT place the drive on the same channel as a CD-ROM or other slow device, such as a Zip drive. Enable DMA for your video and system drives.

■ **Partition and format your drives properly**   Video drives should have a single, FAT32 partition.

■ **Keep the disk defragmented and partially empty**   Windows writes to the inside (slowest) part of the disk last, so leaving it partially empty improves the speed of the drive. A good amount of free disk space is 30 percent.

■ **Close all background programs**   This includes antivirus programs. You might even want to disable the Taskbar clock.

■ **Disable disk caching**   Because video comes in at a steady and relentless rate, software disk caches are useless and should be disabled. To do so, use the following steps.

●   In Control Panel, double-click the System icon.

●   Click the Performance tab, and click File System.

●   Drag the Read-Ahead Optimization slider all the way left (None).

●   Click the Troubleshooting tab, and select the Disable Write-Behind Caching For All Drives check box.

●   Click OK and then restart your computer. (You might want to switch this back when you're not editing or capturing video so that the rest of your system performs faster.)

■ **Configure your capture and editing applications to use the video drive**   Video editing and capture programs should use the video drive for captured movies and preview/temporary files.

■ **Make sure your video drive is fast enough**   Dedicated video drives need to sustain at least 3.5 MBps (worst case). Most hard disks introduced after 1997 are fast enough as a dedicated video drive and 7,200 rpm models from 2000 or later should be fast enough in a single-drive setup, though using multiple drives is much better.

- **Make sure the video drive is big enough** DV consumes 210 MB per minute or roughly 13 GB per hour.

- **Install your sound card and network card in the last two PCI slots** If you have a separate sound card and network card, placing them in the last two PCI slots helps ensure that they don't interrupt the capture process.

- **Install your Small Computer System Interface (SCSI) or IDE controller in PCI slots one or two** If you have a separate hard disk controller (most are on the motherboard), placing it in one of the first two PCI slots gives it the highest performance.

- **Use Windows 98 Second Edition (SE) or Windows XP** Windows 98 SE includes improved support for DV camcorders and generally works better than Windows 98 or Windows Millenium Edition (Me). If your hardware supports Windows XP or Windows 2000, consider upgrading to allow file sizes larger than 2 GB (although upgrading from Windows 98 is not painless, and often times it's better to just buy a new computer with Windows XP preinstalled).

Note Windows 98 has a file size limit of 2 GB, limiting videos to a maximum of roughly 10 minutes. Some capture programs have ways of working around this limitation; others require you to capture and edit in 10-minute chunks.

Backing Up Your Files

It's true, backing up isn't fun, effortless, or cheap, but if your job depends on the data stored in your computer, losing it all could literally mean losing it all.

For this reason, it's vital that you regularly back up your data, if not your operating system and programs. Users of a corporate network probably don't need to worry about backing up anything, as long as they save their files to the proper location (most likely a network share that is backed up nightly). If that's you, go ahead and skip this whole section. If you're not on a network or if you're running your own network, read on (unless playing chicken is one of your preferred pastimes).

Fortunately, as the next sections illuminate, devising a backup strategy isn't difficult. There is a plethora of low-cost backup media to choose from (including CD burners), and using backup software is a piece of cake.

Creating a Backup Strategy

Before you start, determine what you want to back up, as well as how and when.

- **What do you want to back up?**   If you don't mind reinstalling Windows and all of your applications, you can forego backing up everything on your hard disk drive. However, it's vital that you back up your important documents and files.

- **How can you back up the data?**   Most people these days use CD burners, but you could also use DVD writers, tape backup units, or even additional hard disk drives or network drives (as discussed in the next section).

- **When do you want to back up the data?**   How often you back up your computer should depend on how often you change things—either by adding or removing programs or by creating or modifying documents. Some people who don't change things often or don't care much about their data can get away with a full backup once a month and incremental backups every week. Others have important data and files that change frequently, necessitating weekly full backups combined with daily differential backups, as discussed in the sidebar "Backup Types—Full, Differential, and Incremental."

Backup Types—Full, Differential, and Incremental   There are three types of backup jobs—full, differential, and incremental. A *full backup* is a complete backup of the selected files or disk—that is, everything you selected is backed up. When you perform a full backup, each backed up file has its Archive attribute reset, indicating that the file hasn't changed since the last backup.

An *incremental backup* is a partial backup that only backs up files that have changed since the last backup, taking less time and space than a full backup. Incremental backups, like full backups, reset the Archive attribute so that nothing is backed up twice. However, in the event of a disk failure, you first need to restore the latest full backup, and then each incremental backup made since then, in order. Don't perform too many incremental backups in between full backups if you want to minimize the time and inconvenience of a restore.

A *differential backup*, like an incremental backup, is a partial backup that only backs up files that have changed. However, unlike incremental backups, differential backups don't reset the Archive attribute. Because of this, every time you perform a differential backup, *all* files that have changed since the last full backup are backed up—not just the ones changed since the last partial backup. This means that to restore files, you only need the full backup set and the most recent differential backup. This saves time, but means that each partial backup consumes more space.

Most users find the following to be a good strategy, but you should modify it as appropriate for your needs.

■ Perform a full backup of your operating system, programs, and data once a month.

■ Perform a differential backup as often as needed to make the thought of losing your changes manageable. For some this would be once a week; for those who make a living with their data—daily.

■ Keep a full backup set in a safe, offsite location, such as a safe deposit box. Update this set as often as necessary to protect yourself from fire and burglars.

Tip Users who keep all of their important data in a small number of locations (such as My Documents) can maintain separate backup schedules for their data and their software. For example, perform a full backup of Windows and applications once a month, a full backup of your data once a week, and a differential backup of your data at the end of each day (or automated during the night with a third-party backup program).

Selecting Backup Media

Choosing backup media to use is somewhat complicated, with your options including Zip, CD-R, CD-RW, DVD+RW, DVD-RAM, Travan 20 tapes, Onstream tapes, and DAT tapes. Table 12-3 provides a break down of different backup methods, and the following sections discuss which media are best suited to each kind of user.

Table 12-3 Common Backup Media

Media	Size	Speed	Notes
Zip	100 MB, 250 MB, 750 MB	1.2 MBps (4.5 MBps for Zip 750)	Good for small data backups
CD-R	650 MB–700 MB	2.5–5+ MBps	Write once; can create audio CDs
CD-RW	650 MB–700 MB	1.5–2.4+ MBps	Not playable in many CD players
DVD	4.7 GB	1.3–3.9+ MBps	Most can also create video DVDs, playable in DVD players
Onstream tape	15–30 GB	2–2.5 MBps	Proprietary format
Digital Audio Tape (DAT)	12 GB (DDS3), 20 GB (DDS4)	1.1, 2.4 MBps	Requires a SCSI controller
Hard disk drive	20–120 GB	15–20 MBps	External drives require Firewire or USB 2.0 drive for best performance

Average User

The average user doesn't use a whole lot of disk space—perhaps 1 GB to 3 GB for Windows 98 and all programs, and another 100 MB to 1 GB for all user data. Two options make the most sense for the average user.

■ **Backup to Zip disk**   If you already have a Zip drive or other low-capacity backup device, use Microsoft Backup to back up only your data, using 1 to 10 Zip disks.

■ **Backup to CD**   If you have a CD burner or want to back up Windows and your programs, use a third-party backup or hard disk imaging program to back up everything to CD-R or CD-RW discs. (Ahead Software Nero can do this.) This process takes 1 to 6 blank CDs.

Note   Microsoft Backup can't back up to CD-R, CD-RW or any form of writable DVD. You can use the packet writing software (such as Roxio DirectCD) included with your drive to perform a simple copy of data to CD (suitable for backing up user data), but to back up Windows you need a third-party backup program that supports CD-R and CD-RW media, along with disc spanning (so that you can use multiple CDs).

Multimedia User

Someone who has a big MP3 collection, plays games, has a digital camera, or does computer art consumes a lot of disk space. Windows 98 and all programs might consume 6 GB, MP3 files might take 15 GB, and image files another 3 GB. That's 24 GB total.

Your best backup bets are as follows.

■ **Back up to CD**   This is the cheapest, and slowest, approach. A full backup takes 35 discs—and the better part of a day. Supplement yearly or half-yearly full backups with differential or incremental backups as often as necessary. (These should only consume a CD or two.)

■ **Back up to hard drives**   This is the fastest approach and quite cost-effective. If you get two additional drives, perform a full backup to a second internal hard disk drive (or create a disk image) once a week and a differential or incremental backup at the end of each day. Every week or two, when the internal hard disk drive fills up, copy it to an external hard disk drive, erase the internal drive and start over. Store the external drive in a safe, offsite location. You could also use a single external drive if you don't need as much redundancy.

■ **Back up to DVD or tape**   This is more expensive and less convenient than backing up to hard disks but does provide easier portability, and the benefits of a DVD burner (such as the ability to create your own DVD movies). If you choose tape, look at the Onstream and Travan models.

Perform a full backup every one or two weeks and differential or incremental backups as frequently as necessary. Every week or two place the old, full backup set and incremental or differential backups off site, and reuse the offsite disks or tapes for current backups.

Tip   Images, video, and MP3 files are already compressed and can't be compressed more, so look for uncompressed capacity and speeds when comparing backup methods.

Video User

Video, especially DV or captured analog video, consumes more disk space than anything else (12 GB to 22 GB per hour), making it somewhat unreasonable to back up. As such, here are your best options.

■ **Rely on tape logs and project settings**   Perform batch captures from your source tapes and save the capture logs along with your project files. Back up everything but your video (see the Multimedia User section). When you're done with your video, export the project back to DV. If you lose your work or want to go back and edit a project that you already cleaned off your hard disk drive, recapture from the original source tapes.

■ **Back up to hard drives**   If you can't afford to lose a project you're working on, purchase another hard disk drive and back up your project to the disk drive. This is the fastest and least expensive way of backing up a small number of projects (8 to 12 hours should fit on a 120 GB disk drive).

■ **Back up to DAT**   If you need to archive or back up a really large amount of data, DAT is by far the cheapest over the long haul, though be prepared to keep swapping tapes.

DVD Burners—How to Pick the Right One   Currently, the market for DVD burners
is fragmented among a number of competing and incompatible standards. Here's a rundown of the
relevant players, all of which have settled upon 4.7 GB discs (although DVD-RAM and DVD+RW support double-sided 9.4 GB discs):

■   DVD-R discs are the DVD equivalent of CD-R. DVD-R discs are cheap and work in the
    broadest range of DVD players and DVD-ROM drives. Many Macintosh computers include
    DVD-R/CD-RW drives.

■   DVD-RAM discs are rewritable cartridges that can only be read in other DVD-RAM drives
    and some DVD-ROM drives—if you get cartridges that let you remove the discs. Some
    IBM and Gateway systems ship with combined DVD-RAM/DVD-R drives.

■   DVD-RW, the DVD equivalent of CD-RW, is rewritable and compatible with many DVD
    players and DVD-ROM drives. Some Sony computers use it.

■   DVD+RW, the newest standard, is an enhancement of the DVD-RW standard. Write
    speeds are faster, you don't have to format a disc before using it, and it's more compat-
    ible than DVD-RW. Dell and many other companies are switching to this standard.

■   DVD+R is the write-once format for DVD+RW drives. In general, it is just as cheap and
    compatible as DVD-R. The first DVD+RW units (manufactured before April 2002) didn't
    support DVD+R, although some can be upgraded with new firmware (the built-in soft-
    ware on the drive).

As the market for DVD burners matures, expect to see prices drop, speeds increase, and some
semblance of a standard emerge. We expect that DVD+RW will slowly pull ahead, with DVD-RW fad-
ing and DVD-RAM maintaining a loyal, but lesser following. DVD+R and DVD-R will probably coexist
indefinitely as write-once standards.

Using the Backup Wizard

Microsoft Backup comes with a convenient wizard that walks you through backing up your computer. If you want the simplest and quickest way to back up
your files, read on. If you're looking for more control over the backup process,
skip ahead to the Manually Performing Backups section.

Although Windows 98 includes Backup, it is not installed by default. If
Backup is not installed, perform the following steps:

1   In Control Panel, double-click Add/Remove Programs.

2   Click the Windows Setup tab, select System Tools, and then click
       Details.

3 Select the Backup checkbox and then click OK. Restart your computer if prompted.

To use the Backup Wizard to back up your files, follow these steps:

1 Click Start and choose Programs, Accessories, System Tools, and finally Backup. If you don't have a tape backup device, click No when Microsoft Backup tells you that it couldn't detect any backup devices.

2 Select Create A New Backup Job and click OK.

3 To back up your entire computer (everything on all hard drives), select Back Up My Computer. Otherwise, select Back Up Selected Files, Folder And Drives. Click Next to continue.

Caution The Backup Wizard can only back up Windows 98 properly if you select the Back Up My Computer option. To back up Windows 98 and only some of the other files on your hard disk drive, see "Manually Performing Backups" later in this chapter.

---

4 If prompted, select the files and folders you want to back up and click Next.

5 Choose whether to perform a full backup (All Selected Files) or an incremental backup (New And Changed Files) and then click Next.

6 Choose the backup medium, type a file name for the backup and then click Next.

7 Use the two check boxes in the next screen to control whether Microsoft Backup should verify the integrity of the data, which takes additional time, and whether it should compress the data to save space. Click Next to continue.

8 Type a name for the backup job so that you can load these settings another time and review the backup settings.

9 Click Start to begin the backup job.

Caution Anyone who obtains your backup tape or disc can access your files. For this reason, keep your backup media in a secure location and set a password for the backup, as described in the "Manually Performing Backups" section.

Manually Performing Backups

Although the Backup Wizard is a handy way of performing backups, using the main Microsoft Backup interface gives you more control over the process (though it doesn't allow automated backups—you need a third-party backup program, Windows 2000, or Windows XP for that).

To manually perform a backup using Microsoft Backup, use the following steps.

1 Select which folders and files you want to back up, as shown in Figure 12-5.

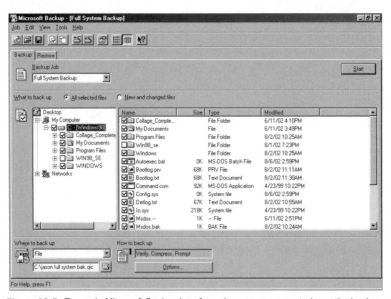

Figure 12-5 The main Microsoft Backup interface gives you more control over the backup process than does the Backup Wizard.

2 In the What To Back Up frame, select All Selected Files to perform a full backup, or New And Changed Files to perform a partial backup.

> **Note** Microsoft Backup automatically performs whichever type of partial backup is set as the default type. To change which type of partial backup you perform, click Options, click the Type tab, select New And Changed Files Only, and then select Differential Backup Type or Incremental Backup Type.

3 In the Where To Backup frame, choose the backup medium and type a descriptive file name for the backup.

4 Click Options to specify such things as backup comparison, compression, password, and whether to back up the Windows Registry (you must select this option to properly back up Windows).

> **Note** New tapes might need to be formatted or initialized before you can use them. To do so, choose Media from the Tools menu and then choose either Format or Initialize.

5   Click Save Job (the floppy disk icon in the toolbar), type a descriptive file name in the Job Name text box, and then click Save.

6   Click Start to begin.

Restoring from a Backup

Two situations generally call for restoring from a backup. The first is when you realize that some files (most likely your data) have become corrupted, and you want to go back to an earlier version of the file when the data is intact. The second is the dreaded "my hard disk drive burst into flames" (or similar) scenario. These situations are covered in the next two sections.

Restoring Files from Within Windows

If you can boot Windows, use Microsoft Backup to restore selected files from your backup set. Here's how.

1   Click Start, choose Programs, Accessories, System Tools, and finally Backup.

2   Select Restore Backed Up Files and click OK.

3   Choose the backup medium, and type the file name of the backup or click the folder icon to browse for the backup. Click Next to continue.

4   Select the backup set from which you want to restore and then click OK.

5   Select the files and folders you want to restore, and click Next.

6   Choose where Microsoft Backup should place the restored files— either the Original Location or an Alternate Location (if you want to compare the files)—and then click Next.

7   Choose when existing files should be replaced (if at all) and then click Start. Insert the requested media and click OK to begin the restore process.

Disaster—Restoring When You've Lost Everything

If a major disaster occurs, the first thing that you should do is try to get Windows running again.

If you can't get Windows to reboot, use the following procedure to boot from your Windows 98 boot disk (grab someone else's if you must) and automatically reinstall Windows.

Tip   If you have trouble getting the System Recovery Wizard to work, perform a normal installation of Windows and restore it using instructions in the previous section.

---

1 Insert a Windows 98 boot disk in the computer's floppy drive and restart your computer. If the computer doesn't boot from the floppy disk, go into your system settings (BIOS) and change the drive boot order to boot from the floppy disk first.

2 Boot with CD-ROM support. Insert the Windows 98 CD-ROM and type the following commands (where D is your CD-ROM drive): **cd d:\tools\sysrec\pcrestor.bat.**

> **Note** If your hard disk is really messed up, you might need to format, repartition, or replace the drive (though this is a last resort).

3 After Windows is finished reinstalling itself, log on and click Next in the first screen of the System Recovery Wizard.

4 Type your registration info, click Next, and then Finish.

5 Select Restore Backed Up Files and click OK.

6 Choose the backup medium and type the file name of the backup, or click the folder icon to browse for the backup. Click Next to continue.

7 Select the backup set from which you want to restore and click OK.

8 Select the files and folders you want to restore and then click Next.

9 Choose where Microsoft Backup should place the restored files— either the Original Location or an Alternate Location (if you want to compare the files) and then click Next.

> **Caution** When you choose Always Replace, any changes made to files after the backup are lost. If you have important changes that aren't backed up, select Replace The File On My Computer Only If The File Is Older. If you're performing a full restore of Windows, the computer might not work properly if you don't select Always Replace Files. If you want to preserve recently altered data files, don't select those files.

10 Choose when existing files should be replaced (if at all) and then click Start. Insert the requested media and click OK to begin the restore process.

11 If you haven't changed your hardware (for example, by replacing your hard disk) or any system settings since the last backup, click Yes when asked if you want to restore hardware and system settings to the registry.

12 Once Windows is functioning properly, use the Restoring Files From Windows section to restore your incremental backups, starting from the oldest backup made after the full backup. To restore a differential backup, restore the most recent differential backup you have.

Dealing with Startup Problems

There are few better ways to start a busy day than to fire up your computer only to find that it won't boot. We can help you get Windows back up and running—just use the following sections.

Using Safe Mode

Safe Mode is your front-line offense against a computer that won't boot. This special troubleshooting mode allows you to boot Windows with the minimum required drivers and system files, maximizing the probability of booting successfully. Once in Safe Mode, you have the full array of Windows programs and utilities at your disposal.

To use Safe Mode, follow these steps.

1 Turn on your computer or restart it.

2 Press and hold the Ctrl key.

3 Choose Safe Mode from the Windows 98 Startup Menu and then press Enter. (If Windows fails to start successfully in Safe Mode, you've got bigger problems—see the section "When Windows Won't Start in Safe Mode.")

4 Restart the computer normally. Sometimes Windows miraculously decides to work again. If not, reboot into Safe Mode again and move on to the next step.

> **Tip** When troubleshooting startup problems, ask yourself, "What's changed?" If you recently added a new device, installed a program, or changed a system setting, this is the most likely cause. Try removing the device, uninstalling the program, or changing the system setting. If error messages appear during boot up, query the Microsoft Knowledge Base (*http://support.microsoft.com*) for additional information about the errors.

5 Click Start, choose Run, type **msconfig** in the Open box, and then click OK.

6 Choose the Selective Startup option on the General tab, as shown in Figure 12-6, and then try the boot options listed in Table 12-4 under Set 1. Click OK and then restart the computer normally.

Figure 12-6 The System Configuration Utility (Msconfig.exe) is the best tool with which to troubleshoot startup problems.

7   If Windows doesn't load, reboot into Safe Mode and try Set 2. If Set 2 doesn't work, try Set 3. The set that enables you to boot Windows normally tells you where the problem is:

●   Set 1 works—The problem is in the System.ini or Win.ini files.

●   Set 2 works—The problem is in the Config.sys or Autoexec.bat files.

●   Set 3 works—The problem is with a program loading from the startup folder.

Table 12-4   Startup Troubleshooting Sets

	Set 1	Set 2	Set 3
Process Config.sys File	Yes	No	Yes
Process Autoexec.bat File	Yes	No	Yes
Process Winstart.bat File	Yes	Yes	No
Process System.ini File	No	Yes	No
Process Win.ini File	No	Yes	Yes
Load Startup Group Items	Yes	Yes	No

8   Choose Normal Startup and then use the following sections to pinpoint and fix the problem. (See "Fixing Other Problems" later in this chapter if none of the sets work.)

Tip   Before editing any files, click Create Backup on the General tab to back up the relevant system files.

Fixing Problems with the Autoexec.bat or Config.sys Files

Windows 98 doesn't need the Config.sys or Autoexec.bat files to function and actually runs faster if these files are empty. If a line in these files is preventing Windows from loading properly, refer to the "Empty the Autoexec.bat and Config.sys Files" section earlier in this chapter for a walk-through on how to empty or streamline these files.

Fixing Problems with the System.ini or Win.ini Files

If the problem is in the System.ini or Win.ini files, click the Win.ini tab, expand the [Windows] section, and then clear the Load= and Run= check boxes.

   If that doesn't fix your problem, disable the entire win.ini file and reboot. If the problem is still there, you know it's the system.ini file; if it goes away, it's in the win.ini file. Use the System.ini and Win.ini tabs to disable lines until you've identified which one is causing the problem. Leave that line disabled. (If it's an important line, research it on Microsoft's Knowledge Base, in newsgroups, or with the help of Microsoft tech support.)

Fixing Problems with the Startup Folder

If the problem is in the Startup folder, open the System Configuration Utility and use the following procedures, starting with the first one and then working down.

■   Click the Startup tab, clear each check box, click OK, and then restart the computer. If the problem goes away, enable each Startup program, one by one, until the problem returns. To fix it, leave the last line you changed disabled, uninstall or reinstall the offending program, or contact the software developer for an updated version.

■   Choose the Selective Startup option on the General tab and enable everything but the Winstart.bat file. If the problem goes away, either back up and then delete this file, or use Notepad to edit the Winstart.bat file, located in the C:\Windows folder. Disable each line in the file, one by one, until you find the offending line. (Type **REM** in front of a line to disable it.)

■ If the problem still persists, a program loading from the Windows 98 registry might be causing the problems. To prevent the program from loading, use the following steps.

Caution   Editing the registry is extremely dangerous and could force you to rein-stall Windows. Always registry keys before editing them and don't make extraneous edits.

---

1 Click Start, choose Run, type **regedit** in the Open box, and click OK.

2 One at a time, select the following keys and choose Export Registry File from the Registry menu.

● HKEY_LOCAL_MACHINE\Software\Microsoft\Windows\ CurrentVersion\Run

● HKEY_LOCAL_MACHINE\Software\Microsoft\Windows\ CurrentVersion\RunServices

3 Delete the key values (NOT the key itself) from among the following that you suspect might be causing the problems.

● HKEY_LOCAL_MACHINE\Software\Microsoft\Windows\ CurrentVersion\Run

● HKEY_LOCAL_MACHINE\Software\Microsoft\Windows\ CurrentVersion\RunServices

● HKEY_LOCAL_MACHINE\Software\Microsoft\Windows\ CurrentVersion\RunOnceEx

● HKEY_CURRENT_USER\Software\Microsoft\Windows\ CurrentVersion\Run

4 Restart your computer. If you find that your deletions broke something else, double-click the backup files you created (the .reg files) to merge the keys back into the system registry.

Fixing Other Problems

If none of the sets fix the problem, try these procedures, starting with the first one and working through them in order.

■ **Troubleshoot protected mode drivers**   Click Advanced on the General tab of the System Configuration Utility and select check boxes one by one, restarting after each one. If Windows boots properly, you've pinpointed the problem. For more information, see Microsoft Knowledge Base Article Q181966 at *http://support.microsoft.com.*

■ **Run the Windows Registry Checker**   Click Start and choose Programs, Accessories, System Tools, and then System Information. Choose Registry Checker from the Tools menu.

■ **Disable PCI bus IRQ Steering**   Double-click System in Control Panel, click the Device Manager tab, expand the System Devices object, and then double-click PCI Bus. Click the IRQ Steering tab and clear Use IRQ Steering. Restart your computer and disable IRQ Steering in your BIOS (if necessary).

■ **Disable all unneeded devices**   Double-click the System icon in Control Panel, click the Device Manager tab, and then disable all unneeded devices (basically everything not under the System heading). To disable a device, double-click it and then select the Disable In This Hardware Profile. Some devices may be listed as Exists In All Hardware Profiles.

   If this fixes the problem, enable each device, starting with COM ports, hard disk controllers, and floppy disk controllers. (Reboot after each device you enable, and use Safe Mode to change display drivers or settings if you have display problems.) When you identify the device causing the problem, remove it, move it to a different slot, or troubleshoot it using the techniques covered in Chapter 9, "Conquering Computer Hardware."

   If the problem still isn't resolved, click Start and choose Programs, Accessories, System Tools, and then System Information. Then choose Automatic Skip Driver Agent from the Tools menu. For more information on this tool, see Microsoft Knowledge Base article Q186588 at *http://support.microsoft.com.*

■ **Check for damaged virtual device drivers (VxDs)**   Restart the computer, hold down the Ctrl key, and then select Step-By-Step Confirmation from the Windows 98 Startup menu, then press Enter. Type **Y** for all prompts up to "Load All Windows Drivers?" Type **Y** for this prompt and then **N** for all subsequent prompts, writing down each item (file name) for which you type **N**.

   If Windows boots successfully, perform this procedure again, but this time type **Y** for the first prompt for which you typed **N** the previous time. Continue this procedure until you identify which line(s) is preventing Windows from booting.

   When you find the offending file(s), uninstall and reinstall the program associated with the file referred to in the problem line. The file in question is a hidden .vxd file in the C:\Windows\System\Vmm32 folder. (Right-click the file in Windows Explorer, choose Properties, and then click the Version tab to view the file association.) If you can't figure out how to uninstall the files causing the problem, move them to a backup folder.

Tip   To display hidden files, in Control Panel, double-click Folder Options, click the View tab, and then choose the Show All Files option under the Hidden Files container.

■   **Use the System File Checker to check for changed system files**
Click Start and choose Programs, Accessories, System Tools and then System Information. Choose System File Checker from the Tools menu, choose Scan For Altered Files, and then click Start. If it finds any corrupted files, follow the prompts or use the Extract One File From Installation Disk option to replace them.

When Windows Won't Start in Safe Mode

If Windows won't start even in Safe Mode, you've got big trouble. However, this situation isn't dire—yet. Try these before you start crying.

■   Boot your computer with an antivirus recovery disk and scan your system for viruses.

■   Turn on your computer and enter the system BIOS (usually by pressing Delete or F2). Check to make sure all settings are correct, and consider resetting them to the default or most conservative settings.

■   Remove all unnecessary devices from your computer. This includes sound cards, modems, network adapters, USB and Firewire adapters, TV cards, and extra RAM modules. If your computer boots successfully, add devices back one by one until the problem returns. Then use Chapter 9, "Conquering Computer Hardware" to troubleshoot the device.

■   Run the Windows Registry Checker. To do so, restart the computer, hold down the Ctrl key, choose Command Prompt Only, type **scanreg,** press Enter, then follow the on-screen prompts.

■   Check the Msdos.sys file for incorrect settings. For information on doing this, refer to Microsoft Knowledge Base article Q118579 at *http://support.microsoft.com.*

■ Boot the computer with a Windows 98 boot disk and type **sys c:** at the command prompt. This writes a new Master Boot Record (MBR) to the hard disk drive.

If you still can't get Windows to boot, install Windows 98 into a new folder. If Windows doesn't install properly, you most likely have a hardware problem. If Windows installs OK, you can either restore from a backup or reinstall your programs and use the new Windows installation from now on. (Delete the old C:\Windows folder when you're sure that you don't have any data hidden within it.)

Dealing with Shutdown Problems

Windows 98 is notorious for freezing up while shutting down. Windows 98 states that it's shutting down but just sits there until you manually shut the computer off (and it never tells you that it's safe to do so). Troubleshooting shutdown problems is similar to troubleshooting startup problems from Safe Mode—here's a quick rundown.

■ Boot your system normally, open the System Configuration Utility, from the General tab choose Selective Startup, clear all check boxes, and then shut your system down. If it shuts down properly, repeat this, selectively enabling options. When you find the file that's causing the problem, use the tabs in the System Configuration Utility to troubleshoot the affected file by selectively disabling lines within it.

■ Disable fast shutdowns. To do so, click Advanced on the General tab of the System Configuration Utility and then select the Disable Fast Shutdown check box.

■ Change the Exit Windows sound to None, using the Sounds tool in Control Panel (as discussed in Chapter 10, "Wielding the Control Panel Tools"). If the problem goes away, you have a corrupted sound file. Replace the file, choose a different sound, or leave it disabled.

■ Disable all unneeded devices and check for damaged virtual device drivers. To do so, see the "Fixing Other Problems" section earlier in this chapter.

■ Check if Advanced Power Management (APM) is causing the problem. Double-click the System icon in Control Panel, click the Device Manager tab, expand the System Devices object, double-click Advanced Power Management, and select Force APM 1.0 Mode and Disable Power Status Polling (if your system uses APM).

■ If Windows still refuses to shut down properly and you're using Windows 98 SE, consult Microsoft Knowledge Base Article Q238096 at *http://support.microsoft.com*. This article includes additional trouble-shooting steps and a link to a software update to resolve this issue.

Key Points

■ Keeping Windows 98 and your other programs up-to-date provides the best stability, security and features—just as long as you don't install updates that you don't need or won't use.

■ The Maintenance Wizard makes it easy to schedule your routine housecleaning chores, such as defragmenting disks, checking for disk errors, and cleaning up unnecessary files.

■ Windows 98 runs best if you have at least 64–128 MB of RAM. Computer artists and video editors should have 256 MB of RAM, but no more than 512 MB.

■ You can make the most of your memory by closing or disabling unneeded programs and services.

■ Let Windows 98 manage virtual memory and its disk cache, despite what various Web sites might report. (However, if you have multiple disks, you might want to reposition the swap file.)

■ Video editing requires different optimization technsiques, such as dis-abling disk caching and using a separate hard disk for video files.

■ Backing up your data really is as important as your mother always said it was.

■ If Windows won't start, hold down the Ctrl key when booting and choose Safe Mode to boot Windows using a special diagnostic mode.

■ Use the System Configuration Tool (Msconfig.exe) to troubleshoot star-tup and shutdown problems.

Chapter 13

Building and Using a Network

Not long ago, networks were the domain of businesses and a few adventuresome home users. Then, in the span of a few short years, the world changed. Computer prices plummeted, the number of households and businesses with multiple computers skyrocketed, and *network* suddenly became a household word.

Today, whenever the same location has more than one computer, it makes sense to consider a network. Networks make the following tasks easy.

- **Share an Internet connection** If you have a broadband Internet connection, or more than one person at a time wants to go online, use a network to share the Internet connection.

- **Share a single printer on a network** Instead of several low-cost models, share one or two really good printers.

- **Share documents, image files, and music files** Access the files you need, regardless of which computer they're on.

- **Easy backups** A single backup device (such as a tape backup or DVD burner) can back up all computers on the network.

Note   Most computers can't be *completely* backed up remotely. For a complete
system backup, run Backup on the local computer and save the backup file directly
to the backup device across the network. If you can't save the backup file directly to
the backup medium (as would be the case for tape drives), back up the system
locally and then use the computer with the backup device to transfer the backup file
to tape.

■ **Multiplayer games**   Multiplayer games are fun, and with a network
   you can play them with friends in the same location.

This chapter covers how to design a network, build it, test it, and secure it
from hackers. Advanced users will feel right at home. However, networking
neophytes shouldn't feel like a duck in Las Vegas. (Just when you find a pond,
it explodes and pirates jump out.) You'll find plenty of tips, hints, definitions,
and background information throughout the chapter.

More Info   For a more thorough discussion of creating a home network, pick up a copy of
Faster Smarter Home Networking by Curtis Frye (Microsoft Press).

Before You Begin: Designing a Network

Designing a network means choosing a network type and selecting an Internet
connection sharing method.

If you're a pro who already has a network design figured out, go ahead and
skip to the "Building a Network" section. Otherwise, read on.

Choose the Best Network Type(s)

To choose the type of network you need, start by looking at the locations of the
computers. If you can easily run cable between all computers, look at a wired
solution—most likely Fast Ethernet. If the computers are widely scattered or if
you want to be able to work on the laptop in the garden, a wireless solution
such as 802.11b (WiFi) might be more suitable.

A Fast Ethernet network is inexpensive, fast, reliable, and secure. An
802.11b wireless network costs more, is slower, slightly less reliable and less
secure—but much more flexible.

Once you've thought about these questions, make a choice from the available network technologies, as described below and shown in Table 13-1 (put
Fast Ethernet, 802.11b, and Home PNA on the short list).

Table 13-1   Common Network Technologies

Technology	Speed	Real-world Speed	Cabling	Max Distance	Other hardware Requirements
Ethernet	1000/100/10 Mbps	200/47/8 Mbps	Cat 5 or 6	328 feet	Hub or switch
802.11b (WiFi)	11 Mbps	6 Mbps	Wireless	1800 feet	Access point
802.11a (WiFi5)	54 Mbps	28 Mbps	Wireless	1650 feet	Access point
HomePNA	10 Mbps	3 Mbps	Telephone wiring	1000 feet	None

Tip   The best solution for the network might be a combination of network technologies. For example, use Fast Ethernet for easily wired computers and 802.11b for the laptops and computers in other locations, or maybe HomePNA if you don't need wireless access.

■ **Ethernet**   The most popular form of networking, Ethernet is fast (100 megabits per second [Mbps] for Fast Ethernet; 10 Mbps for Ethernet, and 1000 Mbps for Gigabit Ethernet), inexpensive and reliable. It's also widely available—the computer might already have an Ethernet adapter installed.

To use an Ethernet network, you need an Ethernet adapter for each computer (available in Peripheral Component Interconnect [PCI], universal serial bus [USB], PC Card, and CompactFlash formats), a central hub or switch into which all computers plug, and Category (CAT) 5 or CAT 6 cabling to connect each computer to the hub (CAT 6 is rated for Gigabit Ethernet, and sometimes referred to as Enhanced CAT 5). Each computer can be a maximum of 328 feet away from a hub.

■ **802.11b (WiFi) Wireless Networks**   802.11b is an extremely popular wireless networking technology that is widely used in businesses and many public places, such as airports, coffee shops, and hotels. It's also available for home use. It's relatively fast (11 Mbps maximum with 2.5-6 Mbps is typical), and has good range (up to 328 feet indoors and 1800 feet outdoors, depending on conditions and the product).

To use 802.11b, you need an 802.11b adapter for each computer (which comes in PCI, USB, PC Card, and CompactFlash formats). If you want to communicate with computers on an Ethernet network, you also need an 802.11b access point (which connects 802.11b wireless networks to wired Ethernet networks), or a cable/DSL router with built-in 802.11b support (a preferred solution for most people).

Caution   All wireless technologies introduce significant security risks. When using wireless networking, always use some sort of security measures, such as Wired Equivalent Privacy (WEP). For more information, see the "Protecting a Network from Hackers" section of this chapter.

■ **802.11a (WiFi5)**   The follow-up to 802.11b, this wireless networking technology is faster (54 Mbps, with 22-28 Mbps real-world speeds) and less prone to interference, operating at 5GHz. Unfortunately, it's not compatible with 802.11b, so look for combination devices (or upcoming 802.11g devices, which are backward compatible). Functionally, 802.11a is identical to 802.11b.

Tip   Purchasing wireless networking gear from the same vendor is a good way to minimize problems and maximize performance, especially if you want to use products that operate at higher than the default 802.11b or 802.11a speeds.

■ **HomePNA 2.0**   HomePNA is a networking technology that communicates with other computers over existing phone lines. HomePNA 2.0 is reasonably fast, with 10 Mbps theoretical speeds and around 3 Mbps real-world speeds (HomePNA 3.0 is slated to increase this to 128 Mbps).

To use HomePNA, each computer needs a HomePNA adapter (usually in USB or PC Card format) and a phone jack on the same phone line (multiple computers can share a single outlet using a splitter).

Try This!   You can easily connect two computers without a network. If both computers have Ethernet adapters, use a crossover cable to connect the two computers without using a hub. (A crossover cable is a special cable with some of its wires crossed—it's used to connect two computers or hubs directly to each other.) Some other approaches are as follows:

■ Two computers with 802.11b adapters can use their ad-hoc mode to communicate wirelessly.

■ Purchase a USB Direct Connect kit to connect two computers using USB cables and proprietary networking software.

■ Use a parallel or serial cable and Windows Direct Cable Connection. Click Start and choose Programs, Accessories, Communications, and finally Direct Cable Connection. (If the program isn't already installed, double-click Add/Remove Programs in Control Panel, click the Windows Setup tab, and select Direct Cable Connection. under Communication.)

Mixing and Matching Networks To use more than one network type, you need a *bridge* to connect the types. Like a bridge connecting two sides of a river, it allows users to communicate with other network types.

Bridges can be hardware, such as a HomePNA/Ethernet bridge or 802.11 access point, a Windows XP computer with two network adapters (one of each network type), or a Cable/DSL router with built-in support for multiple network types. Another device is the 2wire HomePortal, which serves as a firewall and Internet connection-sharing device for networks using any combination of Ethernet, HomePNA, and 802.11b.

Choose an Internet Connection Sharing Method

Sharing an Internet connection is a primary reason people use networks—especially at home. Although Internet connection sharing can be done with a basic dial-up connection, it's most popular when people have a cable or DSL Internet link.

There are three ways to share an Internet connection, each discussed in the following sections.

Additional IP Addresses

With a cable or DSL Internet connection, you can usually lease additional Internet Protocol (IP) addresses—one for each additional computer—from the cable or DSL provider. You will also need an Ethernet hub or switch with an uplink port, into which the external cable or DSL adapter plugs.

With this method, each computer is directly on the Internet, making it easy to host Internet applications such as game servers and videoconferences. It also requires the least amount of hardware and is often the only method officially supported by the Internet service provider (ISP).

The disadvantages include no security against hackers and the additional monthly fee for each extra IP address.

> **Caution**   Install personal firewall software such as ZoneAlarm (*http://www.zonealarm.com*) on any computer directly attached to the Internet to reduce the risk of successful attack.

Windows ICS

Windows Internet Connection Sharing (ICS) is an easy and safe way to share a connection. You'll need a computer running Microsoft Windows 98 Second Edition (SE) to act as host. Plug the Internet connection into a network adapter on this machine, and a second network card on the machine connects to the local network.

> **Note** Microsoft Windows Millennium Edition (Me), Windows 2000, and Windows XP also come with the ICS feature. In addition to ICS, Windows XP includes a personal firewall that provides limited protection to the network (though other firewalls, such as ZoneAlarm, are better and work on Windows 98 as well).

This approach is inexpensive (all you need is a second network adapter). Other computers can be easily added to the network, and the host computer can also easily host Internet applications (because it's directly connected to the Internet).

Unfortunately, this approach exposes the Internet sharing computer directly to the Internet and any hacker who wanders by. Firewall software is necessary on the host computer to protect the network. In addition, the host computer must be turned on for other computers to have access to the Internet.

Cable/DSL Router

A cable/DSL router connects externally to the Internet through a cable modem, external DSL modem, or an external dial-up modem, and talks to the Internet on behalf of your private computers. Internally, it connects to the local network and uses Network Address Translation (NAT) to translate between the private IP addresses the router assigns to the local computers and the router's IP address, which is the only address visible to the Internet. This provides a measure of hacker protection, and many routers supplement it with more sophisticated firewall features.

This solution provides the highest level of security to the computers, makes it easy to connect the computers (because the router automatically provides computers with IP addresses), and doesn't require that a computer be running all the time. It's also low-cost, with many cable/DSL routers costing no more than a hub or access point (which you'd need anyway).

A disadvantage is that setting up Internet applications such as game servers and video conferencing can be difficult, and troubleshooting a broken Internet connection can be more difficult.

Choosing a Cable/DSL Router With countless cable/DSL routers to choose from, figuring out which router to buy can be daunting. Start by doing some research on http://www.pcmagazine.com. Then look for routers that support all the network types you have in use, support the security features you want, and have helpful features such as a serial port for connecting an external modem (in case the broadband connection fails or doesn't exist) or a built-in print server.

Building a Network

To actually set things up, you need to physically plug in the network connections, get the Internet connection working, and then get the rest of the computers talking to each other across the network. If the network is already set up and you just need to add a computer to the network, skip to the "Set Up Client Computers" section.

Tip When setting up a network, keep it simple at the start and enable only what's needed to make the network function. After the network is working properly, you can enable security features such as WEP encryption and any other fancy features you like.

Set Up Network Hardware

The first step is laying cable and plugging things in. Use the following steps as a guide. (You might have additional steps to perform as well—consult the manuals.)

1 Place hubs, switches, access points, and routers in the proper locations. Cable/DSL routers, switches, and hubs need to be placed near the Internet connection and preferably close to the other computers. If you have separate access points, place them as close to a central location as possible without defeating the benefits of being wireless.

2 Carefully run Ethernet cable so that it doesn't bend unduly or run too close to fluorescent lights, uninterruptible power supply (UPS) devices, and anything else that creates strong electromagnetic fields. Also, don't coil the cables.

Caution Cable used under a drop ceiling or under a raised floor must be fire-retardant "plenum-grade" cabling and/or metal conduit. Never use standard cables in these spaces.

---

3 Install network cards (refer to the network card's instructions for help with this).

4 Carefully plug the network cables into all devices. Cables should click in and an activity light should start flickering when the devices on both ends of the cable are on and functioning (additional help is provided in the following sections).

Share the Internet Connection

After setting up the network hardware, the next step is to set up the Internet connection and share it with the rest of the computers. This lets you get back on the Internet quickly and also makes it easy to get the other computers working on the network.

Connect Computers Directly to the Internet

To connect all of the computers directly to the Internet, contact your ISP, lease as many IP addresses as you have computers, and then follow the directions they provide or use the following steps if they leave you on your own.

1   Connect the external cable modem or DSL adapter to the uplink port of the Ethernet hub through a crossover cable (which should come with the cable modem or DSL adapter). See Figure 13-1 for the layout.

2   If the ISP provides static IP addresses, set up each computer with the IP address, subnet mask, gateway, and Domain Name System (DNS) server addresses provided to you, as discussed in the "Set Up Client Computers" section of this chapter. Otherwise, enable automatic addressing so that the computers can obtain their address from the ISP's Dynamic Host Configuration Protocol (DHCP) server.

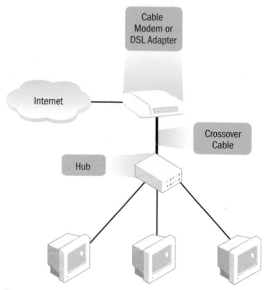

Figure 13-1 Here's an example of a network layout with all computers connecting directly to the Internet.

> ***See Also***   *Definitions of most of these terms are given in the "Setting Up A Cable/ DSL Router" section of this chapter, or you can consult http://www.webopedia.com. Comprehension is strictly optional.*

Using the Windows 98 SE Internet Connection Sharing Feature

To set up Internet Connection Sharing, lay out the connections using Figure 13-2 as a guide. Then follow the steps below.

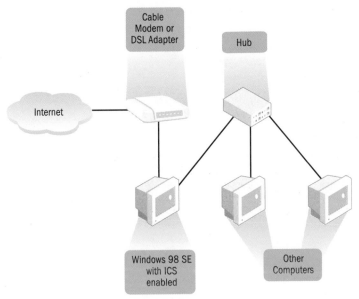

Figure 13-2 Here's an example of a network layout that uses Windows 98 SE Internet Connection Sharing.

1   Follow the ISP's instructions or use the Internet Connection Wizard to set up the Internet access, as discussed in Chapter 6, "Fearless Web Browsing."

> **Note**   If you have an external cable modem or DSL adapter, plug it into the computer's network adapter using the crossover cable provided —a standard Ethernet cable might not work properly.

2   In Control Panel, double-click the Add/Remove Programs icon.

3   Click the Windows Setup tab, select Internet Tools, and click Details.

4   Select Internet Connection Sharing, click OK, and then click OK again.

5   Choose Dial-Up Connection to share a dial-up Internet connection or High-Speed Connection to share a cable or DSL connection, and then click Next.

6   Select the network adapter or dial-up connection through which you connect to the Internet, and click Next again.

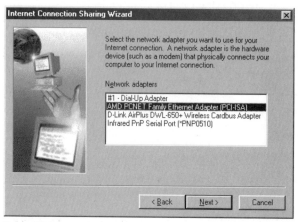

Figure 13-3 Use the Internet Connection Sharing Wizard to select the network adapter you want to use.

Tip   USB network adapters aren't fast enough to keep up with a Fast Ethernet network, but they are fast enough to keep up with a cable or DSL Internet connection. If you have one USB network adapter and one internal network adapter, use the USB adapter for the Internet connection.

---

7   To create an Internet Connection Sharing setup disk for Microsoft Windows 95 and Windows 98 clients, insert a blank floppy disk and then click OK; otherwise, click Cancel. (This disk contains a program that you can run to properly configure other computers' Web browsers.)

8   Click Finish when you're done. Then use the "Setup Client Computers" section of this chapter to get the rest of the computers on the network working.

Tip   To disable ICS, go to Control Panel, double-click the Internet Options icon, click the Connections tab, click Sharing, and then clear the Enable Internet Connection Sharing check box. You can also use this dialog box to change the network adapter used for the local network and for the Internet connection.

Setting Up a Cable/DSL Router

Before setting up the router, plug the Internet connection directly into a computer and get it working properly. Then write down the mail and news server settings, as described in the "Before You Begin: Find The Mail and News Server Addresses" sidebar. The layout for this type of connection is shown in Figure 13-4.

Before You Begin: Find the Mail and News Server Addresses

Before you set up a router, you need to know the fully qualified domain names (the full network address) of the news server, mail servers—Post Office Protocol (POP), or Internet Message Access Protocol (IMAP) and Simple Mail Transfer Protocol (SMTP)—and the proxy server.

Normally, you can find these settings on the cable or DSL installation work order. If you can't find them there, view the mail settings in Microsoft Outlook Express by choosing Accounts from the Tools menu, selecting an e-mail or news account, clicking Properties, and then writing down the server names in the Server tab. Then get the proxy server by double-clicking Internet Options in Control Panel, clicking the Connections tab, clicking LAN (local area network) Settings, and then writing down the proxy server name.

However, if the ISP provided you only with short names such as *mail* and *proxy*, open an MS-DOS Prompt window and type **ping** followed by the first short name you have, for example, **ping mail**. Write down the fully qualified domain name (FQDN) of the server, for example, *mail.attbi.com*, and then ping the next short name. Once the router is set up, replace the short names in Outlook Express and Internet Options with the fully qualified domain names (FQDN).

Although cable/DSL routers differ, use these steps in addition to the device's instruction manual.

1 Plug the Internet connection into the WAN port on the router and plug the individual computers into the LAN ports (as directed by the router's setup guide and shown in Figure 13-4).

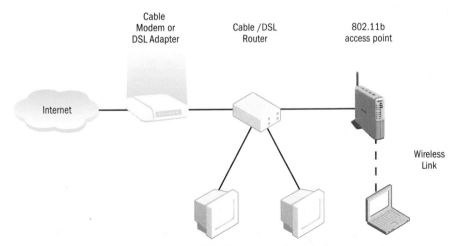

Figure 13-4 This layout includes a wireless 802.11b access point and a laptop.

2   Open Internet Explorer and follow the router's instructions for con-
        necting to the router's setup page (usually by typing **192.168.1.1** or
        192.168.2.1 in the Address bar). If it doesn't connect, you might have
        to configure the computer to use Automatic Addressing—see the "Set
        Up Client Computers" section of this chapter for help with this.

3   Log on using the default password (which is usually blank or **admin**).

After logging into the router, use its setup Web page to enter the following
information. (The setup page from a Linksys router is shown in Figure 13-5; different devices contain different settings, so use the following list as a guide).

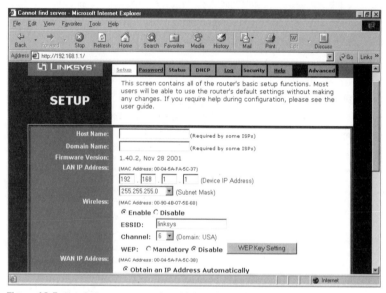

Figure 13-5 Here's the setup page for a Linksys Cable/DSL router with built-in 802.11b support.

■   Change the default password to a more secure password. This is vitally
    important for wireless networks, and a good safeguard for wired net-
    works as well. If you forget the password, simply reset the router to its
    factory defaults.

■   If the ISP provides you with a specific host name such as C893473,
    enter this in the Host Name box.

■   If the ISP provides you with a specific domain name, such as attbi.com,
    type this in the Domain Name box.

■   If the ISP provides you with a static IP address, type it in the WAN IP
    Address box. Otherwise, choose Obtain An IP Automatically, DHCP, or
    a similarly named setting.

Lingo A *Wide Area Network* (*WAN*) is a network that spans a huge geographical area; the Internet is an example of a WAN. A *Local Area Network* (*LAN*) covers a small geographical area within which all computers connect using a relatively high-speed connection.

- If you're using a static IP address, type the subnet mask provided by the ISP.

- If you're using a static IP address, type the IP address of the default gateway, provided by the ISP (a gateway is a server that connects you with another network, in this case, the Internet).

- If you're using static IP address, type the IP addresses of the DNS servers, provided by the ISP.

Lingo An *IP address* (for example, 192.168.1.10) is the network location for a computer (*host*). A *subnet mask* segments a network into two or more *subnets*, or portions of the network. Because IP addresses are cumbersome, the *Domain Name System* (*DNS*) translates user-friendly host and domain names (for example server1.microsoft.com) into IP addresses and vice versa. *Dynamic Host Configuration Protocol* (*DHCP*) servers provide an automated means of giving computers IP addresses.

- If you use a dial-up DSL connection, type the username and password and specify whether the router should automatically connect when needed (Connect On Demand), or attempt to keep the connection open indefinitely (Keep Alive).

- If you want to change the IP address of the router on the internal network, enter the IP address you want to use for the router in LAN IP Address. This will also be the same IP address you use to access the router's setup page.

- If you want to change the subnet mask of the network, choose or type the subnet mask you want to use in LAN Subnet Mask.

- Enter a unique name for the wireless network in Wireless SSID (Service Set Identifier). The name must be 32 characters or less. Change this from the default to make it harder for people to connect to the wireless network.

- Disable the setting to Allow Broadcast SSID to increase security. When enabled, any wireless user within range can see the network and potentially gain access to it. When disabled, users need to know the network is there and type in the correct SSID.

▪ Use the Channel setting to specify which wireless channel the network should use. All devices on the wireless network must use the same channel. Changing the channel from the default makes it harder for unknown users to connect to the network.

▪ Use the DHCP Server setting to enable the router to provide IP addresses to other devices on the network automatically.

▪ The DHCP Starting IP Address is the first IP address you want to assign to client computers on the network. Keep the default unless you have reason to change it. Most users make this number between 5 and 100 numbers higher than their LAN IP Address.

▪ The Number of DHCP Users specifies the maximum number of simultaneous IP addresses the network should support. Leave the default.

▪ The DHCP Client Lease Time setting determines how long each computer or device gets to keep its address before it must renew it. Shorter times mean that addresses are reused quicker and clients get updated DNS server addresses quicker (should they change). Longer times make it less confusing locating computers on the network using IP address, because they change less often. Between 1 day and 1 month is usually the best setting.

Note   Each device or computer on a network needs to have a unique IP address. The easiest way to manage IP addresses is to configure each device to automatically obtain an address (using DHCP) and then set up the router to provide addresses automatically (enable the DHCP server). If you want to use static IP addresses for some devices, make sure that they don't conflict with each other or the router (which must use a static IP address for the local network). They should also be outside the DHCP address range.

Set Up Client Computers

The following steps demonstrate how to connect a Windows 98 computer to an existing network, including Windows NT or Windows 2000 domains.

1 Install an appropriate network card and drivers in the Windows 98 computer.

2 In Control Panel, double-click the Network icon.

3 Make sure the following network components are listed. If they aren't listed, click Add to install any missing components.

● Client For Microsoft Networks

● Ethernet Adapter (or appropriate network adapter)

● TCP/IP->Ethernet Adapter (or appropriate network adapter)

4   Select the TCP/IP component associated with the network adapter you use to connect to the network (for example, TCP/IP -> AMD PCNET Family Ethernet Adapter) and then click Properties.

5   If you're using DHCP on the network to automatically assign IP addresses (as would be the case if you're using Windows ICS, a Cable/DSL router or a Windows Server network), select the Obtain An IP Address Automatically option on the IP Address tab.

6   If you're using static IP addresses, select the Specify An IP Address option, and then type the static IP address you want to use, as well as the subnet mask in use on the network. When you're finished, use the Gateway and DNS Configuration tabs to specify the default gateway and the DNS servers provided to you by the ISP or network administrator. Click OK when you're done.

7   To connect to a Windows domain, select Client For Microsoft Networks from the list of network components, click Properties, select Log On To Windows NT Domain, and then type the name of the Windows domain.

8   Click OK, insert the Windows 98 CD if necessary, and then restart the computer, if prompted.

9   In Control Panel, double-click Internet Options and then click the Connections tab. (If you created an Internet Connection Sharing setup disk, you can use this disk instead in place of the rest of these steps.)

10   Select the Never Dial A Connection option or the Dial Whenever A Network Connection Is Not Present option. If the ISP provides you with a manual proxy server address, click LAN Settings and type the appropriate server name and port (usually 80 or 8080) in the Address and Port text boxes.

11   Open Microsoft Internet Explorer and see if you have connectivity to the Internet. If not, see the "Testing and Troubleshooting a Network" section of this chapter. If you're using a wireless network, refer to the "Connect to Wireless Networks" section.

More Info   Refer to the "Forcing Accounts to Use a Dial-Up or LAN Connection" section of Chapter 7, "Using E-Mail and Newsgroups" for information on changing the Internet connection settings for Outlook Express.

Connect to Wireless Networks

Computers that connect to a wireless network require more steps than wired networks. After following the procedures outlined in the previous section, you need to "associate" with the wireless network. Though the procedure varies from adapter to adapter, here's the general idea.

1   Open the driver software, usually by double-clicking its icon in the System Tray or by right-clicking it and choosing View Available Wireless Networks.

2   Click SiteSurvey, View Available Networks, or similarly named link.

3   Select the network from the list (if the network is broadcasting its SSID) and click Connect. If network name broadcasting is disabled on the network (recommended), click Add or a similarly named button, and enter the appropriate information for the network.

Note   802.11 network adapters have two modes of operation—infrastructure mode and ad-hoc mode. Infrastructure mode is used for connecting to an access point or cable/DSL router with built-in wireless connectivity. Ad hoc mode is for networking directly with other wireless adapters—without using an access point.

Sharing Files on a Network

Not only does a network make it easy to share documents, it also permits such activities as playing the MP3 songs across the network, backing up to a shared CD burner, and copying scanned pictures from one computer to another computer.

Enabling File and Print Sharing

Before you can share files or printers with other computers on the network, you need to enable file and printer sharing. To do so, use the following steps.

1   In Control Panel, double-click the Network icon and click File and Print Sharing.

2   Choose whether to allow other network users access to the files and/ or printers and then click OK.

3   Click the Identification tab and type a unique and (preferably) descriptive name for the computer in the Computer Name box. This name can't contain spaces or punctuation of any type and must be 15 characters or less.

4   Enter a name for the workgroup in the Workgroup box. (This should be the same for all computers on the network.)

5   Optionally type a description of the computer in the Computer Description box, click OK, and then, if necessary, restart the computer.

Sharing a Folder

Once file and print sharing is enabled, you can share any folder on the computer with other users on the network. You can even share the floppy drive or CD burner so that other computers not fortunate enough to have one of these devices can make use of them.

To share a folder with other users on the network, follow these steps.

1 Open Windows Explorer, right-click the folder you want to share, and choose Sharing from the shortcut menu.

Tip Share individual folders instead of entire drives whenever possible. This makes it harder for someone who gains unauthorized access to the network to damage the system or gain access to data you don't want to share.

---

2 Choose the Shared As option and accept the default name for the shared folder, or type a more descriptive name in the Share Name text box. (The name can't have more than 12 characters.)

3 In the Access Type section, choose the level of access you want to allow other users.

4 To require a password to read or modify files, type a password in the Read-Only Password and/or Full Access Password boxes and then click OK.

Connecting to a Shared Folder on Another Computer

To access files on another computer, you must connect to a shared folder on that computer. To do this, use the following steps.

1 Open Network Neighborhood (either from the desktop or in Windows Explorer).

2 Double-click the computer that contains the shared folder you want to access and then double-click the shared folder to open it.

3 To map a shared folder to a drive letter so that you can use it just like any other drive on the system you're connecting from, right-click the shared folder and choose Map Network Drive from the shortcut menu. Choose a drive letter, as shown in Figure 13-6, optionally select Reconnect At Logon to connect to the folder every time you run Windows, and then click OK. (This also permits pre-Windows 95 applications to make use of the shared folder.)

Figure 13-6 Mapping a shared folder to a drive letter makes the folder easier to access.

Testing and Troubleshooting a Network

Testing and troubleshooting networks is a very big subject so we can only hit the high points in the space available. With that said, 95 percent of network problems can be quickly diagnosed using the procedures discussed in the following sections. If you can't get things working properly using this information, try posting to newsgroups (such as *Microsoft.public.win98.networking*), searching the Microsoft Knowledge Base at *http://support.microsoft.com*, or hiring a computer consultant.

Get the IP Address

If you can't connect to the Internet or other computers, start the troubleshooting effort by checking the current IP configuration. This tells you what network addresses (IP address, default gateway, DNS servers, and so forth) the computer is using *right now*, which is useful when troubleshooting connection problems.

To check the IP configuration, follow these steps.

1 Click Start, choose Run, type **winipcfg** in the Open box, and click OK.

2 In the IP Configuration dialog box, click More Info, select the proper network adapter from the box in the Ethernet Adapter Information section and take note of the following fields:

- *IP Address*—This should be in the range of addresses given out by the DHCP server, unless you have a static IP address.

- *Default Gateway*—This is the computer or router through which you connect to the Internet.

- *DNS Servers*—These computers are responsible for translating IP addresses into friendly names such as *www.microsoft.com*.

3 If the IP address listed begins with 169, it means the computer couldn't contact a DHCP server and had to make due without a valid IP address. Click Release and then Renew to make another attempt to get an IP address.

If you can't get an IP address from the DHCP server, check to make sure the DHCP server is responding. (Try performing this procedure on a different computer.) If it's not responding for all clients, reset the router or reboot the computer running Internet Connection Sharing. If only a single computer can't connect, check to make sure that the network adapter is installed correctly and that the network cables are securely plugged in to the computer and hub or router. Try swapping network cables—many network problems lie in cable failures.

Anyone There? Use Ping to Check Connectivity

Once you've verified that you can obtain an IP address from the DHCP server (router or Internet Connection Sharing computer), the next step in troubleshooting a network is to check for basic connectivity to key servers.

To do so, click Start, choose Programs, and then MS-DOS Prompt. Ping the following addresses in order, filling in the addresses you found using the previous section. To ping an address, type **ping** followed by the address, for example, **ping 192.168.1.1.** Windows should report 4 packets sent, 4 received and 0 lost.

Test the following addresses to continue troubleshooting connectivity problems.

- **The loopback address (127.0.0.1)**   This address tests the TCP/IP software in the computer by pinging itself. If any packets are lost, TCP/IP is installed improperly or corrupted. Try uninstalling TCP/IP using the Network icon in Control Panel, or using the System File Checker to check for corrupted files. (For more information, see Chapter 12, "Maintaining a Healthy Computer.")

- **The IP address**   Pinging its own IP address tests whether the network card is installed properly. If any packets are lost, check Device Manager for a hardware conflict, reinstall the network adapter drivers, or try moving the network card to a different PCI slot (if applicable).

- **The default gateway**   Pinging the default gateway lets you know whether the Internet Connection Sharing computer or cable/DSL router is functioning properly. If any packets are lost, check these devices and possibly reboot or reset them.

- **Another computer on the network**   Obtain the IP address of another computer on the network using **winipcfg** and then ping it. If it responds properly, the local network is working fine. If it doesn't, check the cables and network cards, and make sure that all computers have the correct TCP/IP settings.

■ **The ISP's default gateway**   This address is trickier to find—you need to run winipcfg on the ICS computer, or use the router's setup Web page to view the WAN status (as discussed earlier in this chapter).

If the ISP's default gateway responds, you have Internet connectivity. If it doesn't respond or it loses packets, the problem is with the Internet connection. Unplug the power from the cable or DSL adapter for about 30 seconds, plug it back in and then check to make sure that all the proper lights on the cable or DSL adapter are lit. (It might take up to five minutes for this to happen.) If the lights don't come on or you still have problems, it's time to call the ISP.

■ **The DNS servers**   If the DNS servers don't respond or lose packets, the ISP's DNS servers are probably at fault. If the DNS servers respond properly, the problem is probably outside the ISP's internal network.

■ **www.yahoo.com**   If the DNS servers are responding, try pinging Yahoo! or another Web site that responds to pings. (Microsoft doesn't.) If you receive the message "Ping request could not find host…," the problem is with name resolution. (Either the DNS server is having trouble, or you have the wrong DNS server addresses.) If it pings an IP address but packets are lost, the problem is most likely with the ISP's connection to the Internet. Either way, it's time to call the ISP. If the DNS servers aren't responding, don't bother pinging any addresses by name.

■ **An IP address on the Internet**   Try pinging 64.58.76.177 (*http://www.yahoo.com*) or 63.215.198.17 (*http://www.whitehouse.gov*). If the packets are lost, either the ISP's connection to the Internet is down or the IP addresses of the Web sites has changed. (Try pinging them from an Internet connection you know works to double-check.) If the packets get through but DNS didn't work, you've pinpointed the problem—the ISP's DNS servers. Either way, the ISP probably knows about this. You can either wait for them to fix it, or you can call and report it. You can also try adding a tertiary DNS server address from a different ISP so that you have some additional redundancy.

Tip   If the Internet connection is down for an extended period, ask for a credit on the bill.

Test File Sharing

If the Internet works fine but you can't use Network Neighborhood to browse the local network, use the following steps to troubleshoot the problem,

1   Make sure File and Print Sharing is enabled on each computer.

2   Try connecting by UNC name. Click Start, choose Run, and type a local computer's Universal Naming Convention, or UNC name, preceded by two backslashes—for example, \\Antonia.

   If this works, simply connect by UNC name or IP address, or wait until browsing is restored (this problem often fixes itself within 10 minutes or so).

3   Try connecting by IP address. Click Start, choose Run, and type a local computer's IP address preceded by two backslashes—for example, \\192.168.1.101.

   If this works, but UNC names don't, confirm that all computers have NetBIOS Over TCP/IP enabled. To check this setting, in Control Panel, double-click Network, select the appropriate TCP/IP entry, click Properties, and then click the NetBIOS tab.

4   Try using NetBIOS Enhanced User Interface (NetBEUI). Install NetBEUI on all computers and test file sharing again. To install NetBEUI, in Control Panel, double-click Network, click Add, select Protocol, click Add, select Microsoft, then NetBEUI, and then click OK.

Lingo   *NetBEUI* (NetBIOS Extended User Interface) is a Microsoft networking protocol that is easy to set up and fast. Unfortunately, it is no longer supported by Microsoft and is not easy to find in Windows XP. (It's on the CD.) For information on installing it on a Windows XP computer (if you have one of those on the network), see Microsoft Knowledge Base article Q301041 at *http://support.microsoft.com*.

Protecting a Network from Hackers

No network is completely safe from hackers, and even the most closely guarded networks have been invaded. Of course, the most frequently targeted networks have information of considerable value, which lessens the pressure on your network—you probably aren't guarding any nuclear secrets or millions of credit card numbers, and few hackers have your favorite recipe on their most wanted list.

You're not off the hook, however. The Internet has bred a new species of hacker dubbed "script-kiddies" that dabble with hacking by using highly polished hacking programs that lend point-and-click simplicity to network attacks. Throw in a bunch of poorly secured home and business networks attached to the Internet through always-on broadband Internet connection, and you've got a great big sandbox for these kiddies to play in. If you don't want these strangers running barefoot through your files, you must take security seriously.

Securing a Cable/DSL Router

Although most cable/DSL routers advertise their firewall and security features, the majority of these features must be turned on to be effective. Installing a router without adjusting these security settings provides limited protection at best, and literally broadcasts the network to the world at worst (if you have a wireless router).

To secure a network that makes use of a cable/DSL router, take the following measures and refer to the owner's manual for specific help. Also, change the router's password to prevent unauthorized users from changing router settings.

- Disable Remote Management and Remote Upgrade. If you want to manage the router remotely, set up a Virtual Private Network (VPN) connection instead, as discussed in Chapter 14, "Connecting from Home or on the Road."

- Block LAN requests to keep external users from pinging the router to see whether there are any ways to gain access to the network (through open ports). This makes the LAN largely invisible to hackers.

- Enable Stateful Packet Inspection (SPI), if available, to check incoming packets and verify that packets are coming from a location that you previously contacted, such as a Web site, and not from a hacker randomly scanning networks.

- Go to the excellent ShieldsUP! Web site (*http://www.grc.com*) and test the network for open ports. All ports should be closed and in Stealth mode.

Securing a Wireless Network

Wireless network security currently hinges on the WEP encryption protocol. Without it, hacking into the network is obscenely easy and can even be done accidentally. Although WEP is no longer completely secure (tools are available to crack it), it's good enough for all but the most sensitive small networks.

Although securing a wireless network takes a bit of effort, it's essential if you want to prevent hackers or mischievous kids from penetrating the network. The following list of security actions should be taken one at a time. After each action, confirm that all devices on the network are functioning properly before taking the next action. Refer to the owner's manual for the access point device for additional actions you can take.

- First, enable mandatory WEP encryption. To do so, first choose a key length (choose 128 bit if available on all the wireless adapters). Create a key (password) that's exactly 10 digits long (for a 40-bit key) or 26 digits long (for a 128-bit key) and consists exclusively of numbers and the letters A through F (hexadecimal).

- Enable WEP on each wireless device in the network, entering the key in each wireless device. (You might want to type it in a word processor and then copy and paste it.) Microsoft's Wireless Base Station, which includes mandatory WEP out-of-the-box and some of our other recommendations, lets you use a floppy disk to setup each computer with WEP.

> **Tip**   Although many access points support automatic key creation from so-called pass-phrases, we've had trouble getting these to work. Manually creating your own hexadecimal key is the most reliable way to get WEP working. Wireless clients also need to override automatic network handling and manually specify connection settings. (Consult the manual for information on how to do this if you have trouble connecting.)

- By default, wireless networks regularly broadcast their network name, making it easy to connect to them. Disable SSID broadcasting to make casual or accidental access to the network less likely.

- Even if you disable SSID broadcasting, it's relatively easy to guess the default SSID of common model access points. For this reason, rename the SSID to something less obvious. Poor choices include references to the physical location or company name, because these are not only easy to guess but also provide hackers that find the SSID with additional information about you.

- Most access points default to channel 6—choose a different channel to make it harder for people to connect. (Just make sure to change the channel on all the devices.)

■   Each network adapter has a unique Media Access Control (MAC) address that can be used to limit access to the network. Use the winipcfg command to find the MAC address of each computer and then configure the access point to allow only those MAC addresses to associate or connect to the access point.

■   Disabling DHCP and changing the router's IP address and subnet mask makes it more time consuming for hackers to access the network, though it also makes it more time-consuming for you to set up computers; you might consider this optional.

Securing File and Print Sharing

As nice as file and print sharing is, it can also make it easy for hackers to access the files and printers (though not many hackers make unauthorized printouts). Wireless network users should be particularly careful.

To tighten up file and print sharing security, disable File And Print Sharing for all network adapters except the one you use for communicating with other computers on the network. For example, disable File And Print Sharing on the modem, and the network card that connects to the cable or DSL adapter (if you're using ICS). To disable file and print sharing on the network card, follow these steps.

1   In Control Panel, double-click the Network icon.

2   Select the TCP/IP entry corresponding to the network adapter or dial-up adapter that you don't use for File And Print Sharing and then click Properties.

3   Click the Bindings tab.

4   Clear the Client For Microsoft Networks and File And Print Sharing For Microsoft Networks check boxes and then click OK. Click No when asked if you want to select a driver to bind with.

Tip   You can add an additional layer of protection to File And Print Sharing by installing NetBIOS Enhanced User Interface (NetBEUI) and using it for file sharing instead of TCP/IP, though you'll still need TCP/IP installed to use most network applications (such as multiplayer games) and to access the Internet.

Key Points

- Take time to design the network before building it.

- Cable/DSL routers provide the most elegant method of sharing an Internet connection and provide the best security available short of a specialized firewall device.

- Windows 98 SE comes with the Internet Connection Sharing (ICS) feature, which does a passable job of sharing an Internet connection at low cost, though with some security compromises.

- Enable File And Print Sharing if you want to share files and printers with other users on the network; disable it on any network adapter through which you don't want to share files.

- Use the winipcfg and ping commands to find the IP address information and check basic connectivity with other computers.

- Security is extremely important for all networks, and most cable/DSL routers need to be tweaked to provide adequate security.

- Wireless networks provide an unprecedented opportunity for hackers and *must* be secured if you want to avoid attack.

Chapter 14

Connecting from Home or On the Road

Although telecommuting and business travelers can stay in touch through phone, fax, and e-mail (see Chapter 7, "Using E-mail and Newsgroups"), sometimes there is no substitute for a connection to the office network.

Windows 98 provides two ways to connect remotely to a network. You can establish a network connection through a dial-up modem, just like a dial-up Internet connection, or you can connect to the Internet first and then use a Virtual Private Networking (VPN) connection to securely access your office network.

This chapter discusses how to work with dial up and VPN connections, including using the new Microsoft Layer 2 Tunneling Protocol/IP Security (L2TP/IPSec) VPN Client. It also demonstrates how to set up a computer to accept incoming calls so that you can dial in to your own computer when you're away.

Working with Dial-Up Connections

Working with dial-up connections is easy and might even be something you already know how to do (dial-up network connections work the same as dial-up Internet connections). In many cases, your network administrator provides you with a setup disk, detailed instructions, or even sets up a computer for you.

If you have to go it alone, the following sections demonstrate how to create dial-up connections, modify dial-up connection properties, and dial a connection.

Tip   Download and install the Dial-up Networking (DUN) 1.4 update. This update provides increased performance and security when making dial-up connections and is also necessary if you want to install L2TP/IPSec VPN support (discussed later). You can download DUN 1.4 from the Windows 98 Web site at *http://www.microsoft.com/windows98*. You can also find it by searching *http://support.microsoft.com/* for article Q285189.

Creating a Dial-Up Connection

Creating a dial-up connection to your office or corporate network is easy. Many network administrators provide you with a setup disk. If they don't, obtain the phone number and any other necessary settings from your network administrator and then use the following steps to create the connection yourself.

1   Open My Computer and then double-click the Dial-Up Networking folder.

2   Double-click Make New Connection.

3   Type a descriptive name for the connection (such as Connect To Work), select the proper modem, and then click Next.

4   Type the area code and phone number provided to you by the network administrator and then click Next.

5   Click Finish. Your dial-up connection is now complete, although you might need to change some of the settings before you can connect, as described in the next section.

See Also   *To properly access your workplace network, you might need to set up your computer to log on to its Windows domain. To do so, refer to the "Logging On to a Windows Domain" section of this chapter.*

Modifying Dial-Up Connection Properties

After creating a dial-up connection, adjust some settings, such as encryption and which network protocols the connection uses. To adjust dial-up connection properties, use the following steps.

1   Right-click the appropriate connection in the Dial-Up Networking folder and then choose Properties from the shortcut menu.

2   On the General tab, verify that the correct phone number is listed. Clear the Use Area Code And Dialing Properties check box if you want Windows to dial the number exactly as listed.

Tip Area code rules tell Windows which area codes are local and which are long distance. To create area code rules, in Control Panel, double-click the Modems icon, click the Dialing Properties button, and then click the Area Code Rules button. Then use the Area Code Rules dialog box to control when to dial the area code and when to dial 1.

---

3 Click the Server Types tab, as shown in Figure 14-1. In the Allowed Network Protocols area, clear all check boxes except the protocol in use on your office's network—most likely Transmission Control Protocol/Internet Protocol (TCP/IP). Doing so speeds up the connection. If you need to specify a static IP address, click TCP/IP Settings.

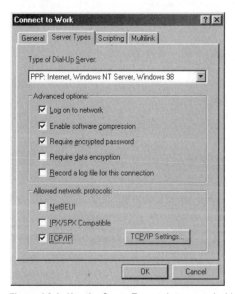

Figure 14-1 Use the Server Types tab to control which protocols are used, as well as encryption options.

4 Use the check boxes in the Advanced Options area to control whether or not encryption and compression are used. Click OK when you're done.

Tip Ask your network administrator whether to enable password and data encryption, or just enable these settings yourself to see if the connection works. (Some connections might not work otherwise.) Compression can be safely enabled on all network connections.

Dialing a Connection

Dialing into a network is no different from manually connecting to the Internet using a dial-up connection. To do so, use the following steps.

1 In the Dial-Up Networking folder, double-click the appropriate connection.

2 Type your user name and password in the familiar Connect To dialog box, (if necessary) and select the Save Password check box if you want to save yourself this hassle next time.

3 Verify that the phone number is correct and click Connect. After Windows establishes a connection, a connection icon appears in the System Tray. Work with the network as if you were directly connected, using Network Neighborhood or whatever network application you use.

4 To disconnect, right-click the connection icon in the System Tray and choose Disconnect from the shortcut menu.

Working with VPN Connections

VPN is a relatively new technology that allows you to safely connect to a business network through the Internet. To use a VPN connection, you first establish a normal Internet connection (through dial-up modem, cable, DSL, and so forth). Then you open a VPN connection, which works similarly to a dial-up connection, except instead of dialing a phone number and connecting over a phone line, it dials an IP address and connects over the Internet.

Before creating any connections, find out whether your company supports VPN connections and what settings you need. Then use the following sections to install VPN support in Microsoft Windows 98, create a VPN connection, modify a VPN connection, log on to a Windows domain, and establish the connection.

Note VPN connections won't work with older cable or satellite connections that use normal telephone lines for uploading. If you have one of these Internet connections, use a standard dial-up Internet connection whenever you want to use VPN.

Installing VPN Support

Windows 98 doesn't install VPN support by default, so you must install it using the Add/Remove Programs tool in Control Panel. There are also two updates that you might need to download and install to use VPN with your company's network. To perform these actions, use the following steps.

1 In Control Panel, double-click the Add/Remove Programs.

2 Click the Windows Setup tab, choose Communications, and then click Details.

3 Select the Virtual Private Networking check box, click OK, and then click OK again. You may need to have the Windows 98 CD in the CD-ROM drive. If you're prompted to keep newer versions of files, click Yes.

4 Restart your computer if prompted and then connect to the Windows 98 Web site (*http://www.microsoft.com/windows98*).

5 Download and install Dial Up Networking 1.4. (You might have to search for this.) If your office network uses Layer 2 Tunneling Protocol/Internet Protocol Security, (L2TP/IPSec), also download and install the Microsoft L2TP/IPSec VPN Client. (Windows 98 uses Point To Point Tunneling Protocol [PPTP] by default for VPN connections.)

Note The Microsoft L2TP/IPSec VPN client doesn't work if Internet Connection Sharing (ICS) is installed. It also won't install properly if 3Com Smart Agent is installed, so if you have a 3Com network card, uninstall this software, install the L2TP/IPSec client, and then reinstall 3Com Smart Agent.

Creating a VPN Connection

Creating a VPN connection to your office or corporate network is usually pretty easy. If your network administrator doesn't provide you with a setup disk, get the proper settings (such as VPN server IP address and whether L2TP/IPSec is required), and then use the following steps to create the connection yourself.

1 Open My Computer and then double-click the Dial-Up Networking folder.

2 Double-click Make New Connection.

3 Type a descriptive name for the connection (such as **VPN Connection To Work**).

4 In the Select A Device section, select Microsoft VPN Adapter (if your network accepts PPTP connections), or Microsoft L2TP/IPSec VPN Adapter 1 (if your network requires L2TP/IPSec connections), as shown in Figure 14-2.

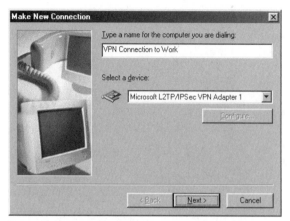

Figure 14-2 You can create VPN connections using PPTP (the default VPN protocol) or L2TP/IPSec, provided you have the Microsoft L2TP/IPSec VPN client installed.

5 Click Next, type the host name or IP address of the VPN server, and then click Next again. Click Finish when you're done.

See Also *To properly access your company network, you'll probably need to set up your computer to log on to its Windows domain. To do so, refer to the "Logging On to a Windows Domain" section of this chapter.*

Modifying VPN Connection Properties

After creating a VPN connection, you might need to adjust some settings, such as which network protocols are used and what host name or IP address the VPN server uses. If you're using L2TP/IPSec, you might also need to specify a shared key or certificate. Certificates (or Digital IDs) are small pieces of software obtained from a certificate authority such as Versign or your company's own certificate server that verify your identity (see the "Get a Digital ID" section of Chapter 11, "Playing It Safe," for more information).

To adjust VPN connection properties, use the following steps.

1 Right-click the VPN connection in the Dial-Up Networking folder and choose Properties from the shortcut menu.

2 On the General tab, verify that the correct host name or IP address for the VPN server is listed.

3 If you need to switch from PPTP to L2TP/IPSec or vice versa, select the appropriate connection method from the Connect Using drop-down box. (Choose Microsoft VPN Adapter for PPTP.)

4   Click the Server Types tab. In the Allowed Network Protocols area, clear all check boxes but the protocol in use on your office's network—most likely TCP/IP (doing so speeds up the connection). If you need to specify a static IP address, click TCP/IP Settings. Click OK when you're done.

5   If you need to change the L2TP/IPSec shared key or default certificate, click Start, choose Programs, Microsoft IPSec VPN, and then Microsoft IPSec VPN Configuration.

6   Set up L2TP/IPSec appropriately for the VPN server to which you want to connect (see Figure 14-3).

- Choose the first option to allow Windows to automatically select a Digital ID or certificate for use with your L2TP/IPSec VPN connections.

- If you have multiple certificates and you want to manually specify which one to use, select Use A Specific Certificate For IPSec Authentication.

- If the VPN server uses a preshared key (a password), select the third option, and type or copy and paste the key in the box provided.

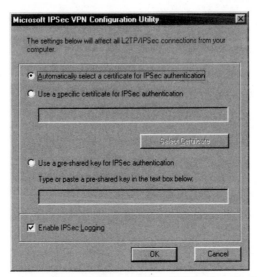

Figure 14-3 Use the Microsoft IPSec VPN Configuration Utility to specify a certificate or preshared key.

See Also   Digital IDs and certificates are discussed in Chapter 11, "Playing It Safe."

Logging On to a Windows Domain

To access files on your workplace's network you probably need to log on to
their Windows domain. This isn't particularly intuitive, but it's necessary. To do
so, use the following steps.

1 In Control Panel, double-click the Network icon.

2 Select Client For Microsoft Networks from the list of network components and then click Properties.

3 Select the Log On To Windows NT Domain check box (see Figure 14-4),
type the name of the Windows domain, and then click OK.

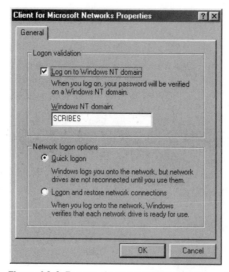

Figure 14-4 To properly access network folders, set up your computer to log on to the
Windows NT or Windows 2000 domain at your work.

4 Restart your computer when prompted. When the Windows logon
screen appears, type the username and password you use to log on at
work. Windows then reports that it couldn't contact the domain. This is
normal—Windows waits until you establish your VPN connection to
log on to the domain, but in the meantime it logs you on to Windows.

Note   If you previously used a different username in Windows, you must recreate some of your
Windows settings for the new user account profile.

Establishing a VPN Connection

Connecting to a network through a VPN works the same as a dial-up connection. To establish a connection, use the following steps.

1   In the Dial-Up Networking folder, double-click the appropriate connection.

2   In the Connect To dialog box, type your user name and password (if necessary), and select the Save Password check box if you want to save yourself this hassle next time.

3   Verify that the host name or IP address is correct and click Connect. After Windows establishes a connection, a connection icon appears in the System Tray. Work with the network as if you were directly connected, using Network Neighborhood or whatever network applications you use.

4   To disconnect, right-click the connection icon in the System Tray and choose Disconnect from the shortcut menu.

Dialing In to Your Computer While Away

Windows 98 comes with the ability to act as a dial-up server, providing a remote user with access to the files on your computer (as long as the computer is turned on and allowed to answer all phone calls). This can be really handy if you need to occasionally phone home to access files you've left behind. However, it's usually more convenient to carry important files with you by copying the files to a disk (CD, Zip, floppy), to your laptop, or by synchronizing your Personal Digital Assistant (PDA). You can also
e-mail yourself important files (if they're small enough) and then check your e-mail while on the road.

If you still want to set up your computer to accept incoming dial-up connections, use the following steps.

Note   Enabling dial-up access to your computer does expose you to an increased security risk, although if you use a suitable password the risk is slight for most home users—not many hackers bother trying to connect to home computers over a phone line, although some high-profile individuals and businesses might be at risk.

---

1   In Control Panel, double-click Add/Remove Programs.

2   Click the Windows Setup tab, choose Communications, and then click Details.

3   Select the Dial-Up Server check box, click OK, and then click OK again. If prompted to keep newer versions of files, click Yes.

4   Restart your computer if prompted. Then open My Computer and double-click the Dial-Up Networking folder.

5   Choose Dial-Up Server from the Connections menu.

6   Select Allow Caller Access, as shown in Figure 14-5, and optionally
        type a description for this connection (such as the phone number of
        the computer).

7   Click Change Password, type a suitable password (see Chapter 11, "Play-
        ing It Safe," for password choosing guidelines), and then click OK.

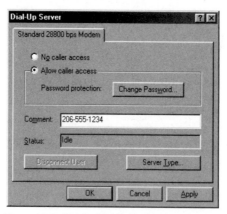

Figure 14-5 Use the Dial-Up Server dialog box to enable and configure incoming dial-up access.

Remote Access and Control over the Internet   Although Windows 98 doesn't
provide any built-in methods of connecting to your computer remotely over the Internet, a couple of
solutions are worth mentioning. The first is Symantec pcAnywhere (*http://www.symantec.com
/pcanywhere*). This program allows you to establish a VPN connection to your computer over the
Internet. It also provides remote control of your computer so that you can use your home computer
over the Internet as if you were sitting right in front of it (though graphics are slow over an Internet
connection).

The other solution worth mentioning is Windows XP Professional VPN and Remote Desktop
features. These features allow you to establish a VPN connection to your Windows XP Professional
computer over the Internet, as well as perform remote control of the computer.

Note that with both solutions, if a Cable/DSL router or a computer running ICS protects your
computer, you must configure the router or ICS computer to allow incoming VPN and remote control
connections. (Read your router's manual or do some searching either in the Microsoft Knowledge
Base or on the Symantec Web site.)

Key Points

- Dial-up network connections work just like dial-up Internet connections.

- You should download and install the Dial-Up Networking 1.4 update for the best dial-up and VPN networking performance and security.

- Windows 98 comes with support for PPTP VPN connections, but can also be configured to connect through L2TP/IPSec by downloading the Microsoft L2TP/IPSec VPN Client (this requires the Dial-Up Networking 1.4 update).

- VPN users probably need to set up Windows to log on to their work domain.

- Windows 98 Dial-Up Server software allows you to dial in to your computer when you're away from home, but most people find it easier to just take important files with them.

- Symantec pcAnywhere and Windows XP Professional both enable you to establish a VPN connection with your home computer while away, as well as to remotely control your computer. (You might have to configure your Cable/DSL Router or ICS computer to support this.)

Index

Numbers

802.11a (WiFi5) wireless
networks, 290
802.11b (WiFi) wireless
networks, 289

A

access points, network setup, 293
accessibility options, 217-20
  general options, 220
  keyboard aids, 219
  sound enhancements, 218
  visibility enhancements, 218
account, Internet service provider
  (ISP), 115
accounts, e-mail
  creating, 115
  defaults, 140-41
  IMAP (Internet Messaging Access
    Protocol) accounts, 141
  setting up, 139-40
  transferring, 115
accounts, newsgroup, 167-69
Ad Aware, 65
adapters, ISDN (Integrated Services
  Digital Network), 200
Add New Hardware Wizard
  digital cameras, 194-95
  scanners, 194
  USB (Universal Serial Bus) ports,
    193
Add Printer Wizard, 185
Add/Remove Programs
  adding printers, 173
  installing software, 56
  removing printers, 175
  uninstalling software, 58-59
Address bar, Internet Explorer
  copying and pasting URLs
    into, 131
  features of, 122-23
  overview of, 121
  searching from, 133
Address Book, 156-59
  creating contacts, 157-58
  creating groups, 158-59
  organizing contacts into folders,
    159
  viewing addresses, 156-57
Address toolbar, 20
Adobe Acrobat Reader, 64
ADSL (asymmetric digital
  subscriber line), 201
Advanced Power Management
  (APM), 285
advanced searches, Web, 134-35
Alt+Tab, to switch between
  programs, 52
America Online (AOL), 114
Anonymizer, 239-40
AnonyMouse, 240
antivirus software, 150, 227-28
APM (Advanced Power Management), 285
Appearance tab, Display Properties
  dialog box, 40
archive property, folders, 75
area code rules, 315
.asp files, 123
asymmetric DSL (ADSL), 201
attachments
  blocking dangerous, 228
  guidelines for polite use of, 156
  opening, 150-51
  sending, 155
  viruses and, 150
  working with, 150-151
attributes, file, 73
auctions, Internet, 245
Auto Arrange, icons, 28-29
Auto Hide, taskbar, 19
AutoComplete feature, 237-39
  changing defaults, 238-39
  clearing, 247
  filling out Web forms, 238
Autoexec.bat
  memory management and,
    258-59
  startup problems and, 281
AutoPlay, CDs, 55-56

B

background pictures, 70
background programs, 268
backing up files, 269-78
  with Backup Wizard, 274-75
  frequency of, 229
  manual, 275-77
  media selection for, 271-73
  network, 287-88
  restoring from, 277-78
  strategy for, 270-71
  types of, 270
Backup, Microsoft
  backing up to CD-R/RWs, 272
  installing, 274-75
  manual backups, 275-76
  restoring from backup, 277
backup media, 271-74
  for general users, 272
  for multimedia users, 272-73
  types of, 271
  for video users, 273
Backup Wizard, 274-75
BIOS (Basic Input Output System),
  264
bits, 113
Boolean searches, 134-35
booting
  defined, 9
  optimizing reboot time, 102
bridges, network, 291
browsing. See Web browsing
bus, defined, 191
buttons,
  Help, 44, 45
  mouse, 8-9, 83, 212
  Start, 4
bytes, 113

C

cable connections, 112, 201-2
cable/DSL (Digital Subscriber Line)
  routers
  Internet connection sharing
    and, 292
  network security and, 308
  setup, 296-99
cabling
  crossover cables, 290
  network setup and, 293
cache, disk, 264, 268

calendar, Outlook, 138
cameras. See digital cameras
CD-ROM drive settings, 192
CDs
   backing up to, 271, 272
   installing programs from, 55-56
certificate authorities, 240-41
chat rooms, 233
client computers, networks, 300-301
Close Program window, 54
closing programs, 52-53
Color Management tab, printing, 180
color profiles
   defined, 180
   display settings, 207
color schemes, desktop, 40-41
command-line access, 12-13
compatibility, of hardware, 189
composing e-mail messages, 153-54
compression, e-mail attachments, 151
compression drivers, 260-61
computer maintenance. See maintenance, computer
computer slowdown, 54-55
Config.sys
   memory management and, 258-59
   startup problems, 281
connection types, 112-13
connectivity testing, 305-6
contacts, Address Book
   creating, 157-58
   organizing, 159
Content Advisor feature, Internet Explorer, 249
Content Protection, Windows Media Player, 226
Contents tab, Windows Help, 45
Control Panel, 211-26
   accessibility options, 217-20
   keyboard options, 215-17
   mouse settings, 211-15
   Scanners And Cameras in, 194
   sound settings, 220-23
cookies, 234-37
   deleting, 246
   Internet Explorer and, 236-37
   overview of, 96-97
   restricting use of, 234-36
copying
   files and folders, 83-84
   floppy disks, 90

copyright law, 226
credit cards
   Internet shopping and, 244
   security of, 234
credit reports, 240
crossover cables, 290
Ctrl+A (Select All), 78
Ctrl key, file selection, 79
Custom toolbars, 21-22
Customize This Folder, 70
Cut command, files and folders, 84

D

DAT (Digital Audio Tape), 271, 273
default e-mail account, Outlook Express, 140-41
default gateway, networks, 305-6
defragmentation, 252, 268
Delete key, e-mail, 152
desktop
   elements of, 3
   eliminating icons from, 100-102
   navigating with Windows Explorer, 82
   schemes, 40-41
   shortcuts for launching programs, 50
   themes, 38-40
   wallpaper, 41-42
desktop icons, 25-31. See also icons
   arranging, 28-29
   Auto Arrange, 28-29
   My Computer, 26
   Network Neighborhood, 26-27
   overview of, 25-26
   Recycle Bin, 27
   size of, 29-31
   system icons, changing, 28
Desktop toolbar, 21
   device drivers. See drivers
Device Manager, 190-92
   CD-ROM drive settings, 192
   device settings, 191-92
   opening, 190
   viewing devices, 190-91
DHCP (Dynamic Host Configuration Protocol) servers/clients, 299-301
dialog boxes, question marks on, 45
dial-up access, 321-22
dial-up connections, 313-16
   creating, 314

   dialing into network with, 316
   download managers and, 136
   forcing use of, 142
   properties, 314-15
   remote connections, 313-16
Dial-up Networking (DUN), 314
differential backups, 270-71
Digital Audio Tape (DAT), 271, 273
digital cameras, 194-96
   downloading photos from, 195
   e-mailing photos and, 196
   installing, 194-95
   managing digital photos, 196
digital IDs
   compared with PGP (Pretty Good Privacy), 242
   e-mail security and, 240-41
digital photos
   downloading, 195
   e-mailing, 196
   managing, 196
digital images, 178
digital signatures, 241-43
Digital Subscriber Line (DSL), 112, 201-2
direct memory access (DMA), 263
directories, online, 233
disaster recovery, 277
disk cache, 264, 268
Disk Cleanup tool
   removing unnecessary files, 103-4
   system tools, 252
   Task Scheduler and, 254
   temp (.tmp) files and, 96
disk compression, 255
Disk Defragmenter, 252, 254
disk drives
   backing up to, 271, 272-73
   disk speed and, 264-65
   display speed and, 268
   formatting, 268
   reasons for not compressing, 255
disk speed, 263-65
   direct memory access (DMA), enabling, 263
   drive replacement and, 264-65
   file system properties, 263
disks, floppy. See floppy disks
display devices, 202-7
   memory management and, 262
   overview of, 202-3
   video cards, 202-3
   video drivers, 203-4
   video settings, 204-7

Display Properties dialog box,
    30, 40
display speed, 266–69
    improvements to, 266–67
    video editing and, 267–69
.dll files
    DLL Help, 107
    boot time and, 266
    critical, 106–7
    recovering, 107–8
DMA (direct memory access), 263
DNS (Domain Name System)
    servers, 306
Documents folder
    clearing history, 246
    clearing list of shortcuts, 105
    working with, 16
DOS mode, 62
DOS programs, 60–62
    running, 60–61
    troubleshooting, 61–62
double-click, adjusting, 212–13
Download Center, Microsoft, 2
download managers, 136
downloading
    files, 135–36
    newsgroup messages, 169–70
    software, 57–58
dpi (dots per inch), 177–78
drivers
    compression drivers, 260–61
    hardware, 192–93
    monitors, 206
    network printers, 184–85
    printers, 174
    protected mode drivers, 282
    video, 203–4
    virtual device drivers (VxDs),
        283–84
drives. See disk drives
DriveSpace feature, 255
DSL (Digital Subscriber Line), 112,
    201–2
DSL routers. See cable/DSL routers
DUN (Dial-up Networking), 314
DVDs
    backing up to, 271, 273
    selecting DVD burners, 274
Dynamic Host Configuration Proto-
    col (DHCP) servers/clients,
    299–301

E

e-mail. See also Outlook Express;
    Hotmail
    account creation, 115
    attachments, 150–51, 155–56
    checking for new messages, 148
    composing messages, 153–54
    deleting messages, 152
    e-mailing photos, 196
    formatting messages, 155
    forwarding messages, 151
    netiquette, 151
    printing messages, 152–53
    reading messages, 149
    replying to messages, 151
    security of, 240–43
    sending messages, 144
    sending/receiving, timing of, 142
    signature files, 145
    spam, 166–67
    spell checking, 146
    transferring accounts, 115
    troubleshooting, 149
encryption, 241–43, 308–9
Ethernet networks, 289
Exchange Server, Microsoft, 138
.exe files, 50

F

F1 key, accessing help, 44
FAT (File Allocation Table) 32,
    254–55
favorites folder, one-click access
    to, 6–7
Favorites list, Internet Explorer,
    125–27
    adding to, 125–26
    importing/exporting favorites,
        127
    organizing, 126
File and Print Sharing
    enabling, 302
    security of, 228, 310
    sharing network printers, 186–87
    testing, 307
file formats, 97, 224
file name extensions
    hiding, 73
    overview of, 97
    Web files, 123
File Transfer Protocol (FTP), 123
file type, editing, 81

files
    associating with programs, 79–82
    attributes, 73
    copying, 83–84
    creating, 75–76
    deleting, advice, 106–8
    fragmentation, 253
    hidden, 95
    moving, 83–84
    naming, 76–77
    overview of, 75
    program files, 96
    properties, 77–78
    recovering from Recycle Bin,
        86–88
    removing unnecessary, 103–6
    selecting, 78–79
    sharing, 307
    system, 94
    system properties, 263
    temp (.tmp) files, 96–97
filtering objectionable content, 248
FilterKeys, accessibility options, 219
Find button, Outlook Express,
    161–62
Find Target, shortcuts, 34
Find tool, 13–15
    combined searches, 15
    saving search results, 15
    searching by date, 14
    searching by file type, 15
    searching by name, 13–14
firewalls, 228, 291–92
floppy disks
    copying, 90
    disabling, 265
    formatting, 90–91
    sending files to Recycle Bin, 85
Folder Options dialog box, 71–74
folder views
    Outlook Express, 162–63
    setting, 68
    Thumbnail view, 71
    Web page view, 68–69
folders, 67–75
    copying, 70, 83
    creating, 68
    customizing, 70
    cutting, 84
    hidden, 95
    overview of, 67
    pasting, 84
    properties, 74–75
    selecting, 78–79

folders, *continued*
  sharing, 303-4
  system-wide options, 71-74
  view settings, 70-71
  Web view, 68-69
folders, Address Book
  organizing contacts, 159
  organizing messages, 160-61
fonts
  display settings, 206
  smoothing edges of, 74
formatting
  disk drives, 268
  e-mail messages, 155
  floppy disks, 90-91
forwarding e-mail, 151-52
fragmentation, 253
frames, of Web pages, 131
FTP (File Transfer Protocol), 123
fully qualified domain name (FQDN),
  297

G

game controllers, 207-9
games
  high-performance, 63-64
  multiplayer, 288
groups, Address Book, 158-59

H

hackers. See also network security
  protecting networks from, 307-8
  stopping, 227-29
hand aids, accessibility options,
  219
hard drives. See disk drives
hardware, 189-210
  compatibility, 189
  Device Manager and, 190
  device settings, 191-92
  device views, 190-91
  digital cameras, 194-96
  display devices, 202-7
  drivers, 192-93
  DSL (Digital Subscriber Line) and
    cable connections, 201-2
  game controllers, 207-9
  ISDN (Integrated Services Digital
    Network) lines, 200-201
  modems, 196-200
  mouse, 207
  profiles, 209-10

scanners, 194
setup for networks, 293
USB (Universal Serial Bus) ports,
  193
hardware acceleration, 206
HCL (hardware compatibility list),
  189
headers, e-mail, 143
help
  F1 key, 44
  button, 45
  menus, 45
  question mark on dialog boxes,
    45
  right mouse button, 44
  Web help, 46-48
  Windows help, 45-46
hidden files and folders, 95
hidden property, folders, 75
High Contrast, accessibility options,
  218
high-performance games, 63-64
History folder, Internet Explorer,
  127-29, 245-46
home page, Internet Explorer, 124
HomePNA 2.0 networks, 290
Hotmail, 141
hot-plugging, USB (Universal Serial
  Bus) devices, 193
.html files, 123
HTML (Hypertext Markup
  Language), 70
hubs, 293
hung programs, 53
hypertext, 68

I

.icc files, 180
.icm files, 180
icons. See also desktop icons
  arranging, 28-29
  eliminating from desktop,
    100-101
  file type, changing, 81
  hiding, 73-74
  shortcuts, 4, 34
  Use Large Icons option, 206
ICS (Internet Connection Sharing),
  291-92, 295-96
IDE (Integrated Drive Electronics)
  controller, 269
identities, Outlook Express, 146-47
identity theft, 240

IM (instant messaging), 233
IMAP (Internet Messaging Access
    Protocol)
  accessing e-mail on server, 141
  defined, 113
  folder synchronization settings,
    Outlook Express, 143-44
  mail servers, 297
Import/Export Wizard, 127
Index tab, Windows Help, 45
Inkjet printers, 179
Install New Modem Wizard, 196-97
Install on Demand programs, 136
instant messaging (IM), 233
Integrated Services Digital Network
    (ISDN) lines, 200-201
interface, Outlook Express,
    147-48
interface, Windows 98. See
    Windows 98 interface
Internet. See also Web browsing
  auctions, 245
  connecting automatically,
    117-18
  connecting manually, 118-19
  disconnecting from, 119
  objectionable content, 248
  remote access/control, 322
  shopping, 243-45
  searching for help, 46
Internet Connection Sharing (ICS),
    291-92, 295-96
Internet Connection Wizard
  e-mail account setup, 139-40
  ISP account creation/transfer,
    115
  LAN (Local Area Network)
    connections, 116
Internet Explorer
  Address Bar, 122-23
  AutoComplete, 237-39
  Content Advisor, 249
  cookie handling, 236-37
  desktop icon, 26
  e-mailing Web pages, 130-31
  Favorites list, 125-27
  features, 120-21
  History folder, 127-29
  home page, 124
  printing Web pages, 131
  saving Web pages, 129-30
  security of download scripts,
    228-29
  slow loading pages, 123-24
  versions of, 120

Web addresses, 122
Web searches, 132–35
Windows Update and, 16
IP (Internet Protocol) addresses
  defined, 299
  ICS (Internet Connection Sharing)
    and, 291
  network troubleshooting and,
    304–5
IP configuration, 304–5
IPSec (IP Security), 313, 318
ISDN (Integrated Services Digital
  Network) lines, 200–201
ISPs (Internet service providers),
  114

K

Kb (kilobit), 113
Kbps (kilobits per second), 113
keyboard, 215–17
  Print Screen key, 175
  shortcuts, 7, 216–17
  Speed tab settings, 215–16
Knowledge Base, Microsoft, 46

L

L2TP/IPSec (Layer 2 Tunneling Pro-
  tocol/IP Security), 313, 318
LANs (Local Area Networks),
  116–17
  compared with WANs (Wide Area
    Networks), 299
  connecting through, 116–17
  defined, 116
  forcing use of LAN connections,
    142
Large Fonts, 206
lasso selection method, 79
launching programs. See programs
Layer 2 Tunneling Protocol/IP Security (L2TP/IPSec), 313, 318
licensing, 226
Links toolbar, 20–21
load time, Windows, 265–66
loopback address, 305
lurking, newsgroups, 170

M

MAC (Media Access Control)
  addresses, 310
mail servers, 297

maintenance, computer, 251–86
  backups. see backups
  conversion to FAT 32, 254–55
  disk speed, 263–65
  display speed, 266–69
  Maintenance Wizard tasks,
    252–54
  memory management, 256–62
  processors, 266
  shutdown problems, 285–86
  software updates, 251–52
  startup problems. see startup
    problems
  Windows load time, 265–66
Maintenance Wizard tasks, 252–54
manual backups, 275–77
manuals, installation instruction,
  56–57
mapping network drives, 73
Master Boot Record (MBR), 255
Mb (megabit), 113
MB (megabyte), 113
Mbps (megabits per second), 113
MBps (megabytes per second), 113
MBR (Master Boot Record), 255
McAfee VirusScan, 228
Media Player. See Windows Media
  Player
megabit (Mb), 113
memory management, 256–62
  compression drivers, disabling,
    260–61
  Config.sys and Autoexec.bat files
    and, 258–59
  display settings, 262
  network components, removing
    unneeded, 257–58
  RAM (random access memory),
    256–57
  startup programs, removing
    unneeded, 259–60
  system tray programs,
    eliminating, 257
  virtual memory settings, 261–62
memory, video cards, 202
Menu bar, selecting help from, 45
Message Rules dialog box, 165
message rules, Outlook Express,
  164–66
Microsoft Backup. See Backup
Microsoft Download Center. See
  Download Center
Microsoft Exchange Server. See
  Exchange Server

Microsoft Internet Connection Shar-
  ing (ICS). See Internet Con-
  nection Sharing (ICS)
Microsoft Knowledge Base. See
  Knowledge Base
Microsoft Network (MSN), 114
Microsoft Office. See Office
Microsoft Profile Assistant. See
  Profile Assistant
Microsoft Windows 2000. See
  Windows 2000
Microsoft Windows 3.x. See
  Windows 3.x
Microsoft Windows 98 interface.
  See Windows 98 interface
Microsoft Windows 98 Second Edition (SE). See Windows 98 SE
Microsoft Windows NT. See
  Windows NT
Microsoft Windows XP. See
  Windows XP
modems, 196–200
  dialing properties, 199
  installing, 196–97
  removing, 197
  replacing, 198
  settings, 198–99
  speed of, 114
  troubleshooting, 199–200
monitors. See also display devices
  dpi (dots per inch) outputs and,
    178
  installing, 206
  replacing, 206
mouse, 211–15
  button configuration, 212
  double-click speed, 212–13
  left mouse button, 83
  motion settings, 213
  overview of, 207
  pointer settings, 213–15
  right mouse button, 8–9
  single click operation, 8
MouseKeys, 219
MP3s, 224, 272–73
msconfig.exe (System Configuration
  Utility), 280, 285
MS-DOS. See DOS programs
MSN (Microsoft Network), 114
multiple users, 10–11
My Computer, 26, 36–37
My Documents, 25

N

naming
  files, 76–77
  shortcuts, 33
NAT (Network Address Translation), 292
navigation
  desktop with Windows Explorer, 82
  paths and, 51
NetBEUI (NetBIOS Enhanced User Interface), 307, 310
Network Address Translation (NAT), 292
network cards, 293
network components, 257–58
network interface card (NIC), 201–2
Network Neighborhood
  desktop icons, 26–27
  eliminating icon for, 100–101
  sharing folders, 303–4
network printers
  adding, 184–86
  sharing, 186–87
network security
  cable/DSL (Digital Subscriber Line) routers, 308
  File and Print Sharing, 310
  wireless networks, 308–10
networks, 287–311. See also remote connections
  bridges, 291
  cable/DSL routers, 296–99
  client computers, 300–301
  designing, 288
  direct connections, 294–95
  Faster Smarter Home Networking (Frye), 288
  File and Print Sharing, 302
  hardware setup, 293
  sharing connections, 291–92, 295–96
  sharing folders, 303–4
  speed of, 113
  troubleshooting, 304–7
  types of, 288–90
  wireless, 301–2, 308–10
New Mail Rule dialog box, 164–65
news servers, 297
newsgroups
  account setup, 167–68
  downloading messages, 169–70
  getting help from, 47

  maintenance and clean up, 171–72, 247
  posting messages, 170
  subscribing to, 168–69
  synchronizing, 171
NIC (network interface card), 201–2
nonresponding programs, 53–54
Norton Antivirus, 228
notification area, of taskbar, 4

O

objectionable content, Internet, 248–49
Office, Microsoft, 252
Office Update, 252
Offline Browsing Pack, 126
online directories, 233
online printers/service bureaus, 180–81
Online Services desktop icon, 26
online services defined, 114
onstream tape, for backups, 271
opening programs. See programs
operating systems, 49
Outlook, compared with Outlook Express, 138
Outlook Express
  account setup, 139–40
  Address Book, 156–59
  attachments, 150–51, 155–56
  checking for new messages, 148
  composing messages, 153–54
  default e-mail account, 140–41
  deleting messages, 152
  desktop icon, 26
  digital IDs and, 241
  digitally signed or encrypted e-mail, 242–43
  finding messages, 161–62
  folder views, 162–63
  formatting messages, 155
  IMAP (Internet Messaging Access Protocol) folder synchronization settings, 143–44
  importing settings and messages, 138
  interface, 147–48
  message rules, 164–66
  multiple identities, 146–47
  organizing messages into folders, 160–61
  photo attachments, 196
  printing messages, 152–53

  reading messages, 149
  replying/forwarding, 151
  saving messages outside of, 161
  sending messages, 144
  server, accessing messages on, 141–42
  signature files, 145
  spam, 166–67
  spelling checker, 146
  timing of sending/receiving messages, 142

P

Page Setup, printing, 175
paper selection, printing, 179, 180
partitions, 268
passwords
  adding to screen savers, 43–44
  guidelines for good, 230–32
Paste, files and folders, 84
patches, Windows Update, 251
paths, 51
pcAnywhere, 322
PDAs (Personal Digital Assistants), 138
performance. See system performance
Performance Monitor, 55
personal information, protecting, 232–34
PGP (Pretty Good Privacy), 242
photo printers, 177, 179, 180
photos. See digital photos
physical security, 229
ping, 297, 305
pixels, 178
pixels per inch (ppi), 178
Plug and Play, 191
pointer settings, mouse, 213–15
Point-to-Point Protocol (PPP), 201
POP (Post Office Protocol)
  accessing e-mail on server and, 141–42
  defined, 113
  mail servers, 297
ports
  printers, 188
  USB ports, 193
Post Office Protocol. See POP (Post Office Protocol)
posting messages, to newsgroups, 170
ppi (pixels per inch), 178

PPTP (Point To Point Tunneling
    Protocol), 318
Pretty Good Privacy (PGP), 242
Print dialog box, 176, 179
Print command, File menu, 153,
    175
Print Preview, 175
print queue management, 182–84
Print Screen, on keyboard, 175
printing
    adding network printers, 184–86
    basic process for, 175–77
    capturing ports, 188
    color management, 180
    cost savings, 181
    default settings, 182
    e-mail messages, 152–53
    installing printers, 174–75
    online printers/service bureaus,
        180–81
    paper selection, 179
    photos, 177
    print queue management,
        182–84
    quality settings, 179
    removing printers, 175
    resolution, dpi, and size, 178
    sharing network printers, 186–87
    types of printers, 179
    wizard, 185
privacy, 229–34
    cookies and, 234–37
    passwords, 230–32
    personal information, 232–34
privacy policies, 232–33
.prn files, 177
processors
    optimization, 266
    tracking performance of, 54
Profile Assistant, Microsoft, 239
profiles, hardware, 209–10
profiles, user, 10–11
program files, 103
Program Files folder, 96
programs, 49–66
    associating with file types, 79–82
    closing, 52–53
    computer slowdown and, 54–55
    DOS, 60–62
    essential third party, 64–65
    executable file (.exe) and, 50
    high-performance games, 63–64
    installing, 55–58
    launching, 50–51

nonresponding, 53–54
switching between, 51–52
uninstalling, 58–59
Windows 3.x, 60
Windows NT/2000/XP, 63
properties
    dial-up connections, 314–15
    displays, 30, 40, 205
    files, 77–78
    folders, 74–75
    modems, 199
    overview of, 28
    shortcuts, 33–34
    sound, 220
    VPN (Virtual Private Network)
        connections, 318–19
protected mode drivers, 282
proxies, third party, 239–40
proxy servers
    defined, 116
    mail servers, 297
    settings, 116–17
    streaming media and, 225

Q

question marks, on dialog boxes, 45
Quick Launch toolbar, 20, 50–51
QuickTime Player, 64

R

RAM (Random Access Memory), 50,
    256–57
reading e-mail, 149
read-only property, folders, 74
Real Jukebox, 224
Recycle Bin
    bypassing, 85–86
    eliminating from desktop, 101–2
    emptying, 89–90, 247
    floppy disk files and, 85
    overview of, 27, 84–85
    recovering files from, 86–88
    settings, 88–89
regedit.exe, 98–100, 282
registry
    associating file types with
        programs, 80–82
    defined, 79, 98
    editing, 282
    eliminating Network Neighbor-
        hood icon, 100–101
    eliminating Recycle Bin, 101–2

Optimizing the Windows Registry
    (Ivens), 102
    overview of, 97–98
    Registry Checker, 98–99
    safeguarding, 98
remote access
    dial-up, 321–22
    over Internet, 322
remote connections, 313–23
    dial-up access to computers,
        321–22
    dial-up connections, 313–16
    methods for, 313
    VPN (Virtual Private Network)
        connections, 316–21
remote control, 322
resolution
    display settings, 205
    icon size and, 29
    printing and, 177, 178
restoring, from backups, 277–78
right mouse button
    contextual help with, 8–9, 44
    copying files and folders, 83
root directory, 265
Run command, 12–13

S

Safe Mode, 279–81, 284–85
ScanDisk
    system tools, 252
    Task Scheduler and, 254
scanners, 194
Scanners And Cameras, Control
    Panel, 194
screen savers, 42–44
    adding password to, 43–44
    overview of, 42
    selecting, 43
script-kiddies, 308
scroll boxes, proportionate size
    of, 38
SCSI (Small Computer System
    Interface), 269
Search Bar, Web searches with,
    133–34
search engines, 132
Search tab, Windows Help, 45
searches. See Find tool; Web
    searches
searches, Outlook Express
    messages, 161–62

security
  anonymous surfing tools, 239–40
  AutoComplete feature, 237–39
  cookies, 234–37
  credit reports, checking
    frequently, 240
  e-mail, 240–43
  hackers and viruses and, 227–29
  Microsoft Profile Assistant and,
    239
  objectionable content, 248–49
  passwords, 230–32
  personal information, 232–34
  physical, 9
  privacy, 229–30
  screen saver passwords and,
    43–44
  shopping, 243–45
  for social security numbers, 234
  tracks, covering, 245–47
Select All, Edit menu, 78
Send tab, Outlook Express, 144
Send To menu, 35–36
Serial Line Internet Protocol (SLIP),
  201
service bureaus, 180–81
Set Up The Microsoft Network
  (MSN), desktop icon, 26
sharing connections, 295–96
sharing folders, 75, 303–4
sharing printers, 186–87
ShieldsUP!, 308
Shift key, file selection with, 79
shopping, on Web, 243–45
shortcuts
  adding to Send To menu, 35–36
  arrow indicator in icons, 31
  compared with icons, 4
  creating, 32–33
  documents list and, 105
  find target of, 34
  icon for, 34
  keyboard, 7, 216–17
  launching programs from, 50
  naming/renaming, 33
  organizing, 5–6
  overview of, 31–32
  properties, 33–34
ShowSounds, accessibility options,
  218
shut down
  overview of, 11–12
  problems, 285–86

signature files, Outlook Express,
  145
size, printing and, 178
SLIP (Serial Line Internet Protocol),
  201
Small Computer System Interface
  (SCSI), 269
SMTP (Simple Mail Transfer
  Protocol), 297
software
  Add/Remove Programs, 56
  downloading, 57–58
  installation manuals, 56–57
  installing from CD, 55–56
  updates, 251–52
sound cards, 269
Sound Recorder, 222
sound schemes, 221
sounds, 220–23
  acquiring new, 221
  accessibility options, 218
  creating, 222
  schemes, 221
  Sound Properties dialog box,
    220–21
  special effects and editing,
    222–23
SoundSentry, accessibility options,
  218
spam
  spam-proofing e-mail account,
    233
  steps for reducing, 166–67
Speed tab settings, keyboards,
  215–16
spell checking, e-mail, 146
SPI (Stateful Packet Inspection),
  308
splash screen, disabling at bootup,
  265
Star Downloader, 136
Start button, 4
Start menu, 12–19
  accessing with Start button, 4
  adding to, 18
  deleting form, 18–19
  Documents folder, 16
  Find tool, 13–15
  launching programs from, 50
  Run command, 12–13
  Windows Update, 16–18
Startup folder
  launching programs, 51

removing unneeded programs,
  259–60
startup problems and, 281–82
startup problems, 279–85
  Autoexec.bat or Config.sys and,
    281
  Safe Mode and, 279–81,
    284–85
  Startup folder, 281–82
  System.ini or Win.ini files and,
    281
startup processes, 9–11
  logon, 9–10
  user profiles, 10–11
Stateful Packet Inspection (SPI),
  308
StickyKeys, keyboard options, 219
streaming media, 225
subscribing, to newsgroups, 168–69
switches, network, 293
synchronizing newsgroups, 171
System Configuration Utility
  (msconfig.exe), 280, 285
System File Checker, 107
system files, 94
system icons, 27–28
System Monitor, 54, 55
system performance
  disk speed, 263–65
  display speed, 266–69
  memory management, 256–62
  processor management, 266
  Windows load time, 265–66
system property, folders, 75
System Recovery Wizard, 277
system tray, 4, 257
System.ini files, 281

T

tape backups, 271, 273
Task Scheduler, 254
taskbar
  adjusting toolbar size and
    location, 22–23
  appearance of, 19
  overview of, 4
  placement of, 19
  switching between programs on,
    51–52
  toolbars on, 19–22
  visibility of, 19

TCP/IP (Transmission Control Protocol/Internet Protocol), 315
telecommuting, 313
temp files, 96–97, 103–4, 246
themes, desktop, 38–40
themes, Windows Themes, 266
third-party proxies, 239–40
threads, newsgroups, 169–70
Thumbnail view, folders, 71
.tmp files, 96
ToggleKeys, accessibility options, 219
toolbars
  adjusting size and location of, 22
  types of, 19–22
tracks, covering, 245–47
troubleshooting
  e-mail, 149
  modems, 199–200
  networks, 304–7
  start up, 280

U

Update Device Driver Wizard, 206
updates, 251–52. See also Windows Update
URLs (Universal Resource Locators)
  copying and pasting into Address Bar, 131
  Web navigation and, 122
USB (Universal Serial Bus) ports, 193
user profiles, 10–11

V

versions, Windows 98, 2
video
  advanced configuration, 205–7
  backing up, 273
  drivers, 203–4
  resolution, 205
video cards, 202–3
video drives
  dedicated, 267
  eliminating Windows swap file from, 268
  size of, 269
video editing, 267–69
view settings, folders, 70–71
virtual device drivers (VxDs), 283

virtual memory settings, 261–62
viruses
  preventing, 227–29
  scanning downloaded files for, 57
visibility enhancements, accessibility options, 218
VPN (Virtual Private Network) connections, 316–21
  creating, 308, 317–18
  establishing connection, 320–21
  installing VPN support, 316–17
  logging on to Windows domain, 320
  properties, 318–19
  remote connections, 316–21
VxDs (virtual device drivers), 283

W

wallpaper, 41–42
WANs (Wide Area Networks), 299
WAV files, 221–22
Web addresses, 122
Web browsing, 111–36. See also Internet Explorer
  account creation, 115
  account transfers, 115
  connecting to Internet automatically, 117–18
  connecting to Internet manually, 118–19
  connection types, 112–13
  disconnecting from Internet, 119
  downloading files, 135–36
  Internet service provider (ISP) selection, 114
  local area network (LAN) connections, 116–17
  searches, 132–35
Web forms
  AutoComplete feature, 237–39
  Microsoft Profile Assistant, 239
Web pages
  e-mailing, 130–31
  printing, 131
  saving, 129–30
  slow loading, 123–24
Web page view, folders, 68–69
Web searches, 132–35
  Address Bar, 133
  advanced, 134–35
  Search Bar, 133–34
  services, 132–33

Web surfing tools, 239–40
Web views, disabling, 266–67
WEP (Wired Equivalent Privacy) encryption, 308–9
Wide Area Networks (WANs), 299
WiFi (Wireless Fidelity). See wireless networks
Windows 2000, 63
Windows 3.x
  network printers and, 188
  programs and, 60
Windows 98 interface
  desktop, 3
  icons and shortcuts, 4
  Start button, 4
  taskbar, 4
  versions, 2
Windows 98 SE
  compared with Windows 98, 2
  Internet Sharing Connection (ICS) and, 295
  video support in, 269
Windows Critical Update Notification, 18
Windows domains, VPN connections to, 320
Windows Explorer
  adding to Start menu, 18
  compared with My Computer, 36–37
  deleting unused files/documents, 106
  desktop navigation with, 38
  opening multiple windows, 37
Windows Help, 45–46
Windows key + Tab, switching between programs with, 52
Windows load time, 265–66
Windows Media Player
  buffer range and, 225
  Content Protection, 226
  files types, 224
  overview of, 223–24
Windows NT, 63
Windows Registry Checker, 283
Windows Themes, 266
Windows Update, 16–18
  checking for available updates, 17
  downloading latest version of Internet Explorer, 120
  Internet Explorer and, 16–17
  Windows Critical Update Notification, 18

Windows XP
  ICS and, 292
  NetBEUI (NetBIOS Extended User
    Interface) and, 307
  programs, 63
  video support, 269
Windows XP Professional
  personal firewall, 292
  VPN and Remote Desktop, 322
Win.ini files, 281
winipcfg, 304
Winzip, 64
wireless connections, 112

wireless networks
  802.11a (WiFi5), 290
  802.11b (WiFi), 289
  connecting to, 301–2
  security of, 308–10
wizards, 5. See also specific wizard
  names
World Wide Web. See Internet; Web

X

X.509 certificates, 242. See also
  digital IDs

Z

Zip disks, backing up to, 271, 272
ZoneAlarm, 292

Sharon Crawford

Sharon Crawford is a veteran, even grizzled, writer of many computer books, including *Windows 2000 Pro: The Missing Manual*, *Windows 2000 Professional for Dummies* (with Andy Rathbone), and *Microsoft Windows 2000 Server Administrator's Companion* (with Charlie Russel). She also writes a regular column on using Windows XP for the Microsoft Windows XP Expert Zone at *http://www.microsoft.com/windowsxp/expertzone*.

Before becoming a book author, Sharon was a waitress, student, payroll clerk, housewife, telephone operator, pharmaceutical salesperson, bookkeeper, proofreader, taxi driver, subway electrician, and editor. When writing seems too tough, she thinks back on this checkered career and quickly finds it very easy to return to the task at hand.

Jason Gerend

Jason Gerend has written, contributed to, and edited numerous computer books, including *Microsoft Windows 2000 Server Administrator's Companion* (with Sharon Crawford and Charlie Russel), *Microsoft Help Desk for Microsoft Windows 98* (with Microsoft Product Support Services) and the *Effective Executive's Guide to Microsoft Outlook 2002*.

Jason became interested in computers back in the days of MS-DOS 2.0 and has been a professional Webmaster since 1995. He sold computers while getting his degree in psychology, and then dodged graduate school and psychology research to write books full time. Jason is also a Microsoft Certified Systems Engineer (MCSE) and freelance computer and network consultant.

The manuscript for this book was prepared and submitted to Microsoft Press in electronic form. The pages were composed by nSight, Inc., using Adobe FrameMaker+SGML for Windows, with text in Garamond and display text in ITC Franklin Gothic Condensed. Composed pages were delivered to the printer as electronic pre-press files.

Cover Designer:	Tim Girvin Design
Interior Graphic Designer:	James D. Kramer
Compositor:	Mary Beth McDaniel
Project Manager:	Tempe Goodhue
Copy Editor:	Marcia Allen, Robert Saley
Technical Editor:	Bob Hogan
Proofreaders:	Jennifer Carr, Katie O'Connell
Indexer:	Jack Lewis

Get a **Free**
e-mail newsletter, updates,
special offers, links to related books,
and more when you

register on line!

Register your Microsoft Press® title on our Web site and you'll get a FREE subscription to our e-mail newsletter, *Microsoft Press Book Connections*. You'll find out about newly released and upcoming books and learning tools, online events, software downloads, special offers and coupons for Microsoft Press customers, and information about major Microsoft® product releases. You can also read useful additional information about all the titles we publish, such as detailed book descriptions, tables of contents and indexes, sample chapters, links to related books and book series, author biographies, and reviews by other customers.

Registration is easy. Just visit this Web page and fill in your information:

http://www.microsoft.com/mspress/register

Microsoft

- -